Keeping the Dalai Lama Waiting
& Other Stories

An English Woman's Journey to Becoming a Buddhist Lama

By Lama Shenpen Hookham

Lama Shenpen Hookham

Published by
Shrimala Publishing
Shrimala Publishing name and logo are copyright of the
The Shrimala Trust
Criccieth, Gwynedd UK
© 2021

First edition published May 2020

This edition: November 2021

ISBN: 978-1-3999-1049-1

The Shrimala Trust is a registered charity (no. 1078783)
and a limited company (no. 3880647)
that supports the activity of the Awakened Heart Sangha.
The Awakened Heart Sangha is a spiritual community
under the direction of Lama Shenpen Hookham.

www.ahs.org.uk
Email: info@ahs.org.uk

All images (unless otherwise stated) are hard copies from the author's personal collection. Where photographers are unknown, permission has been sought and every effort has been made to contact copyright holders, but if any have been overlooked the author and publishers will be pleased to make the necessary arrangement at the earliest opportunity.

Cover image:
Main photo of Snowdon from Llyn y Dywarchen by Tara Dew.
Lama Shenpen Hookham as a nun, 1977, author's collection.

Recommendations for
Keeping the Dalai Lama Waiting

'Lama Shenpen Hookham is an inspiring figure in the world of Tibetan Buddhism with her great knowledge of the precious Buddhadharma and mastery of the Tibetan language. *Keeping the Dalai Lama Waiting* chronicles some of the most exhilarating and compelling stories of Lama Shenpen's extraordinary life as a Buddhist nun and translator for great Tibetan masters and her own rich spiritual journey. It is so wonderful that she has chosen to share these poignant and personal experiences. May they inspire and encourage others along their own exploration of innate wisdom.'

> — *Her Eminence Khandro Rinpoche, teacher in the Kagyu and Nyingma lineages of Tibetan Buddhism. Author of 'This Precious Life'*

'Lama Shenpen Hookham is not only an acclaimed scholar but also a well-known and highly respected teacher of Tibetan Buddhism. She tells here the entertaining and inspiring stories of her extraordinary journey where she encounters some of the greatest Tibetan Masters of the 20th century.'

> - *Ringu Tulku Rinpoche, Buddhist monk, teacher and author*

'This is a fascinating personal account of a young English woman finding a connection with Tibetan lamas and nuns during and after the 1970s in India and Nepal. Shenpen lived in nunneries and Dharma centres and her story highlights her close relationship with several eminent Karma Kagyu lamas in Europe where she served as a translator. This includes her own inner struggle between life as a nun and as a householder. In time Lama Shenpen has set up her own community in Wales which presents the Dharma for Westerners in a way that is both authentic and yet relevant to the students' own needs and cultural background.'

>   – *Jetsunma Tenzin Palmo, author of 'Into the Heart of Life' and 'Reflections on a Mountain Lake'. Founder of Dongyu Gatsal Ling Nunnery*

'The Golden Age of Tibetan Buddhism in the West, when many of the most realised lamas from traditional Tibet were with us, has come and gone. Shenpen Hookham lived through this unique period in history and offers us a poignant and beautiful memoir of her experience with these remarkable people. In addition, hers is an important historical document: vivid, moving, and compelling in its exquisite portraits of truly realised people. I cannot recommend this book too highly to anyone interested in Buddhism, Tibetan Buddhism or the spiritual life in general. An outstanding accomplishment.'

>   – *Reginald Ray, author of several books including 'Touching Enlightenment'. Co-founder and spiritual director of Dharma Ocean Foundation*

'Lama Shenpen is an intrepid, lifelong spiritual explorer, and a wry and engaging storyteller. The combination prompted this reader alternately to burst into tears and laughter, and rightly so. If you too care to laugh and cry for all the right reasons, and expand your horizons in the process, you will want to read this book. In Tibetan we call a lama's life story a 'namtar', which means a model or exemplary life that frees your mind. This is such a story.'

> — *Tulku Sherdor, author of 'A Path Strewn with Flowers and Bones', translator of 'Mahamudra Teachings of the Supreme Siddhas' by the Eighth Situpa*

'For half a century Lama Shenpen has been a dear heart friend and the living example of a true Bodhisattva's activity endowed with authentic devotion to the Buddhdharma. Her lofty and inspiring autobiography is full of lovely stories, profound philosophical insights and deep teachings through examples of awakened activities. It offers an inner vision on Buddhist communities settling and growing in the West. From heart to heart I recommend it to all Dharma practitioners.'

> — *Lama Denys Rinpoche, Head of the Shangpa Rimay Community, Former President of the European Buddhist Union*

'Lama Shenpen is not just a highly-qualified Buddhist practitioner and teacher, but someone who really cares about her students' welfare and progress on the path. Her approach to transmitting the traditional Indo-Tibetan Buddhist teachings in a way that makes them truly accessible for the hearts and minds of people in this so very different day and age is skilful, committed and innovative. This approach also shines through in her book, which not only includes very delightful and instructive episodes from her own Dharma journey, but also profound insights and methods on how to present Buddhism to contemporary audiences. Last but not least, it is such a joy that a capable female teacher raises her voice in her very own way in the otherwise male-dominated Tibetan tradition. May her gentle yet determined lioness's roar be heard everywhere!'

> — *Karl Brunnholzl, translator and author of several books including 'The Heart Attack Sutra' and 'Luminous Melodies'*

'Keeping the Dalai Lama Waiting' is a delightful memoir of a Western woman's training in the Tibetan Buddhist tradition. I was moved by Lama Shenpen's humility and directness and by her extraordinary discipline, both in meditation and in study. I especially enjoyed reading about her personal encounters with some of the most extraordinary teachers of Tibetan Buddhism of the last century. Shenpen really evokes what it is like to be a Dharma student. Her book focuses on living experience, not dry theory. Shenpen points to the power of seemingly ordinary student teacher encounters, and how much transpires in intimate, tender, humorous moments of connection so central to the spiritual path.'

> — *Judy Lief, student of Chögyam Trungpa Rinpoche, editor of many of his books and author of 'Making Friends with Death'*

'Lama Shenpen has written an engaging account of her spiritual journey from its earliest stages as a small child who wanted to be a nun to her present life as an acknowledged teacher of Mahamudra in the Kagyu tradition and founder of the Awakened Heart Sangha.

The tale is plainly told and leads us through her very unusual experiences as a young Buddhist nun in North India, studying with many prominent lamas of the Tibetan Kagyu tradition, including the 16th Karmapa himself. This was at a time when very few Tibetan teachers had been to the West or knew English and the Western mentality, and very few Westerners, women especially, were able to talk with them.

This is one of the most interesting aspects of her story: her own struggle to understand what she was being taught, given her completely different cultural outlook. She faces this with honesty and intelligence – and very strong faith. Indeed, her faith and determination stand out and make this book a source of inspiration and encouragement to any Buddhist practitioner who reads it. Perhaps women will find it especially stirring, for she went very boldly into an environment that could be quite dangerous for a single woman, travelling and living alone. She is clearly a woman of great and fierce courage.

I would recommend this book for its inspiration and example of courage, faith and determination, and for its revelation of a particular phase in the translation of the the Dharma into the Western cultural context and the emergence of Western Dharma teachers. We owe such pioneers as Lama Shenpen a great debt of gratitude.'

> -   *Subhuti, Preceptor and Former Chair of the College of Public Preceptors of the Triratna Buddhist Order, Author of ' Sangharakshita: A New Voice in the Buddhist Tradition', 'Seven Papers', with Urgyen Sangharakshita, and more.*

'Lama Shenpen tells a good story, and she has a very inspiring and enjoyable story to tell. She is one of a pioneering generation of Westerners who went to Asia determined to learn about Tibetan Buddhism and seriously practise it. That meant engaging with some of the greatest lamas of the 20th century, and her anecdotes and reminiscences really bring them to life. It is also a tale of great dedication, effort and sacrifice, as first she devotes herself to her own practice and then to passing on what she has learnt to other Westerners.'

> — *Vessantara, author of several books including 'A Guide to the Buddhas', 'A Guide to the Bo-dhisattvas' and 'A Guide to the Deities of the Tantra'*

Contents

Maps of India & Nepal...x

Foreword by the Author xiii

Acknowledgements...xiv

Prologue xv

One: How I Became a Buddhist.. 1

Two: Living the Life of a Nun in India 21

Three: Learning from Karma Thinley Rinpoche 38

Four: New-found Independence 59

Five: Learning from Bokar Rinpoche 85

Six: Pilgrimage, Ordination and Retreat................................... 111

Seven: What is the Nature of Mind?........................... 131

Eight: Keeping the Dalai Lama Waiting 149

Nine: Return to the West 158

Ten: Becoming a Translator 170

Eleven: Meeting Khenpo Rinpoche & Disrobing 201

Twelve: Becoming a Scholar at Oxford 234

Thirteen: Marriage & Reconnecting to Trungpa Rinpoche 246

Fourteen: What is Buddha Nature? 274

Fifteen: Becoming a Lama 291

Glossary of People.. 316

Glossary of Terms... 326

The Teachings of Lama Shenpen Hookham 335

About the Author...336

Publisher's Note 337

Maps of Places Referred to in the Book

India & Nepal

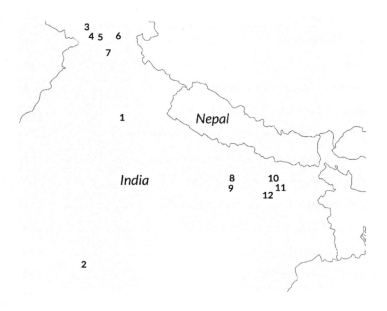

1. New Delhi
2. Ajanta Caves
3. Dalhousie
4. Tilokpur Nunnery
5. Dharamsala
6. Manali
7. Tso Pema Monastery
8. Sarnath
9. Varanasi
10. Patna
11. Rajgir
12. Bodhgaya

Detailed Map of Northern India, Sikkim & Nepal

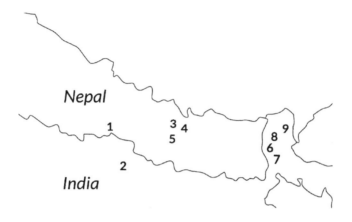

1. Lumbini
2. Kushinagar
3. Swayambhunath, Kathmandu
4. Boudhanath, Kathmandu
5. Asura Cave, Yanglesho/Pharping
6. Darjeeling
7. Sonanda
8. Rumtek, Sikkim
9. Gangtok, Sikkim

Foreword by the Author

My life has spanned a fascinating era in the history of Buddhist ideas coming to the West. Fifty years ago, the idea of a Westerner calling themselves a Buddhist was a source of amusement for many people, while now it is far more respected and respectable. People from all walks of life talk about liking to meditate sometimes, and Buddha images are used as a symbol for peace and tranquillity to such an extent they appear in pubs, shops, garden centres and television advertisements. Mindfulness, like meditation, has become a household word in modern society.

Since mindfulness and meditation are central to the Buddhist path, it seems to me to be a tremendous leap forward that here in the West people now recognise them as important and useful, although it remains to be seen to what extent this will lead to more people adopting the whole Buddhist approach to life. It has been the life's work of pioneers like myself to try to bridge the gap and help Westerners connect to an oriental spiritual tradition. I am hoping my stories will go some way to helping to introduce more of the cultural context into which those spiritual teachings fit.

Everyone's life contains riches and encounters that make wonderful stories. I miss out many events, people, angles and facets of my own life which somehow didn't come into the foreground as this narrative emerged. I would like to express my apologies to the people concerned, and my regret for the stories missed. Maybe I will tell them another time.

Lama Shenpen Hookham

Acknowledgements

Since the stories in this book span the seventy-four years of my life, there are too many people involved in it to acknowledge and thank for their contribution to both my life and the book, so I will restrict myself to those who helped bring this book together. In the 1980s Katie Morrow typed out the handwritten vignettes of my time in India. Twenty years later I started to compile them into a book with the help of Silvina Milstein. Six years later Jonathan Shaw picked up the project and about ten of my students read through the work done so far and made comments to which I responded. All the readers enjoyed the stories so much they just wanted more. They also wanted more context of my life as a whole that they could fit the stories into.

Four years later Elizabeth Cochrane was given the project of turning the book into a narrative spanning my whole life and preparing it for publication. This meant shaping and shortening it. From then on, the work was talked of more as an autobiography than as a collection of stories or vignettes, yet I still wanted to call the book 'Keeping the Dalai Lama Waiting and Other Stories', in order to retain the spirit of its original form. Naomi Levine gave me some useful advice at a point where I was really flagging and finally Tara Dew helped Elizabeth and me bring together the final draft that Gonzalo Perilhou, Dashu, Jo Bourke and their team prepared for publishing. Meanwhile Gabriele Reifenberg (Yeshe Palmo), Alan Fealdman and Leslie (K-Tso) Peters prepared the audiobook. Thank you to all of you for keeping me going with your consistent encouragement, patience and hard work. May this book, the result of all our efforts, bring enjoyment to all its readers and inspire them on their path to Awakening.

Prologue

It is forty years since I returned from the East and disrobed as a Buddhist nun. I am an old lady now, living in semi-retreat in the wilds of north-west Wales.

This is a sacred land steeped in ancient myths and legends of gods, saints and chieftains including King Arthur who is said to have been born and died here.

From my window I am looking into the distance at the twin peaks of Snowdon emerging from the clouds as the sun rises from behind them. It is where King Arthur's knights are said to lie ready to rise up at the hour of our greatest need.

In the foreground are fields of sheep and woodlands and to the south the drowned kingdom lying under Cardigan Bay. To the north is the Island of Anglesey where the Druids made their last stand and to the west the holy Island of Bardsey that some say is Avalon.

I look out at all this from Ynys Graianog, the Island of Stones, known also as the Hermitage of the Awakened Heart, where stands a fully consecrated Buddhist stupa proclaiming peace, freedom and prosperity for one and all. It is a ten-foot high monument symbolising the Buddha, the Awakened One, and contains the relics of Enlightened beings.

'When the current of spiritual tradition starts to weaken and run dry, it is good for it to be revived from a source from elsewhere,' remarks a local Welsh church-goer. 'The people here are disenchanted with the church and chapel, but have a natural spirituality that is looking for a means of expression,' remarks a Welsh-speaking writer and broadcaster.

Is this why the great Enlightened master Dilgo Khyentse Rinpoche directed us to this area to build a stupa?

At the last moment of its consecration in 2011, the clouds parted and the sun burst through as if to symbolise the Buddha's spiritual Awakening that dispels the confusion obscuring our heart's primordial wisdom.

The story that follows tells you how I ended up here and, even more importantly, introduces you to the people who inspired me along the way, that they might inspire you too.

One

How I Became a Buddhist

As a child all by myself in the playground, I did a handstand against the school wall. As I stood up, the thought came to me out of the blue that I was not going to be like other people. I was going to be a great nun. It was as if the voice of God Himself had called me, but could I be sure and what could it mean?

The sense that I had been called to be a nun never left me, but I was far too embarrassed to ever mention this to anyone. I'd never met a nun and hardly knew what a nun's life was like but logic told me that if God existed, was almighty and compassionate, the only thing that made sense was to give one's life to him. Being a nun seemed an obvious choice. I wondered if it meant praying all day. Could I do that? Maybe it would be easier and just as good to be a missionary. What about Gladys Aylward in the film 'The Inn of the Sixth Happiness', courageously leading a singing band of orphaned children through the Chinese mountain passes to safety? I imagined myself like that, feeling uplifted with a sense of mission as I sang to myself again and again the school hymn:

> He who would valiant be
> 'Gainst all disaster
> Let him in constancy
> Follow the Master!

I sometimes woke up at dawn and sang hymns really loudly just because I loved words like glory, holy, almighty, and stirring lines such as these, from another hymn we sang at school:

And let me set free with the sword of my youth
From the castle of darkness, the power of the Truth!

My poor brothers in the next room yelled at me to shut up and let them sleep. 'If you must sing, then at least don't sing flat,' they wailed. I wondered what 'flat' meant and just carried on regardless.

I was growing up in Essex just after the Second World War in a terraced house in Westcliff-on-Sea with my parents and two brothers. My father worked in London as an engineer and my mother was a housewife with a gift for looking after young children. They both brought us up to be confident and independent-minded. In many ways I couldn't have wanted for better parents. Only very occasionally as I grew up did the topic of nuns come up but whenever it did both my parents remarked in no uncertain terms that being a nun was a waste of a life, so there was no way I was going to tell them what I thought. Since my father didn't believe in God, I could understand why he thought as he did, but my mother was a believer, so what was she thinking?

My father's atheism bothered me and I wanted to convert him. At fourteen I thought I had found a knock-down argument proving God existed. My first opportunity to try to convince my father happened to be while he was on the loo. Speaking from outside the lavatory door I told him I could prove God existed. 'Go on then,' he said. I started with the premise the vicar had used in our confirmation classes, which I presumed must be all right. 'Everything has a beginning, doesn't it?' I said. Straight off, my father replied, 'Why do you assume that?' and with that question, I realised my whole argument had collapsed – a salutary and humbling lesson in clear thinking.

There seemed to be no limit to my urge to convert. I heard on the radio that the Dalai Lama, the god-king, was escaping from Tibet. 'He is probably a good person,' I thought, 'but one day I should go and tell him that he is not a god.' In the sixth form at school we discussed Buddhism in the RE class. 'It sounds good to me,' I said. Someone asked why I was not a Buddhist then. 'Jesus came after the Buddha, so his must be the most recent revelation from God,' I said. 'Why should that make Christianity more true?' replied a classmate. I had no answer but was still slow to give up my view.

My teenage years were not easy due to my mother's mental illness. She had chronic arthritis from her early twenties and now suffered increasingly violent mood swings, later diagnosed as schizophrenia. Vivacious and intelligent, she had married at eighteen, during the war, and she felt trapped by her choices in life made so young. She railed against my father and myself as if her misery were our fault, sometimes keeping the whole family awake at night as she stormed around the house acting out her frustration and fury. Her illness and suffering were constantly on my mind. I longed to find some way to understand and relieve them. Could my prayers actually heal her if I had enough faith? Such questions haunted me.

Cycling home from school one day, I was happily asking myself another question – how did I know I existed? It took me to an amazing and strange place of not knowing. Wanting to share this experience with my mother, I innocently asked, 'How do you know you exist?' It was more than my poor mother's fragile state of mind could handle. 'Don't you ever ask me a question like that again!' she exclaimed with a cry of alarm, leaving me feeling quite puzzled. What had I done wrong?

My father would reach his wits' end at times but mostly just told us children to be kind and understanding to our mother. Once, though, he came home from work to find my mother and myself distraught after some sort of scene. Without knowing what had gone on, having calmed my mother down, he came to where I was in tears on my bed, tousled my hair and told me it would all change and be forgotten by tomorrow. The contrast with my mother's constant needling was stark. I recognised the profound wisdom in his words and yet wondered how an atheist could be so wise.

Normally for me it was God that kept me sane. I prayed almost daily, but it wasn't just an attempt to cope with difficulties. I associated prayer with a sense of well-being and joy, and I just couldn't imagine how others managed without it. God was my name for that sense of an all-pervading benign presence that I could open to and align with.

I loved thinking. After leaving school I had spent a year doing voluntary service on the South Atlantic island of St Helena. One of the other volunteers and I had spent many a star-lit tropical evening, in the company of local children and passers-by, sitting on our doorstep looking out over the main street talking endlessly about deep questions such as the nature of awareness and what it meant to be more aware.

At Reading University in 1965, I still had the mission to convert others. The truth is that I ended up a Buddhist out of my zealous wish to prove Christianity was the one true religion! I began attending the meetings of other faith groups and was inspired by many of the people I met, especially some of the Sudanese and Somali Muslims. These were deeply spiritual people and it was clearly not going to be easy to even understand their religion let alone show them the error of their ways.

One evening, I attended a University Buddhist Society meeting at which the evening's speaker was a shaven-headed, brown-robed Buddhist monk. He impressed me by his presence. Slowly and deliberately, he said, 'The mind has great power. Look at your mind,' and had us sit and look at it in silence for a few minutes with him. I found this was extraordinary. Even though my mind could scarcely hold an object in focus for any length of time, I believed what he was saying about its power. I was intrigued as to what this might mean.

I had been looking at my mind since early childhood. Cycling uphill to school against the wind in the driving rain, hot and panting, glasses steamed up, feeling miserable, it would suddenly occur to me to ask 'Who is feeling miserable?' I didn't know and somehow this brought me an unexpected sense of relief. Walking home from senior school one day, I was looking at my mind, wondering whether it was possible to think without words. I was so engrossed that I wasn't looking where I was going and nearly bumped into a lamp-post! So looking at my mind was something I was familiar with, but not like this – not as a whole important discipline in its own right. Being given it as a serious practice and sitting in silence with a roomful of people doing it together was a whole different ball-game. As far as I was concerned the only honest thing to do was to take up the challenge and look at my mind. I was hooked.

My friends and I decided to meditate together in my college room. It was a far-out thing to do in those early days and we were taking it very seriously. We carefully hung a notice on my door saying 'Do not disturb. Meditation in progress', with the added note 'for five minutes'. I was impressed with how many thoughts I could have at one time and wondered if I was unique in that.

I was not attracted by the exoticism of Buddhism. I wasn't even particularly attracted by the Buddha image – partly because my idea of compassion meant looking tortured and distraught. Compared to Jesus the Buddha looked too content and self-satisfied, so I didn't associate him with compassionate action in the world. Instead, I took Buddhism to be a system of knowledge based on the truth of direct experience. Because it wasn't presented as a belief system that you accept without question, it seemed to be more like science than religion. What really appealed to me about it was that it was a rigorous quest for truth and there was a path to Enlightenment you could actually follow, with the help of *teachers.* I was very excited about this last possibility.

When I read in a Buddhist scripture called the Dharmapada that the mind is fickle, I immediately recognised that this was the truest thing I knew about my mind. I had never been quite convinced about my being a sinner but I *knew in my direct experience* that my mind was fickle. If a whole system of deep thought could be based on such a simple truth, how could I not pursue it? The Buddhists say that although the mind may be fickle, it can be tamed. The way to do that is through meditation. I had already started meditating most days, but now I upped my game and started attending more events. On a Zen weekend retreat at the London Buddhist Society, the Roshi told us to meditate on Mu. At my personal interview with him I had nothing to say. He said to me, 'Mu is the spirit of God,' and something in me opened up.

At Christmas, I spent a week at the Thai temple in East Sheen sleeping in a shed, one of a row of them, in the garden. On the back of the door was a timetable telling me to meditate from five in the morning till eleven at night, so I did. I sat in the main house shrine room all day watching my abdomen rise and fall, my mind wandering, nearly dropping off from time to time as the hours went by. Each day I went for a meditation interview with the abbot, called the Chao Kuhn, and he asked, 'How are you getting on?' Since I assumed he knew my mind without my saying anything, all I said was, 'Better than yesterday.' I kept this up day after day. In fact, nothing much happened till one night, a light flashed on and off in the darkness of the shed. There was no light – it was my mind! Stumbling back to the house in the dark, I found some Westerners who told me, 'We have to go through all kinds of madness on our way to Enlightenment.' I returned to my shed reassured. After a good night's sleep, things seemed to settle down and a day or two later I got back to college. Back in my room I lay on my bed only to find my body shaking involuntarily for half an hour. It was alarming but I thought, 'This experience, like all other experiences, must be impermanent,' and it was. For days after that I felt blissfully happy.

An artist friend, Peter, who was the chairman of the University Buddhist Society, loaned me a book of Zen Buddhist sayings called 'Zen Flesh Zen Bones'. It was full of enigmatic little phrases and riddles, the famous koans that are used for meditation in the Japanese tradition. Pointing to an intuitive reality beyond reason, there is an elusive simplicity about them, both profound and immediate. The possibility of a new faculty of vision that goes beyond ordinary thinking was opening up, a new dimension to experience – fresh and alive. I *loved* the book and I had a deep feeling that something crucial was happening to me. Within a week or so I was no longer Christian and I thought of myself as a Buddhist.

There was no crisis of belief or any sense of backlash. I just went smoothly from being Christian to being Buddhist. My interest was to find out what direct experience meant. I responded very readily to the suggestion that God was just an idea that I was clinging onto and let that idea go. It seemed to me that Buddhism was offering me a way of knowing that wasn't just about my own made-up ideas. Had I ever really believed in the Christian God or had it always been my name for all that was most inspiring and nearest to truth in my life? Words like glory, holy and almighty had always been about a truth that went beyond words for me, as expressed in these lines from George Herbert:

'A man that looks on glass, on it may stay his eye;
  Or if he pleaseth through it pass, and then the heaven espy.'

It seems I had always been inspired by another way of looking. If as it says in St. John's Gospel, God was in me and I was in Him, how could I be a miserable sinner? Although part of me had tried to take on board a whole package of religious beliefs, I cannot have been all that convinced by them since I gave them all up so easily.

I took my leave of God praying my last prayer something like this, 'Dear God, this is my last prayer to you. I have followed you to the best of my ability and am grateful for your love, teaching and protection. If you are there, you know it is through your grace that I have arrived at the wonderful teachings of the Buddha. If you made me, then you made my intelligence and my intelligence tells me that this is the way to go. If I am making a mistake then you must show me, but do not think that to appear in a vision will impress me. Visions are just creations of the mind.' I added that last bit because the books on Buddhism warned against visions as likely to be deceptive. There were no indications from God that I was taking a wrong path and there was not much discontinuity between my Christian and Buddhist self except for the fact prayer and faith had lost their meaning. Instead I now meditated on a regular basis for anything up to an hour a day.

That is how it all started. Not only did I not think in terms of having faith in the Buddha, I wasn't interested in fundamental Buddhist ideas such as karma and rebirth. I was only interested in the path to Enlightenment and how to reach it as quickly as possible, as if it were some kind of elevated state of perfection in which you had perfect knowledge.

I imagined a well-trodden path to deeper knowledge, something I never suspected existed as a Christian. Best of all there were Enlightened beings, called Buddhas and Bodhisattvas, who could teach and guide you to Enlightenment. The philosopher in me heaved a sigh of relief. The job had been done. The truth was known. It had already been discovered two and half thousand years ago by the Buddha. I had found the path and I was determined to follow it through to the end.

Meanwhile, I was doing so well in Philosophy, my subsidiary subject for the first year of my BA, that my tutors told me to make it my main subject. My father forbade it, telling me it would be useless when it came to finding a job. He wasn't to know the direction my life was going to take and that studying Philosophy would have served me well. I didn't feel strongly enough about it to oppose him at the time. Since I saw the way forward as meditation and looking directly at the mind, I felt no need for Philosophy any more. Nonetheless, I continued with my joint honours degree in Sociology and Geography.

I started helping Peter run the Buddhist Society and we invited eminent teachers to give talks. One of these teachers was Sangharakshita, an English monk with shaved head and saffron robes. He had just arrived back from India where he had trained for around twenty years since he was a young man. He was now trying to set up a Buddhist movement for serious practitioners in the West. His talks were always packed. One evening he gave a talk entitled 'Mind – Reactive and Creative', having brought with him a small team of people to record it. The idea of recording a talk was unusual and struck us as very exciting. Sangharakshita had an aura of authority and grandeur about him, to the extent that we had to be reminded that even he needed to go to the loo sometimes. He was a clear and arresting speaker, so the room was spellbound as he explained that our mind can respond or react. At that very moment a late-comer started to open the door and all our heads turned to look. 'That is the mind reactive,' he observed with a gentle smile and then he expanded on the meaning of the mind responsive – a mind free to choose.

My friends and I decided to hitch up to London and back to attend his meditation classes once a week in Monmouth Street. They took place in a small room that held about ten to fifteen people, in the basement of an oriental lacquer shop. It was dimly lit and yet felt strangely peaceful and spacious. Sangharakshita led the meditation by chanting for about five minutes in the Pali language and we alternately sat and walked in meditation, watching our breath, for about an hour. Eventually we gave up going to London when it occurred to us we could just as well meditate at home in Reading.

At around this time I had a breakthrough in my thinking. It suddenly became blindingly obvious to me that time is mind and mind is time. They seem like two separate things, but in fact they are both aspects of one reality. Time is a movement or shift in the mind. It is not something other than mind. The mind only knows anything because it is also time, the time that allows knowledge to appear to itself. I was sure this was a major and significant discovery and couldn't wait to tell my fellow students, thinking maybe I had come up with one of the greatest revelations of our time. No-one was especially interested though.

Sangharakshita came a number of times, sometimes eating with us in our attic flat. I told him about my experience at the Thai Temple and he advised me that the methods used in the Far East to intensify concentration are good for people who are very relaxed, but not always good for people like us Westerners who tend to be rather tense in comparison. His answer confirmed my belief that these Buddhist teachers knew what they were talking about. He suggested to me that I take meditation instruction from Trungpa Rinpoche, a Tibetan lama whom I assumed was Enlightened.

I had noticed in his talks Sangharakshita always spoke modestly about how *we* unenlightened beings behave. I took this to mean that he didn't claim to be Enlightened himself. Disappointedly I concluded that since he wasn't Enlightened, he wasn't going to be able to enlighten me. It seemed only right that he should point me to Trungpa Rinpoche who would.

On a sunny summer's day in 1967, my heart was singing as I cycled to the outskirts of Reading to the modest home of a middle-aged couple who were hosting Trungpa Rinpoche. I was excitedly anticipating the day ahead in the company of an Enlightened master and already thinking in terms of surrendering my life to him.

Our first encounter was relatively low key as we spent the day chatting about this and that. He was in the traditional maroon robes of a Tibetan monk, quietly spoken, yet relaxed and interested in everything. I felt at ease in his company, though a little startled when towards the end of the day he commented that I never wasted a moment. He had clearly been observing me! I wondered what he meant but didn't ask. Was he noticing that I was trying to be awake and aware all the time? Or was it simply that I was busy knitting a sweater for my boyfriend as we talked?

There was a quality to his presence, his attentiveness to detail, his poise, openness and thoughtful clarity that satisfied my longing for someone I could trust to guide me. At the dinner table, somebody asked him what, as a Tibetan refugee, he thought of the Chinese. He didn't answer straightaway; it seemed he was gathering his thoughts. The conversation moved on, so it was about ten minutes before she remembered her question and repeated it. I was struck by Trungpa Rinpoche's patience in waiting to be asked again before speaking. He clearly had his answer prepared this time as he immediately said, 'The Chinese think you can change society and that this will alter people's minds and behaviour, but I believe you have to change people's minds and behaviour first, after which society will naturally change.' He observed that the West has something called a social conscience and expressed regret that such a sentiment didn't exist in the East. 'People believe in karma and rebirth and tend to act in order to secure happiness for themselves in this and future lives. It stops them developing the strong sense of social responsibility that you have here in the West. It is something the East could learn from the West.'

His comments struck a chord. My social conscience troubled me greatly. For as long as I could remember I had been torn between whether to devote myself to the contemplative way of life or social action. I knew most people found it hard to think a contemplative life was compassionate. For me it was a matter of principle. If there was a higher purpose to life and the contemplative was privy to it, then that way of life had to be the most direct and powerful way of helping humanity. As Trungpa Rinpoche had made clear, we had to change ourselves in order to change society.

The meeting in the evening was packed. As we sat in the dimly lit common room where Trungpa Rinpoche was about to speak, I felt an aura of deep peace, ease and authority about him. It wasn't so much that I believed in him as that I had no doubts. I was sitting on the floor right in front of him, looking up into his somewhat strange face that was hard to read, which lent it an air of mystery. He seemed to be talking about how the world began, how it emerged from primordial space or emptiness and how everything came to be – how we all came to be – as if he were talking, at the same time, of my own most intimate experience of being. In retrospect I realise he must have been talking from the perspective of some of the innermost teachings of Tibetan Buddhism, the Dzogchen teachings about how the world of appearance arises from the primordial ground. I was dumbfounded, propelled into a whole different mind-space without being able to say a thing about what it was I had just heard, except that it was profoundly significant and what I had always wanted to hear.

He came several times to talk to the University Buddhist Society and as secretary I was there to welcome him. I also went at least three times to visit him at Samye Ling, his retreat centre in the middle of nowhere among the hills of Dumfriesshire. It had been founded just the year before my first visit and was one of the earliest Tibetan Buddhist centres to be established in the West.

At dawn, on my first trip to Samye Ling, after a wearying overnight coach ride from Reading I was met in Dumfries by a tall Texan sent to pick several of us up. After a twenty-six-mile ride through wild and rugged countryside we reached our destination and were met at the door by a friendly Tibetan man who carried my bags up to my bedroom. I thanked him and held out my hand, introducing myself as Susan Rowan. He took my hand and introduced himself as Akong. I thought he must have been one of the staff working as a guest assistant, but it turned out that he was one of the lamas that escaped from Tibet with Trungpa Rinpoche and was also referred to with the title 'Rinpoche', meaning precious one. He was much less formal than Trungpa Rinpoche, acting more like a servant than a teacher, and didn't wear monk's robes. I asked him if he thought Buddhism would enable me to help my mother and he said 'yes'. I thought, 'At last, a way to help her!' It was a tremendous weight off my mind.

I was still young and impressionable – everything was so fresh and new that I was scarcely aware that it was the same for everyone there. I was among its first flush of visitors, a handful of residents and guests from various countries and backgrounds, eating our meals in the ramshackle kitchen with Akong Rinpoche, whose enigmatic remarks struck me as both startling and profound. I admired the fact that when we rose at dawn the hand-washed sheets of the guests were already hanging out in the morning mist to dry. This was all Akong Rinpoche's doing. He seemed to do everything, including serving Trungpa Rinpoche, who only occasionally appeared from his room upstairs.

The front room downstairs was referred to as the shrine room, and it was where we all meditated together morning and evening. There was an altar with offerings in front of Buddha images and a high throne to one side for the

Karmapa. I was told he was the head of the Karma Kagyu spiritual lineage to which Trungpa Rinpoche belonged. He was obviously held in high regard. They said he knew the three times, past, present and future, but I didn't understand what that meant. I stared bemusedly at a cheap looking woman's brooch with glistening paste stones reflecting various colours placed on the altar, among the other offerings of flowers, candles, incense, rice and water. Through the lens of my own conditioned thinking, it looked completely incongruous. Trungpa Rinpoche clearly didn't share my concepts of 'cheap, nasty and poor taste'!

I was asked if I wanted a personal interview with him. This was a novelty for me and I accepted the invitation. It didn't occur to me that in Tibet easy access like this to such a great being would have been a rarity. As I entered the rather dark room for my first formal interview, Trungpa Rinpoche was sitting quietly silhouetted against the window. I sat down opposite him. He talked to me about meditation and told me to meditate outside, gazing into space, using the image of being immersed in an ocean of awareness. Interestingly, when my friend Peter asked whether he should also do this, Trungpa Rinpoche said no – that he should meditate inside. It was clear that he was tailoring his advice to each student individually.

Rinpoche explained how in meditation one should greet thoughts as guests, welcoming each guest without lingering so long on one guest that one neglects the next one. Welcoming thoughts means to recognise thoughts as thoughts, appreciating them as such and simply being aware of them without reacting. As I reflected on this I found it affecting my whole attitude to life and my relationships with people, both those I found easy to be with and those with whom I had difficulty. Just as I could welcome all thoughts, good and bad, I could welcome all people.

I told him that I didn't know anything about Buddhism and asked him if there was anything I should read. He thought for a moment or two, and then suggested I read Meister Eckhart, a great medieval Christian mystic, and Krishnamurti, a non-denominational 20th century Indian teacher. I didn't take up his suggestion straightaway. In fact, it was many years before I read their works. Had I done it at the time I am sure I would have responded to the natural depth and resonance of the language in them. It was as if he saw into my soul and knew how at home I always felt with God-language.

Early one morning, standing on the porch of the main house, listening to the gentle tinkle of the wind chimes, I looked out at the swirling mist that filled the valley as the dawn sunlight started to break through. Then as if from nowhere, I heard the distant sound of a wild duck flying across the expanse of the sky from right to left, quacking as it went, coming in and out of view through the fast-moving clouds. I followed it with my eyes until it was out of sight. At dusk that day in the failing light, back in the meditation room, someone read aloud Trungpa Rinpoche's poem the 'Silent Song of Loneliness', which he had just written, and which was published a few years later in his collection 'Mudra'.

> The wild duck, companionless,
> Cries out in desolate loneliness
> And flies alone, wings outspread,
> Soaring in the boundless sky.

It was as if something or someone was calling to me from beyond time and space with an image that spoke to the very depths of my heart.

Another evening he gave a talk that later appeared in his book 'Meditation in Action'. He used the image of throwing clay on a potter's wheel, saying that if one throws it well, it creates a perfect pot every time. The image made such a strong impression on me that, at a personal interview, I asked him what it meant. He simply repeated what he had said, leaving the image to tantalise and haunt me for years to come. He explained when we can throw our clay like that, effortlessly, our every action will be perfect every time. Decades later, I am still contemplating this image, having asked several lamas about it. They have always hesitated to explain it.

He had just published his first book, 'Born in Tibet', about his life and training as a reincarnate lama in Tibet and his escape to India. On reading it, I realised that his life in Tibet had been austere and lonely in many ways and his escape from the Chinese horrific. I associated him with all the contemplative life was about – the sacred, the simple life and serenity.

On my last visit to Samye Ling, I sensed something strange in the atmosphere. I had shared a room with two giggling teenage girls whispering to each other all night in muffled voices. I could only make out the names 'Akong' and 'Trungpa' uttered in decidedly familiar terms. I was left feeling very puzzled, but successfully put aside my misgivings.

Back at University, as an expression of my wish to do something active about the state of the world, I joined the United Nations Student Association (UNSA) and helped to run it. At that time, the Vietnam War had been raging for some years, and I persuaded my fellow students in UNSA that we should campaign against it. We decided to investigate prevailing attitudes, and distributed a questionnaire amongst our fellow students, only to find an appalling degree of ignorance. A fair proportion of the students did not even know who the main protagonists in the war were, let alone what constituted British policy. I found the apathy around me disturbing. Why wasn't everyone up in arms about the cruelty and wanton destruction shown in documentary films of the time?

Somehow it felt wrong to experience any happiness at all while others suffered that way. I found relief when I could weep about it, but having cried myself to sleep one night, I was surprised to find that I woke the next morning feeling really happy. That worried me. Why would the heartfelt sense of other people's pain bring with it any kind of joy, or even relief? How could it be that the more deeply I felt compassion for the sufferings of others, the happier I felt in myself? It was only decades later I came to realise that when we feel compassion we are in alignment with our true nature, which is naturally joyous.

My friends and I in UNSA mobilised demonstrations against the war in Vietnam. So few people came that we were hardly mentioned in the press and it felt as though we were swimming against the tide. Then, in March 1968, in the build-up to the famous Grosvenor Square riots outside the US Embassy in London, we arrived for a UNSA meeting that we had organised at the college to find a huge excited crowd around the door, waiting to attend. The room was hardly big enough to hold everybody and discussions were loud and passionate. We had been taken over by left wing activists and anarchists. Suddenly bus-loads of demonstrators were being organised to descend on London for the demonstration the next day. Things seemed to be really moving for once – but the talk was aggressive and angry, going against everything I believed in.

On the bus ride into the city the next day, the ring-leaders told us how to divert police violence and avoid arrest. I had never encountered such people before: strongly politicised young men and a few women, passionate and clearly used to police tactics in a big demonstration like this. The situation felt ominous and I was having strong misgivings. What was going on? Did I trust these people? I had only ever heard my communist grandfather talking in such anti-establishment far-left terms and I had never taken him seriously. Surely England was a peaceful country ruled by just laws, the establishment trustworthy and the police there to protect us?

As we demonstrators marched, linked arm in arm, shouting slogans, I was dismayed to see above our heads a murderous message, 'Kill Johnson'. I drew aside and stumbled along the kerb by myself, upset and unsettled, chatting a little to the amiable young policeman escorting us. My friends, so apathetic for so long, were radiant with the excitement of the crowd, shouting, laughing, even dancing up and down waving their arms. I hardly recognised them. I felt alienated and forced to think. No, this was not demonstrating the values that I had come to stand up for. Yet I felt powerless to make my voice heard.

The next day we read in the national newspapers about the mounted police riding into crowds of demonstrators outside the Embassy and realised our nice young policeman had diverted us away from the trouble in the nick of time.

What was that all about? Was this the best one could hope for when standing up for peace? This became the turning point of my life. My uncertainty as to whether to choose an active or a contemplative life came abruptly to an end as I decided an active life trying to change the world externally was likely to be all in vain. We cannot control the outcome of our activism. At any point, whatever we try to do in the outer world can be destroyed overnight. A contemplative life, however, is never wasted if devoted to the path to Awakening. If what I do is good and wholesome it will have positive results regardless of what other people do. I was beginning to think like a Buddhist, but not quite. I was not thinking of future lives and I still didn't have much idea what Enlightenment meant. The point was that I was turning away from the futility of the conditioned world that I was experiencing around me towards what I believed would be ultimately meaningful.

I hadn't forgotten what Trungpa Rinpoche had said about a social conscience. I still believed it was possible to follow the path to Enlightenment or Awakening at the same time as leading an active life – but I was not sure I personally could do both. The only thing in life that made ultimate sense to me was the path to Awakening, and if there was such a path, then I had to pursue it full-time without getting distracted. I was convinced this was the best way to serve the world. This was what I was going to do. For this I was going to have to turn inwards and look at my own mind.

I wrote to Trungpa Rinpoche asking if I could come and join him in Samye Ling on a permanent basis to learn about my mind. The reply from Trungpa Rinpoche took me by surprise. He said I should go to Tilokpur nunnery in India to learn meditation from his friend and colleague, Lama Karma Thinley Rinpoche. He suggested that I write to Ani Kechog Palmo ('Ani' means nun), who was an English Buddhist nun and the Abbess of the nunnery. I was excited about having such a definite sense of direction. I loved adventure and this looked like a really big one.

I was quite unaware that Trungpa Rinpoche normally emphasised to his students that they integrate Buddhism into their lives, rather than jet off as spiritual tourists attracted by the exoticism of the East. Did he have some kind of super-knowledge that told him that I was so strongly Christian in my previous lives that I needed exposure to Eastern culture to open me up to the Buddhist world view and influence? Or was he sending me away because he intuited that if I stayed around him too long, I would be shocked and put off by his, at times, quite outrageous behaviour?

I considered dropping out of University, but something in me said that if you start something, you should finish it, so I stayed on for my final exams and completed my degree, during which time I corresponded with Trungpa Rinpoche from time to time. In one of his letters he mentioned that when you go to a foreign country it is important to respect its culture and not try to convert people to your way of thinking. I found this remark startling, given my childhood fantasies about becoming a missionary.

As soon as I finished my finals, I took on various jobs to raise money for my trip to India. I ended up in north London, from where I travelled daily to my filing job at County Hall. I was once travelling back on the underground with Sangharakshita from one of his talks and I told him about my plan to go out to India and join Ani Kechog Palmo at her nunnery. He cautioned me to think carefully about what I was doing. It was to no avail. My mind was made up. I was going to India to learn meditation from Karma Thinley Rinpoche.

Before going, Trungpa Rinpoche told me to meet him at the London Buddhist Society where he was going to give a talk. I rang up to arrange a meeting, but the receptionist said there would be many people waiting to see him, so it probably wouldn't be possible. I was already torn between that event and going out with Mike, my boyfriend, and the uncertainty about meeting Rinpoche tipped the balance away from going to the Buddhist Society. What did that say about my avowed intention to follow the master? I hardly noticed the irony. Although I was completely changing the direction of my life on Trungpa Rinpoche's instructions, I was so casual and unemotional about missing a chance to see him one more time before I went!

Many years later, I visited Trungpa Rinpoche at his home in Boulder, Colorado, and asked him why he sent me to India. He said quite sweetly, 'To absorb the vibes.'

Two

Living the Life of a Nun in India

All I knew about Ani Kechog Palmo was that she was one of the first Western women to have taken ordination as a nun in Tibetan Buddhism and had been ordained by the Karmapa. She had replied to my request to stay at the nunnery, one of the very first Tibetan Buddhist nunneries in India and was expecting me to work there as a volunteer. It was 1969, less than ten years since the Tibetans had fled from their homeland in the face of the Chinese takeover. They were busy re-establishing in India the monasteries that had been destroyed in Tibet, but nothing much had yet been done for nuns.

Sangharakshita, who had known her from his days in India, told me about Tenzin Palmo, a young English nun who had already been out in India for six years. She has since become well-known from the biography of her life 'Cave in the Snow'. He gave me the address of her mother and I spent an enjoyable evening with her as she regaled me with strange tales of ghosts and miracles experienced in India while visiting her daughter. I was grateful for her sound advice over what to expect and what to take with me. How understanding, supportive and admiring she was of her daughter and her chosen way of life!

In contrast, my parents showed no interest in my plans and why I was going. They simply expressed their disapproval and their opinion that I should be trying to get a proper job and follow a conventional pattern of life. Yet I sat up late into the night, talking about it with my adopted aunt Mollie, a lodger in my maternal grandmother's house. She had known me since my earliest childhood and questioned me about why I was going. On hearing the full account, she insisted, 'You must go. You must find out for yourself or you will never be happy,' and wished me well.

While earning the money for my fare to India, I answered advertisements in the newspaper and newsagents put out by people looking for fellow travellers going overland along the hippy-trail to the Far East. This looked like the cheapest option, but then suddenly the Indian landlord of the bedsit I was renting announced that he could get me a cheap airfare to Delhi with the Asian Music Circle.

I was so focused on my mission that I didn't think about what I would be leaving behind. My boyfriend Mike and I had been together for three happy years. We had met at the International Voluntary Service (IVS) HQ in Reading and often worked on projects helping local people. He was an exceptionally kind and generous person, caring not only for me but all my friends too. He worked in Reading as a telephone engineer and was a great dancer. About a year after I became Buddhist, he decided that he was too and was supportive of my plans to go to India. It didn't occur to me that splitting up with him would be painful for both of us. It wasn't until we, with my best friend from infant school, arrived at the airport that the emotional impact of the parting hit me. Suddenly I realised that I was not going to be seeing him again like this and I was totally amazed to find myself overwhelmed by grief.

My cheap ticket was a plane filler and turned out to be First Class Air India! Here I was leaving for India in style after all those months of contemplating dodgy overland options. The food that was put before me looked exceptionally delicious – but I couldn't eat a thing because of the great lump in my throat. I cried for a week once I got to India, but I didn't waver in my determination and intention. In spite of the tears I was enjoying the sense of adventure, of going into the unknown without ties or obligations, feeling deliciously free.

Descending from the plane in Delhi was like stepping into a steam bath. The heat and the humidity suddenly slowed everything down; everyone was half asleep. Gone was the rushed sense of urgency I had become used to in Europe. Time stopped and didn't speed up again till I set foot in Heathrow airport five and a half years later.

All I had was the name of someone who lived in Delhi, who had offered to pick me up from the airport. The plane touched down in the early afternoon, and I waited at the airport for some hours, not at all sure if anyone would come to meet me. It was the end of the working day when a neatly dressed young office worker turned up and politely introduced himself to me. He was simple and straightforward, taking care of my luggage and making sure I was comfortable riding pillion on his motor scooter. Clearly, he saw it as his duty to take care of me on behalf of his brother, who in turn had only heard about me through friends. This was my first taste of the graciousness of the Indian sense of duty to which I was to owe so much. He and his family humbly opened their home and hearts to me – a total stranger.

I found myself astride his motorbike holding on to him for dear life as dusk descended, weaving through the dust and noise of the jostling late rush-hour traffic. It was a little scary, but I was too tired to take much in. My main feeling was relief that I hadn't been left stranded at the airport.

He and his wife lived in the suburbs with their two school-age children and a small baby. Even though he had a good job, his standard of living was very low by Western standards. It was a one-roomed house, that accommodated the whole family including me, their guest. Chirruping sparrows flew in and out of the windows. Cooking took place on a primus stove on the floor in a little side room where there was a tap and a hole in the floor through which water could drain. There was a squat-loo just outside that was served with a tap and bucket rather than a cistern. The bucket was the nearest there was to a shower – so the tiny room did for everything including bathing and laundry. We ate and slept on simple string beds either in that single room or in the courtyard under the stars.

The family insisted I stay for a number of days, during which time I barely went out and had nothing much to do except sit quietly watching them get on with their lives. Much of the time I just sat staring into space, feeling tearful about Mike and wondering how he was. At last the father informed me that he would take me to the station late that evening for the night train to Pathankot. As I was about to discover, the timing was perfect.

Jung called it synchronicity and I gradually discovered that Tibetans call it auspicious connection (*tendrel*). No sooner was I settled in my seat in the ladies' compartment, having said good-bye to my Indian host, than my attention was drawn to one of the occupants of the carriage, a young American woman with a very loud voice who was shouting angrily at the porter dealing with her luggage. I didn't venture to talk to her straightaway, but then in the middle of the night the ticket inspector came by and asked for our passports. Looking at hers, he read out the name 'Michael Abrahams'. I couldn't believe it! A week or so before I left London, a kindly well-wisher at a Buddhist event had given me the name of his friend, Michael Abrahams, who I assumed was a man. Could this woman be the person he meant? I cautiously asked her if she knew the man I'd met. She did, and exclaimed with delight at having news of her dear friend. As we chatted, I started to see quite a different side of this lady. By some miracle, she was travelling to Tilokpur herself, and so could accompany me there. It was a tiny wayside village on the road up to Dharamsala and she was familiar with it. She was able to tell me about the places and people I was about to meet among the refugee Tibetan lamas and the monastic communities that they were beginning to build.

The next day we descended the train at Pathankot and changed to a bus for our onward journey. I was horrified to find myself surrounded by clamouring beggars, many with tiny babies on their hips, all with their big brown eyes focused on my face and their open hands held out towards me. It was a shock the first time it happened and I never got used to it.

The bus ride from Pathankot to Tilokpur was delightful, if somewhat squashed, bumpy and noisy, with villagers getting in and out with their bundles and livestock at the many stops all along the way. The scenery was glorious, with the Himalayas on the sky line in the distance, flowering trees along the roadside, and a lush and varied landscape under a clear blue sky. As we neared our destination, the road ran alongside a river flowing through paddy fields and pastures. It was idyllic, etching these early impressions of the foothills of the Himalayas indelibly on my mind.

On arrival at the nunnery, I was immediately ushered into a small, bare room where Karma Thinley Rinpoche was sitting on a mattress on the floor. He had been expecting me and asked me some questions about my journey in his idiosyncratic broken English, and I answered as best I could. I was trying to be open to whatever transpired. My initial interview with the Lama was short, since I was tired and hadn't really arrived sufficiently to know what I wanted to ask. My first impression of him was not disappointing. He had a warm, authoritative presence, bright honest brown eyes and an open expression I instinctively trusted. He was a thick-set and well-built man in his mid to late thirties and, in spite of the heat, wore the heavy woollen maroon robes of a Tibetan lama. He hadn't shaved his head for a while so he had a full head of thick black hair about half an inch in length. I looked forward to meeting him again once I was feeling a little less disorientated. Apparently, no sooner had

I left the room than he turned to the young English nun beside him and remarked, 'She big Christianee.' I hadn't said anything to him about having ever been a Christian.

I was to share living quarters with a young English nun called Wongmo who was about my age and had come overland to India following the hippy trail. She had only been in Tilokpur a few months but had already taken nun's ordination despite being very new to Buddhism. She showed me our simple house with its mud floor, shutters rather than windows and a veranda on two sides big enough to sleep out on. It had no kitchen, bathroom or toilet – not even a tap, but was otherwise fairly comfortable, with a lovely breezy atmosphere, placed as it was where the land levelled off above the gentle wooded river valley below.

She led me down to the nearby sacred spring where, at dawn and dusk, the Indian village women wearing brightly coloured saris or tunics and baggy pants gathered, carrying huge pots on their heads, as they collected water and chatted. A mass of water gushed through spouts into the sturdily built stone bathing houses, one for men and one for women. Outside was a pool from which the women filled their pots. I glimpsed a way of life that must have changed little for perhaps thousands of years.

Immediately above the spring was another building and a large flat flagged area. It had been kindly loaned by the villagers to a group of about ten Tibetan nuns to use because their own wattle buildings had gone up in flames just a few months prior to my arrival. It was a public stone building, presumably meant as a place of worship and not for living in, being open to the elements on all sides. I discovered that this was where I was to eat with the nuns. Kitchen facilities were basic: a large clay pot of water and a clay hearth where an Indian villager on her haunches deftly worked culinary miracles of rice, dhal and chapattis, and sometimes also vegetables. Toilet facilities were even more basic. I had it explained to me that you went for a bit of a walk away from any buildings with a small brass pot of water to clean your-self afterwards, making sure to do so with your left hand.

To my relief, I quickly received a letter from Mike, telling me not to worry about him. Having prepared himself for the wrench, he had made sure he went off walking with his friends. He was fine and was getting on with life.

A week or so after my arrival the whole of the nunnery de-camped and travelled with Karma Thinley Rinpoche on a rickety bus over pot-holed roads to the hill station of Dal-housie. I was told that we were going to receive something called 'empowerments' (Skt. *abhisheka*, Tib. *wong*) from a great Enlightened lama called Kalu Rinpoche. This turned out to mean sitting on the floor squashed together with one or two hundred people in a hall not much bigger than a large reception room, listening to him reciting texts from his throne from nine in the morning till six at night, every day for the following three months. Many lamas and monks, old and young, from near and far, were assembled to receive these empowerments – and about twenty Westerners, most of whom had arrived via the overland hippy trail, their inter-est in Buddhism having been aroused by experiences on drugs.

There I was sitting at the feet of Kalu Rinpoche, gazing up into his serene and saintly face, basking in the power of his presence. I kept wondering if this was what sitting at the feet of Jesus had felt like. Every now and then the monks and lamas packed in around the foot of his throne crowded forward to receive the empowerment which he gave by touching our heads with some ritual object or other. I had only a vague idea of what an empowerment was supposed to be, but there was something very impressive about the conviction with which it was being given and received. Rinpoche looked very old and frail, though he was only about sixty.

It was very hot in the crowded room and many of the monks were dozing off as they sat there supposedly listening. Someone started squirting a water pistol into their faces from time to time to wake them up. We wondered who had the cheek to be doing that and gradually realised it was Rinpoche himself as he sat there solemnly reading out the sacred texts. There was just the hint of a smile on his face when he realised he'd been rumbled.

I was staying with Ani Tenzin Palmo, Wongmo and an American woman called Lodro in one room in a flimsy wooden chalet with a corrugated iron roof, perched just below the road and facing out over a dramatic, deep, steep-sided mountain valley with tall, dark coniferous forests rising on both sides. The walls were thin like a garden shed and lined with newspaper to keep out the draughts. Tenzin Palmo and Wongmo had shaven heads and wore the maroon robes of Tibetan monastics. Lodro, like me, had not taken ordination. She wore a traditional Tibetan dress (*chuba*), with her hair scraped back in a single plait. An intrepid Dutch lady, Eugenie, fresh off the hippy trail, moved into the room below.

Unconsciously, yet very quickly, I began to take Ani Tenzin Palmo as my role model. She had come out to India when she was twenty, five years previously. I was twenty-three, so she was just a couple of years older than I was. She was full of fun, unassuming and obviously a completely dedicated Dharma practitioner. I was starting to use the word 'Dharma' for the first time. It is not quite synonymous with Buddhism because it is not an 'ism'. It is the truth that the Buddha taught, the path and the goal. Buddhists listen to Dharma, practise Dharma, realise the Dharma, worship and take refuge in the Dharma.

After a few weeks I decided to have my head shaved too, because I discovered that this is customary for someone like myself devoting at least a period of their life to celibacy and formal Dharma practice. Very quickly the Tibetans started to call me 'ani' and the Westerners around followed suit. Having my head shaved was a strangely moving experience. I felt as if for the first time in my life people could really see me for who I was, a nun – and their kind acceptance of me touched me deeply. One felt so beautiful and clean with a freshly shaved head. Mercifully there weren't any mirrors around, because I am sure I looked awful, like a plucked turkey.

Kalu Rinpoche spent his every waking moment helping others. As well as eight hours a day in the ritual reciting of texts to us, he saw people morning and evening before and after sessions to answer their individual queries and problems. On top of that he spent an hour each evening talking to us Westerners. For him it was a new experience trying to teach people so culturally unprepared for the teachings. He explained to us the nature of samsara, our confused condition of existence that causes us to be reborn again and again in various states of suffering, and he talked about the different possible states in samsara. These states are called the 'six realms' and are populated respectively by hell demons, hungry ghosts, animals, humans, gods and demi-gods. He emphasised to us the different kinds of negative actions that are supposed to cause us to be reborn in them.

I was disappointed. This was not what I had come all the way to India to hear. Did he expect us to believe all this blindly? What had this got to do with investigating one's own direct experience? When I had asked Sangharakashita about rebirth he had just told me not to worry about it, which I hadn't. I had come to India to learn about my mind and about verifiable truth; I was not interested in all this doctrinal stuff being trotted out as if I was just going to swallow it whole. I asked Kalu Rinpoche through his translator why he was telling us all this. He replied that it would stop us just wandering off to the bazaar instead of staying in retreat to meditate. I knew that he was wrong. It wouldn't have that effect for me. Firstly, I had more interest in meditation than in the bazaar and secondly, these stories about the six realms didn't convince me.

Then one day out of the blue he asked us whether, when we were sitting listening to his chanting and our mind wandered off home to the West, our mind was now in the West or the West was now here? This question grabbed me immediately. I considered it from time to time throughout the day as I listened to him chanting. Does the mind go anywhere? Does anything come from somewhere else into the mind? Does the mind stay in one place? If it does, where is that? If the mind is always in one place, how does it seem to go to other places? Rinpoche's question was a seed sown on fertile ground. The more I considered the matter, the more I realised I didn't have an answer – which in itself was a revelation. He was pointing something out to me and yet I couldn't see it. It was tantalising and I was drawn on to explore further. *This* was what I had come here for!

While in Dalhousie I didn't get to speak a lot to Karma Thinley Rinpoche, although he was there every day, sitting very close to the foot of Kalu Rinpoche's throne, listening intently and from time to time taking brief notes on little bits of paper he had about him. However, one morning, we Westerners were sitting in our house wrapped in blankets, holding large steaming enamel mugs of tea between our freezing hands and taking turns to toast sliced bread over the open flame of a kerosene wick burner. We had been woken as ever by the rasping cries of crows as they made their noisy landings on our corrugated iron roof. The rising sun was already lighting up the other side of the deep valley that dropped away hundreds of feet below us. Suddenly there was a clatter of feet on the loose boards of the bridge and balcony that led from the road down to our doorway. After a pause, the door was rattled violently. Someone jumped up to open it, and there stood Karma Thinley Rinpoche.

'Oh, you eaty breakfast I see,' he announced, as if he'd merely called in to see what we were doing. We invited him in for tea, and he took the seat that was offered, planting his feet firmly apart in their unlaced battered shoes, and wrapping his heavy woollen maroon robes more closely around himself for warmth. He surveyed us with his intelligent bright brown eyes. After a while he said, 'I want some bread.' We asked him if he wanted butter on it and he responded, 'Do you think slugs like butter?' 'Slugs?' we all exclaimed in unison. 'What they called then? Those long black and orange animals. Many outside. You mustee know.'

'They no legs,' he continued. 'I think very difficult. Not like worms – well, like worms – but I think they very difficult. They on the road and there no food on the road. They might get walk on – people go walk – they very difficult with no legs.' He looked so genuinely concerned that I thought he must be joking. 'I think they don't like butter,' he continued thoughtfully. 'I think butter no good for them. I think just bread enough.' We were incredulous, not least because cut white bread was a relative luxury in India, but he raised his thick black eyebrows, opened his eyes wide and said very seriously, 'They likee bread. I soak for them in my mouth like this.' He showed us how he masticated the bread for a moment or two, spat the imaginary food out onto his hand and then broke it up with his fingers, holding it out to the floor as if offering a tiny creature a morsel.

Someone protested that slugs don't eat bread and he asked, 'What they eat then?' Someone suggested grass and leaves, but Rinpoche protested, 'No, they not eat grass. If they eat grass, why they not stay on the grass? They go on road. They looking for food. It very difficult for them without legs.' He seemed quite persuaded by this, and rejected all our protests, since we clearly didn't know any better than he did what slugs ate. Someone gave him a bag with the last few slices of our bread in it. He took it in the manner of a man with a purpose, and clomped out and off up the rickety bridge onto the road.

There is a sequel to this story. Some years later, I was relating this incident to a group of friends when one of them suddenly let out a cry of astonishment. 'Then it's true after all,' she laughed. 'All these years, I've been telling this story about how my husband once got so drunk in Dalhousie that he came home late one night telling me he had met a Tibetan lama on the road feeding slugs with bread and talking to them. Now from what you are saying it seems it was probably true!'

All the time Kalu Rinpoche was giving us empowerments I kept asking people what they were exactly. This being a technical matter my question was not easy to answer. I was told they were a blessing, yet nobody could really explain what a blessing was either. To everyone else it seemed self-evident but to me it was not. Nevertheless, the question never arose as to whether, given my ignorance, it was suitable for me to receive the empowerments. Karma Thinley Rinpoche clearly expected me to attend them and since everyone was telling me it was a rare and precious opportunity I was happy to do so.

In order to receive empowerments I was supposed to have taken Refuge. I didn't know what this meant but Ani Tenzin Palmo told me it was what made me officially a Buddhist. Taking Refuge in the Buddha, Dharma and Sangha (the community of the Buddha's followers) meant to commit myself to following the Buddha, his teachings and those who teach them. Since I had decided I was a Buddhist I didn't mind doing what Buddhists do to show they are Buddhist, so I signed up for taking Refuge the next day, having no idea what to expect.

Taking Refuge is the central act for any Buddhist and is taken very seriously. You would think therefore that a Buddhist teacher would make sure a student understood what it meant before encouraging them to make such a formal life commitment. You might have expected that I would have to go through some kind of training and probationary period in preparation for such an important step. Strangely, in my case this didn't happen. All I was asked to do was to come along to the shrine room at a particular time on the first day before the ceremonies began. I joined several other Westerners in a corner of the room as Kalu Rinpoche chanted and we joined in, when prompted by a nearby attendant, we repeated the lines of the Refuge vow after the Lama. It was all over so quickly that it felt more like a formality than anything profound. Why was that necessary in order to discover the true nature of mind?

I was having misgivings about whether I had come to the right place after all. I was just being fed ideas to believe in with next to no explanation. Even Tenzin Palmo, the most experienced of us Westerners, couldn't answer my questions satisfactorily and there were no books around to help me. Yet everyone was proceeding with such conviction that I decided to give the whole thing more time. Kalu Rinpoche explained that being present at the ritual was like planting seeds in fertile ground that would bear fruit later on. I was going to have to wait for the answers and that was all right by me. If a respected Buddhist teacher like Kalu Rinpoche thought I should take Refuge and empowerments to reach Enlightenment, who was I to argue?

As is customary when one takes Refuge, Kalu Rinpoche gave me a Tibetan Refuge name, Karma Sonam Hlakyi, the last two names of which mean 'happy goddess of good fortune' (Skt. *Sukha Punya Devi*). Karma means Buddha activity and in this context indicates a student of the Karmapa's lineage. I used this name from that day on until I returned to England five and a half years later.

Along with Refuge comes the training in following the five fundamental Buddhist rules of conduct against killing, stealing, lying, sexual misconduct and taking intoxicants. I had only learnt about these the evening before taking Refuge. At first glance they sounded straightforward enough but then I started to ask questions. What about killing pests and creatures that threaten human life? What counts as lying? What about situations in which telling the truth might do more harm than good? What does sexual misconduct mean exactly, at a time when societal norms are changing? Does the fifth precept include any kind of intoxicating substance and is it a problem if you drink in moderation? There was nobody to answer my questions, at least nobody who spoke English, so I decided to just take the one precept against stealing.

As if that were not enough, in order to receive the empowerments, I had to take the Bodhisattva vow. This I learnt was the vow to reach Enlightenment in order to benefit all beings. This seemed straightforward to me. As an eight-year-old child, when blowing out the candles on my birthday cake, I was told I could make any wish I wanted. I quickly worked out that whatever else I wished for, what I *really* wanted was to be happy. Just before committing myself to that one wish, I realised that I couldn't be happy if everyone around me was not happy, so I wished for *everyone* to be happy. After that, I always made the same wish. It was as if all I was doing now was formalising that wish. However, my world view at that time was so narrow that, had I thought about it, I would have found I didn't really believe I would ever be able to save *all* beings. I didn't stop to consider this because I was so happy with the general sentiment. I took the vow and from then on took it as given that I was on the Bodhisattva path.

After some weeks, Kalu Rinpoche introduced a new meditation practice to his Western students. He showed us a picture of a white, rather effeminate male figure dressed in a skirt, with long black hair and four arms, and said, 'This is Avalokiteshvara. Think of Avalokiteshvara as sitting on the crown of your head and recite the mantra *Om Mani Padme Hum*.' I had no idea how to take this. The figure looked so bizarre. I was just starting to relate to the image of the historical Buddha Shakyamuni, whose form, though pretty stylised, at least looked human. What sort of being was Avalokiteshvara supposed to be?

Rinpoche explained that Avalokiteshvara was the essence and union of the compassion of all the Buddhas, which was an attractive idea, but what could it possibly mean? Did it mean he was not a person? As for the image – what did a four-armed white person have to do with compassion, or with Buddhas for that matter? Kalu Rinpoche told us to pray to Avalokiteshvara and ask for his blessing. It sounded as if he was supposed to be some kind of god, but I had become Buddhist because I had given up belief in my Christian God, so why would I now start worshipping a Buddhist one? Furthermore, because of my new Buddhist beliefs I didn't know how to pray any more.

Tenzin Palmo explained that every empowerment we received related to a corresponding god-like form which might have any number of heads, arms and legs, either peaceful or wrathful, in various colours. I was appalled. I had never signed up to a belief system involving multiple gods. She explained that Avalokiteshvara was not a god, but a Bodhisattva, meaning a person who was advanced on the path to becoming a Buddha. But nothing had prepared me for the idea that I should pray even to Buddhas, let alone Bodhisattvas. All I could do was reserve judgement as I joined in with everyone else in opening myself to some kind of force for good that was clearly emanating from Kalu Rinpoche.

I found everything about the practice a problem. Why think Avalokiteshvara was on the crown of my head? Why dissolve Avalokiteshvara into myself at the end of the practice? Why recite the mantra *Om Mani Padme Hum* over and over again? Perhaps even more importantly I was asking how? How do you conjure up images like that sending out light to all beings, human and non-human throughout the Universe and so on? I couldn't make my mind do things like that and I just felt stuck. Reciting the mantra *Om Mani Padme Hum* was like a constant irritation. How to recite it so that it was in some way pleasant and inspiring? I was beginning to try to feel things I didn't feel and imagine things that I didn't want to imagine. I wondered if I should leave and travel on to Japan to the simplicity of Zen? My aesthetic sensibilities were drawn far more by Japanese art forms than Tibetan. Was I in the wrong place altogether?

Trying to do the practice as instructed left me feeling so bewildered and disconnected that I just ended up in tears. Despite such difficulties, I persevered, because of the wonder of Rinpoche's presence and the fact that from time to time he threw out hints of more direct experience-based teachings. Everyone assured me that Kalu Rinpoche was Enlightened, and for my part I could find no reason to doubt it. Nevertheless, I was learning that communicating subtle things to people from a different culture speaking a different language was challenging even for an Enlightened being.

Whenever I asked anybody whether a Tibetan or Westerner, what was going on, I was told I was receiving a great blessing. If you say blessing in English it is not at all clear what is meant, whereas the word *adhishtana* in Sanskrit, like its Tibetan equivalent *chinlab*, is fundamental to the whole way Buddhists think about their world. You could say it means a benevolent spiritual influence or energy, but this doesn't convey the cosmic context of the term. In a culture where one is exposed to ideas like *adhishtana*, karma and its fruits, connections *(tendrel)* and so on from childhood, it is easy to just go along with things you don't understand without really thinking much about it. Without that cultural background, it was hard for someone like me to take on practices that fitted a conceptual framework I simply didn't have. My view of the world was not only conditioned by the distortions that all beings have, but also by my cultural conditioning that prevented me just going along with things that I didn't understand. Nonetheless, I adopted what I could, provisionally, with the hope that real understanding would follow.

In this spirit I kept giving the Avalokiteshvara practice a go. Having made some attempt at thinking of Avalokiteshvara on my head, I went to Rinpoche and asked about it. I explained, 'When I am thinking of Avalokiteshvara on my head, there is me here looking up, and also me somehow looking at Avalokiteshvara as if from in front of him, and also the one on top of my head looking outwards. Which is my mind?' My question was basically whether I had to take different standpoints from which to imagine or visualise someone on top of my head and whether when visualising him, I was somehow within him looking out. I suspected that my whole approach was wrong and hoped my question would reveal this, so my misunderstanding could be corrected. I paused and waited for an answer through the translator. I didn't have much hope of a clear answer because the translator's English was very limited. Rinpoche gently replied, 'It is all your mind.'

His answer was surprisingly helpful. He was pointing out something about the nature of mind and although I didn't understand it, I sensed it was profound. I was going to have to reflect on the fact that 'mind' included a whole range of shifting perspectives. Although I didn't quite realise it at the time, this challenged my whole way of thinking of one and many, inside and outside, self and other. What reassured me about his answer was that he clearly didn't regard my question as silly. I was on the right track and I pursued the practice further with his answer in mind.

Three

Learning from Karma Thinley Rinpoche

The three months of empowerments came to an end and I went back to Tilokpur with the rest of the nuns. Now, at last, it was time to learn meditation from Karma Thinley Rinpoche as Trungpa Rinpoche had instructed me to do. I returned to the house in Tilokpur where I had been living before and which I would continue to share with Wongmo. Each morning for quite a few months Wongmo and I went separately for an interview with Karma Thinley Rinpoche to talk about our spiritual practice. He would sit on his bed, reading or writing as I entered and prostrated and then sat on the floor in front of him, at which point he might look up and start talking – or he might continue reading, until in his own good time he started the interview.

'How your meditation going?' he asked amiably one morning. I told him I'd done eight hours the previous day. 'That a lot meditation – very good.' After a pause, he asked, 'Did you see Enlightenment Mind?' I remarked that this must be quite far off and Rinpoche replied, 'Enlightenment Mind – your mind – not far off.' I persisted with my point. 'Surely it must take a long time to see that?' He conceded, 'Yes, that take long time – *really* see take long time – but little see – something coming maybe – that not so long.' Encouraged, I said, 'Yes I think something is coming, a little bit,' and then wondered to myself if that was true. After a long pause, Rinpoche started again. 'Eight hours very good – you good energy – good effort – very good. Tomorrow you do ten – okay?' I said okay. I was well up for a challenge.

He continued, 'My uncle, he meditate all day and all night. He had long hair. He tie it up like this' – and here he demonstrated – 'to roof the cave. Then when he fall sleep, his head drop and hair pull – and wake up' – another demonstration – 'just keep wake up. Then he meditate all the time – never sleep. You do like that you be great meditator.' There was another long pause as I tortured myself wondering how many more good nights' sleep I was going to have in my life.

Then he started to speak again. 'Have you learn Tibeti letters yet?' 'I've not had time, I've been meditating,' I replied, a little non-plussed. 'You not learnt yet? You very slow. Wongmo she learning Tibeti letters very good – both meditation and Tibeti letters.' Somewhat dismayed, I said, 'Surely meditation is the only important thing,' to which he replied, 'No, learn Tibeti very important. All texts in Tibeti letters – all lamas teach in Tibeti. You mustee know Tibeti.' I left the room determined to learn Tibetan.

At my next interview I could boast of having learnt the Tibetan alphabet. This time he kept praising Wongmo as a great meditator. He spoke of her prowess and progress in such glowing terms that my only recourse was to decide to meditate more and study Tibetan less. When I got back to my room she was sitting on her bed studying the alphabet, starting to put letters together to make words. 'I wish I could study and learn like you,' she said, and I replied that I was sure she was much better than I was. 'No, I keep forgetting them. I am so fed up.' 'Well it's all the meditation you are doing. Rinpoche tells me you are wonderful at meditation.' She looked astonished. 'Really? How odd. He's always telling me how good *you* are at meditation – so much better than me – and that you are also better at learning to read Tibetan.' 'That is what he tells me about you,' I said, and we both realised we had been had. We cracked up and had a good laugh at ourselves. 'I came all the way from England,' said Wongmo, 'hitching overland with only £10 in my pocket, to leave all that stuff behind. Yet here I am, playing *exactly* the same old game.'

While Karma Thinley Rinpoche was away in Delhi one time, Wongmo realised that she was *really* missing Kalu Rinpoche. She mooned around talking about her incredible devotion and faith in him. 'Kalu Rinpoche's my guru, you know,' she told one of the nuns, who replied, 'That's good – he's a wonderful lama. You can't get a higher lama than Kalu Rinpoche. He's Avalokiteshvara himself, the Buddha of compassion.' 'Yes,' said Wongmo, 'Avalokiteshvara is my practice, I got it from Kalu Rinpoche. He's really, really my guru.' The nun's prayer beads clicked as she murmured the mantra *Om Mani Padme Hum*. She nodded encouragingly to Wongmo to follow suit on her own prayer beads. After a while Wongmo sighed distractedly. 'Oh, I miss him so much. He's really my lama and I miss him.' The nun patted her reassuringly on the knee and went to get us all a cup of tea. I offered her a hand. 'Anyone would think Kalu Rinpoche was only *her* guru,' she confided. 'He's all our guru – it's just that we don't keep going on and on about it.'

Eventually Wongmo found her situation so unbearable that she left Tilokpur and travelled all the way from north-west to north-east India to see Kalu Rinpoche at his monastery in Sonada, about ten miles down the road from Darjeeling. After a month or so she wrote to me from there saying, 'It is all magical and Kalu Rinpoche is *really* my guru. No superlatives suffice to describe life here.' Something seized my heart and I quickly totted up my credentials. Reassured that I was doing at least as well as she was, I convinced myself that I was happy for her. Karma Thinley Rinpoche was returning to Tilokpur that day and I happened to meet him on the footpath. With a big smile I told him about Wongmo's letter and her news. Opening his eyes wide, he lent back and gazed at me in wonder. 'Oh, she more lucky than you then,' he said. I dropped my forced smile. Looking into his kind and honest face as he beamed warmly at me, I knew he knew what I was really feeling and that it was all right.

Trungpa Rinpoche and I exchanged letters several times while I was in Tilokpur. I told him about living as a nun and he congratulated me, saying, it was good that I was living as a nun even if I gave it up later. In response to something I had said in my letter to him he said, 'You are quite right that you have to learn to be humble and develop deep devotion to the sangha. That doesn't mean worshipping their personality, but the beauty of their characteristics, which are the quality of Dharma. You should be careful not to be caught up in this, which a lot of Westerners tend to do. And one has to completely absorb oneself in the general atmosphere so that there is no feeling of novelty based on Western criteria.' I wasn't sure what he meant by this. Sangha could mean the monastic community but could just as easily mean any community of Buddhist practitioners. I suspect he was referring to our tendency as Westerners to worship *any* oriental in robes without any real sense of what they might or should stand for. He might even have meant Buddhist teachers.

Karma Thinley Rinpoche made similar points about the right way to relate to teachers. For example, he said, 'The teacher is like a flower you take honey from – the flower itself is no use to you. The honey is the teaching – like a bee, take the honey and fly away, put the teachings into practice.' He added that the Karmapa warned those who were constantly hanging around him that they would never gain Enlightenment – for this you had to take the honey and quickly go away to practise. The point was to not get attached to the teacher like a kind of groupie. He didn't mean one shouldn't stay around to help the teacher if needed. The problem with staying too close to the teacher is that you start to see faults in them. He told me to always be like a dog that looks up to the good qualities of others and not like a pig that looks down in the dirt for their faults.

Although Ani Kechog Palmo was the abbess she was not in residence at the nunnery and seldom visited. She travelled the world seeking financial help for the nunnery and for Tibetan refugees generally. She sent me letters from time to time telling me what she wanted me to do. As well as some secretarial work, writing to potential donors and so on, she wanted me to help take care of the young nuns – about eight little girls between the ages of five and ten. In the event I didn't do much for the children because they lived with an old Tibetan couple whom Kechog Palmo had employed to look after them in a mud and wattle house about 100 yards away. We volunteers tried from time to time to take the children down to the spring to wash or to tend to their sores that wouldn't heal. The old couple blamed the problem of the sores on our taking them too frequently to bathe in the spring. We blamed it on an insufficiency of same.

Ani Kechog Palmo's letters with instructions on what I should do were mystifying and unworkable. She told me that the children should be brought down to the house we were living in and our room be converted into a dormitory. She even sent drawings of how the beds were to be arranged and what each child should be provided with. I didn't know where she thought we and the old couple were supposed to live. I ignored the instructions, and we carried on as we were.

It struck me as wrong that these little girls were already singled out to be nuns when they were far too young to know what that could possibly mean. For the most part their parents were poor refugees from Tibet and unable to care for the girls, or at least thought they stood a better chance of a good education and training at the nunnery than with their families. For sure they thought this was a blessing for the children. I found it hard to imagine that this struggling little community of nuns would one day grow into a flourishing nunnery.

Ani Kechog Palmo appeared out of the blue one day, having arranged for some lamas to come and do special rituals and prayers for the proposed site of a new building to replace the one that had burned down. Her nun attendant Ani Pema Zangmo came the day before her arrival to warn us she was coming and to get things ready. We volunteers had to move out onto the veranda on mattresses in order to make room for them. My first impression of Ani Kechog Palmo was of a somewhat portly lady with bright blue eyes, fair skin and a silvery halo of stubble on her shaven head. Dressed as a Tibetan nun, she swept into our quiet little world like a whirlwind. She had so many ideas of what could and should be done, it was dizzying, and as far as I could see, impractical and at times high-handed. The Indians and Tibetans were bowing respectfully to her. Many of them had every reason to be very grateful to her as she was able and willing to pull many strings to get help for them. To me she was warm and friendly, but she didn't give me much opportunity to speak. I found myself disagreeing with her on all sorts of levels, so decided to give her a wide berth. Nevertheless, whenever she saw me, she issued me instructions including what Dharma practices I should be doing. There was definitely something of the 'Memsahib' about her which fitted with her being deferred to by everyone as 'Mummy'. I felt uncomfortable about the way she talked to the nuns, especially those many years her senior, as she constantly busied herself with the queues of people lined up to see her, very often to seek her help.

The proposed site was within the walls of the old ruined fortress that stood proud against the sky-line looking down the cliff to the river below. A huge, brightly coloured tent had been set up in the fortress courtyard with rows of seats for all the grand lamas due to come. The nuns ran up and down to the fortress from their headquarters down by the spring all day long to prepare the space and to carry up saucepans of food.

The next day, Khamtrul Rinpoche (Ani Tenzin Palmo's lama) arrived with a number of other monks, lamas and highly realised practitioners referred to as yogins or togdens. He led the way up to the ruined fort, followed by the four great togdens with their matted hair wound like huge felt hats on their heads. I was standing by the entrance to the fort as they all passed by, and as I turned to go, I suddenly found myself before the togdens' elderly teacher, Apho Rinpoche. He was right at the end of the procession, dressed just like the other togdens, in a white lower robe and red and white striped upper robe, a mass of matted grey hair on his head and a long beard. He was a little bent in posture, and as I bowed my head before him, he took it in his hands. They felt warm and gentle as they cupped my head and held it for a few moments. It was an intimate and powerful gesture. I was left shaken as he moved away towards the tent – I found myself sobbing and I had to sit down on the step. I didn't know why I was crying, but was glad I was on my own to savour the moment. It was his compassion that had moved me so deeply. It penetrated to the heart of my being, causing a spontaneous and strong up-welling of devotion such as I'd never felt before. However, in spite of this strong emotional response I was not tempted to change my chosen direction. I was going to stick with Karma Thinley Rinpoche and continue to learn meditation from him.

Ani Kechog Palmo's visit lasted only a few days and then everything settled down to normal again. One afternoon, a nun ran up to me and anxiously asked me to fetch Karma Thinley Rinpoche because there was a snake in the children's room and the Indians were going to kill it. Since I had not been in India long, I had no idea what one did about snakes. What would Karma Thinley Rinpoche know about it? I hurried off down the cobbled village path in the afternoon heat, and as I passed our house, Rinpoche called down to me from the shady side of our upstairs veranda, overlooking the street. I told him about the snake, expecting him to leap up and follow me back up the hill. 'What they doing to it?' he enquired suspiciously. I didn't know. 'You mustee save it. It your mother in past life. You mustee save it.' I hesitated. His manner told me he meant to be taken seriously, but I couldn't quite believe it.

I asked him how I should save it. 'You get a box and a stick,' he explained, 'and you push it in with stick and then close the box and take a long way away.' I argued that it might become annoyed and shoot off somewhere and bite some-one. He suggested a sack instead of a box. I protested fur-ther, but I was still not sure he wasn't joking. I thought about how the Buddhist teachings say that we have all had every possible relationship to each other during the course of our endless past lives, and so all creatures must have been our loving mother in some life or other. I didn't like being accused of just standing by, letting my own mother be killed, but to rush up the hill brandishing my stick and tell the mill-ing crowd to stand back as I single-handedly saved the day seemed like the latter-day heroics of a sun-struck English memsahib. Whatever I did it was going to be either dishon-ourable or foolish. Why wasn't the lama sensitive enough to see my dilemma and let me off the hook? I wanted him to direct me in the way my reason told me he should. Couldn't he point out some deep spiritual meaning to justify not interfering in the situation?

He did nothing to lessen my discomfort. I didn't know what was worse, to stay here with him or rush off to try to save the snake. I looked at him helplessly and longed for him to clarify my moral dilemma. 'You mustee go quickly or they kill it – they kill your mother, you mustee help!' He screwed up his face in agony and horror. 'Also they Indians make bad karma killing the snake. They Tibetee nuns they do nothing – they pretend not want it kill but hope Indians kill for them. I know them. They very big lie and not compassion. You mustee help – quickly.' I realised that in spite of all my high aspirations to be a good disciple and do all the guru ordered, I was not going to obey him. I was puzzled and asked him,

'Why don't you save it? It's your mother too.' His eyes opened wide as with disarming honesty he replied, 'I frightened – you do it.'

I gave up. What else could I say? It was not my way to admit to being afraid. It was not how I had been brought up. I turned away and walked slowly up the hill. The Indians were crowded around the door of the little mud house where the snake was lurking, discussing what to do. The Tibetans were huddled along the edge of the green with their backs to the proceedings, muttering the mantra *Om Mani Padme Hum*, and were clearly very upset. They kept looking over their shoulders to see what the Indians were doing, but nothing happened for a long time and I followed the nuns down the hill to the kitchen.

Later that day, the nuns told me the Indians had killed the snake. They were shaking their heads at how wrong it was for them to have done that, yet clearly relieved that the snake had been dealt with. They didn't want to be implicated in the killing of it, any more than I did. I could sympathise with that, in spite of the hypocrisy, but I was not going to let myself off the hook so easily. Karma Thinley Rinpoche was right. I should have done something. I hadn't even tried to find another solution. Subsequently I discovered the villagers knew perfectly well how to remove snakes without killing them. Had I not been so afraid of making a spectacle of myself, I would have found that out.

That night I tossed and turned and took a good long look at myself. I hadn't had enough compassion even to open my mouth to try to save the snake. I hadn't had enough faith in my teacher to give it a try. What kind of student was I? Here I was giving up everything and coming all this way thinking I would be the perfect, devoted disciple and yet at the very first hurdle I had shied away like a frightened horse. It was humbling, but at least it was forcing me to be a bit more honest with myself. In so many ways Karma Thinley Rinpoche was like a mirror reflecting me back to myself.

One day he was working away in a small storeroom, peering into little wooden boxes containing little metal pieces with tiny Tibetan letters in reverse embossed on them. They were for arranging into wooden frames so they could be pressed into an ink pad for printing texts. As I approached, he looked up and said, 'Come, you mustee help me. This important work. Make Dharma books. This Dharma work. Very important.' I saw he was sorting the contents of a big bag of mixed letters into boxes of individual letters. He was fiddling with a small piece of frame trying to arrange some letters on it into words. I asked him how I could help as I started to take letters out of the mixed bag to put in the individual boxes. 'No, no – you don't touch,' he snapped bossily. 'You don't know – you *wait* and I show.'

He kept me waiting until I got fed up and decided to leave. Then, with a beam, he said, 'Here, I done it – very, very good – look,' and showed me the row of letters he'd just arranged. I examined them carefully. It was quite hard to read them back to front, but soon I got the hang of it. 'It says Sangjay!' I proclaimed proudly. I'd only been learning Tibetan for a few weeks but had recognised the word for Buddha. 'Oh, you very clever,' he exclaimed delightedly. 'You so clever, so quick learning – and read backwards too. How you know that? How you learn so quick? I not learn so quick English – I do many years English – no good – not coming good.' He screwed up his face in disgust at himself. 'But you so good – so quick. You Westerners – you much more clever than us Tibetans.' It was all rather exaggerated and silly, but he continued his lavish praise until the conversation started to bore me.

I turned to the boxes again and exclaimed 'Hey, they are still muddled. Even in the boxes where you said you had sorted them.' 'I never say I sort them – I not sort them. Other people sort them. I just take them out of bag – like this,' he said, showing me the bag and how he took letters out of it. 'So who is sorting them then?' I asked. 'I am,' he said. I gave up. He looked at me with a fond smile and laughed. 'You thought I muddled them – didn't you? But it not me – it is you mistake!' The joke was definitely supposed to be on me. I was beginning to feel a bit irritated. 'You very silly,' he said, beaming at me fondly. 'You not really clever. You Westerner but not clever – you mistake.' He continued to laugh in his exaggerated and absurd way. I stared out of the door, wishing myself somewhere else.

'You not stand there,' he commanded. 'You mustee help – it is Dharma work.' I tried again. The same sort of thing happened. 'Look, you put this one wrong,' he said, holding up the offending piece in indignation. It wasn't a big deal but he made out it was and accused me of being bad and careless. 'Mistakes in Dharma book very bad. It big sin, make Dharma wrong – you go hell.' He stared at me to see if I had taken in the enormity of my crime. I told him I didn't believe I'd go to hell for making a mistake. He insisted it was showing disrespect for Dharma. I argued that it was not disrespect, it was a mistake.

Suddenly he made an about-face. 'That true – it only a mistake. It not disrespect of Dharma – you right. You very good understanding Dharma.' He stepped back and stared at me, wide-eyed, admiringly, but so exaggeratedly that I had to smile. 'You very good Dharma mind – your mind naturally Dharmakaya mind!' He gazed at me in what seemed like genuine wonder. I cheered up and resumed sorting out the letters.

'You must go later to West and teach Dharma,' he said, this time in a reasonable tone that I couldn't help taking seriously. 'It is very early days yet,' I said modestly. 'First I have to get Enlightened myself.' He agreed: 'Yes, that true – you mustee get Enlightened Mind. That very important. You not think about teaching – you right. You very good thinking.'

We continued sorting the letters in silence, with me in an increasingly cheerful frame of mind. After a while, he enquired, 'Why you say I bad and I muddle letters? This is Dharma work – I very careful. You do muddle sometimes – that's why you think I muddle – but I not muddle. You very bad.' He stopped work to stare at me, screwing up his face in disgust. Down come my spirits. Why was he being so silly again? 'You no clever – and you say I am bad when it your mistake.' He was being very provocative. I was very bored with it all and wanted go and do something else. He held me there with his chatter.

After a while I said, 'I didn't say you muddled them, I just said they were muddled.' There was a pause. Then, 'Yes, you right – you said that. That's right, you not mistake – I mistake. You right – they muddled. Someone muddled them and you found it – that's good.' I felt somewhat cheered again. He continued in this vein for an hour or more, alternately praising and criticising me. My spirits lifted and fell as by a mere flick of a button. Even though part of me knew his exaggerated praise and blame were about winding me up, I still fell for it emotionally every time. However short-lived and meaningless it was, my spirits went up when I was praised and down when criticised. It was a lesson for me. It had forced me to notice the way my mind worked and how easily it was swayed by praise and blame. How boring! How ridiculous!

The daily routine for the nuns at the nunnery was morning and evening *puja*. *Puja* is an Indian word for worship. Whenever the Indians saw Tibetan monastics at their prayers they referred to it as puja, and the Tibetans and their Western disciples had followed suit.

I was not interested in pujas and the associated rituals so never joined the nuns as they gathered in their tiny shrine room twice a day to chant, beat drums, clash cymbals and blow trumpets and horns. What did all that have to do with realising the true nature of mind? I asked Karma Thinley Rinpoche about it. He looked at me thoughtfully for a moment or two and then said it was all a lot of nonsense and not to bother myself about it. From that moment on, I became more interested in what they were doing. I didn't believe he really thought it was nonsense, but his remark had relieved me of any sense of pressure.

Sometimes he called me his sister, teasing and annoying me, seemingly deliberately. He seemed to like to just hang out, telling me stories about Tibet and talking about world affairs. It was 1969 and the Americans had just landed on the moon, and he kept asking me how I knew it wasn't a hoax. He was looking at photos taken on the moon and asking me how I knew that they weren't actually taken on the earth. Then the poet in him bemoaned the fact that astronauts were walking on the moon's surface, treating it like dirt, when traditionally it had always been praised as made of light and as a palace of the gods. 'Anyway,' he said, 'we Tibetans have been going there for centuries. Yogins just fly there.'

At times he was clearly using me as a sounding board to expand his knowledge of the world by asking me questions about the West. Often he asked really odd questions and made quirky remarks such as, 'There *must* be a creator god, because look how beautifully our eyes and eyelashes are made.' Then all of a sudden he seemed to transform into a full-blown guru figure pointing out the nature of mind. One day, seemingly out of the blue, he asked me what colour my mind was. My first impulse was to say no colour. But if mind had no colour, what was colour other than the mind? I didn't know if what I saw as a colour was what you saw as colour. I told him that the mind was the colour of whatever colour was appearing in it at any given moment. He didn't reply to this but continued to ask me questions such as where do sounds happen. Do they happen outside in the world or in the ear that hears them or somewhere in-between?

These questions had a profound effect on me as they cut through the very assumptions that my world was built on. I sensed that they were very significant but I didn't find I came up with answers. I just kept going back to them again and again in my meditation. Each time I found myself thinking colours or sounds were somehow *not* my mind I got confused. Where and what were they, then, and how did I know them? But whenever I thought they *were* the mind I felt even more confused. It couldn't be true that everything was just my mind. That would be madness. There must be something *outside* my mind – but how would I know? These questions really woke me up. There was something wrong with the way I was thinking, I was sure. I could let the wrong thinking go for a fraction of a second, but then it just came back. Was there another way of knowing?

I instinctively knew that when Rinpoche asked questions like this, he was helping me to see something about my direct experience that could lead to Enlightenment. The effect was rather like having something pointed out – something about the true nature of mind.

In various ways he was also helping me get the right touch and have a relaxed mind. One day he asked, 'What make your mind relax?' I told him, 'Swimming in the sea – throwing myself into the big waves without a care in the world like I did as a child.' With wide-eyed amazement he told me that would frighten him. A few days later I accompanied him and one of the young nuns to the post office in the next village, and before coming home we wandered along the riverside in the blazing morning sun, looking at the light dancing off the waves and relaxing. 'You swim in the river?' he asked. 'I don't have a swimming costume,' I said sadly. 'You swim in underskirt then. You show this nun how to swim and relax.' So the nun and I stripped off our upper garments and drew the elasticated waists of our underskirts up under our arm-pits to cover our bodies. Then we lay down in the shallow water, letting it wash over us. It was wonderfully warm. We rolled over and looked up into the clear blue sky above and it felt like heaven. 'Are you coming in too?' we called.

He didn't join us but stood watching us happily. As we dried ourselves off afterwards, he told us, 'That very good. You mustee remember, you need very relax mind for meditation. You very relaxed mind today.' He chuckled happily to himself as we made our way back to the bus stop and home to the nunnery.

Karma Thinley Rinpoche sometimes let me sit alongside him all morning. One particular morning I remember sitting there hoping he would turn his attention to me and teach me something but instead he seemed to be ignoring me as one nun after another, young and old, came in to talk to him. They didn't seem to have anything urgent to ask, yet he seemed more interested in just hanging out with them than engaging in anything important. He got very enthusiastic about cutting out paper patterns with one of the younger nuns and tried to get me interested. I felt very frustrated because I had come to learn about my mind. I needn't have come all this way to just hang out and mess about with paper cut-outs. He clearly noticed that I was getting frustrated but was not going to be influenced by that. I was not sure how to take this so I said, 'Whenever I start to ask Dharma questions you change the subject, but if I talk about something trivial you are all ears.' He looked at me wide-eyed and said, 'Yes – that is true.'

There was nothing for it but to drop any attempt to control the situation and yet to remain open. Nevertheless, I still got impatient. He told me to go to his room at the top of the hill and he would come. I waited around for hours but he didn't come. When eventually I saw him again he was not bothered about having kept me waiting. This was how I learnt that impatience and preconceived ideas were not going to get me anywhere. I either had to give up my expectations or go away. It was sobering.

My relationship with Karma Thinley Rinpoche was on his terms only. He had nothing to lose – he was not hiding anything. If I were to walk off, I would lose and that was all there was to it. Something about his uncompromising genuineness held me there. I didn't think he was deliberately testing me. He was just being completely open with me, as if to say, 'This is the moment, this is how I am and this is how it is. You either learn from that or you don't.' Even my getting impatient and feeling irritated was just how it was. No problem. He was showing me my mind here and now. The situations he created mirrored my own habits of mind back to me in very telling ways. His lessons were often extremely subtle, as he drew my attention to false assumptions and ways of thinking that we normally take totally for granted.

One afternoon I was awoken from what I took to be a daytime nap by the sound of Karma Thinley Rinpoche stomping up the stairs calling my name. When he saw me lying down, he opened his eyes wide in surprise. 'Oh, you have woke up at last! We thought you were never going to wake up. We were very worried about you. You have slept a very long time!' I said it couldn't have been that long as the sun was still well up in the sky. He then told me I had been asleep for more than 24 hours. 'You were asleep last night and all this morning. We worried. You not come down for breakfast or lunch!' I found this very hard to believe, but how did I know that 24 hours had not passed? I asked if he was joking and he insisted that they had all been very worried, and that he'd already tried once to wake me. He seemed really relieved to find I was all right.

It felt very, very strange. I sensed so strongly that I had only dropped off for ten or fifteen minutes, but how did I know? How did I ever know? Karma Thinley Rinpoche was staring at me intently as if trying to work out what was the matter with me. He told me to go and ask the nuns, if I didn't believe him. It was not easy trying to establish whether it was that day or the day before, as every day was the same in the nunnery. I asked if I had been at breakfast and lunch that day. Eventually I became convinced that Karma Thinley Rinpoche had indeed been joking but I was left with an eerie feeling. How do we know the past is the past, other than a kind of feeling or flavour of it?

His disarmingly child-like manner could be quite deceptive. He could suddenly switch and you got a blast of power as he took on the role of the Primordial Buddha. What dignity and presence! It felt natural to me to always prostrate to him as if to the Buddha, even though I didn't really understand what this meant. Yet when he acted like a child, wondering at things or shamelessly expressing his fears and hesitations, I found myself talking to him as if he were a child. His simplicity revealed to me the child-like nature of fearlessness. It held up a mirror to my own subtle attempts to give a good impression of myself and the limits this put on my imagination and understanding.

Karma Thinley Rinpoche's imagination knew no limit. One of his big ideas was to put a Buddha image on the moon. Since the moon can be seen from everywhere on earth, such an image would be able to bless everyone. I now think this is a brilliant idea but back then I tended to dismiss his notions as amusing and childish and hadn't the insight or understanding to believe it would have any benefit. When he told me to write to the American embassy, to ask them to help him put an image of the Buddha on the moon, I dragged my feet. 'They will just dismiss us as cranks,' I told him, but Rinpoche was deadly serious about his mission. He sent several letters to the American embassy and even went there in person. They very sweetly explained to him that the problem with taking a religious image was that it meant taking an image from every religion, which would get too heavy. They suggested he ask one of the astronauts to take the image in their personal luggage. Rinpoche got very excited about this idea and had it in mind to ask the next American astronaut that came to India. As it happened he and I were both in Delhi at the same time as one of them was visiting and I should have told him but I didn't. I suppose I was still

afraid of being taken for a crank. What a missed opportunity! No wonder Rinpoche was annoyed with me.

Eventually I got a letter from him saying, 'To my sister Susan,
Today only myself go and see embassy of USA. He said can't
put in the moon. Then I said doesn't matter you leave in
Apollo please. Then he has take my Buddha. If he sent letter
there for me please send here. So I will come after twenty
days to Tilokpur see you and others. I send you my Dharma
Mind and loves – your Mind and my Mind all meditation one
O [he had made a drawing of a big circle]. Please you look
carefully. Karma Thinley.'

One afternoon I saw a side of Rinpoche I had never seen before. We looked up to see a huge dark cloud was nearly
upon us, and hurried for shelter. An Indian neighbour came
running up to Rinpoche and begged him to stop the rain because he was having a huge feast and celebration that evening and all they had was a light cloth canopy for protection.
To my surprise, Rinpoche agreed to do his best – though he
warned that it was much harder to stop rain than create it.
Half an hour later the heavens opened. There were dozens
of adults and children gathered for our neighbour's celebration, huddled together under the cloth canopy as the rain
poured down, but then within minutes it had ceased completely and without more ado the evening's celebrations resumed. It had been so quick that the cloth canopy had sufficed. Our neighbour was very satisfied – and I was amazed!

A letter arrived for me from Ani Kechog Palmo. 'The Karmapa will be in Delhi for a few days and I want you to come
and meet him,' she wrote. I had been in awe of the very
thought of the Karmapa ever since being in the presence of
his picture on the throne at Samye Ling. He was the head of
the Karma Kagyu lineage to which Trungpa Rinpoche, Karma
Thinley Rinpoche and Kalu Rinpoche all belonged. Spiritually
the position of Karmapa ranks on a par with the Dalai Lama
and like him he is regarded as an emanation of Avalokiteshvara.

It was exciting to be setting off for Delhi by myself on the night train from Pathankot, even though I was unsure about where I would stay in the city. The whole carriage was kept awake all night by the incessant talking of a middle-aged Indian lady with a very loud voice. She provided my first encounter with how Indians think about spirituality. She considered herself a deeply religious person because she bathed herself at least four times a day, fasted two days a week and rose at four every morning to worship God at her shrine. Even though she was visibly taken aback, when I told her how little I washed in comparison with her, she nonetheless recognised in me a kindred spirit and very kindly invited me to stay. In fact she offered to host me whenever I was in Delhi, so over the years I got to know her very well. Her name was Mrs Jerrat.

On this first occasion she was very keen to meet my guru and so I arranged for Karma Thinley Rinpoche to join her and her husband for dinner while I was there. Her husband didn't consider himself a religious person at all, though this didn't mean he didn't *believe* in religion. It meant he didn't think he made as much effort as he should to follow it. Like every Indian I subsequently met, he had an intuitive feel for what a holy person was, and so he liked Karma Thinley Rinpoche very much. During the dinner, he asked Rinpoche, 'Why is it that even though we are all God by nature we find it so hard to keep Him in mind and instead prefer worldly things?' Rinpoche gazed at him thoughtfully for a while and simply said, 'Your question comes from a very deep place.' I was very moved by the simple honesty of the exchange.

I was to meet the Karmapa at the Oberoi Hotel. The owners were close friends of Ani Kechog Palmo and were now disciples of the Karmapa. After so many months of simple living it felt weird to be stepping into the relatively opulent Oberoi with its modern comforts and somewhat colonial style of service.

As I arrived, the very way I was dressed told the reception I was one of the party of dozens of monks, nuns and lamas assembling in the foyer and elsewhere waiting to meet the Karmapa. I found Karma Thinley Rinpoche and he very kindly accompanied me for my first ever interview with the Karmapa. He was an impressive, good-looking and well-built man with a radiant smile and a lot of charisma. He was sitting cross-legged on the bed and we sat on the floor looking up at him. Karma Thinley Rinpoche translated for me. I had no idea what to expect or what to say. The Karmapa looked at me very kindly for a moment or two as if he was taking me in. Then he said something I found incredible. 'When you are beyond meditation and non-meditation you will be able to help everyone effortlessly.' It was as if he had seen my whole life trajectory and how since childhood I had been torn between an active and a contemplative life. It was as if he could see into the depths of my being and was promising me what I had always longed for with all my heart. I recognised that what he was saying was profound and it was not going to be easy to find that place beyond meditation and non-meditation, but the Karmapa's words reaffirmed for me that I was on the right path.

Back in Tilokpur I found the house I was living in too much of a public highway because it functioned as the main guest house for visitors. I wanted a quiet place to stay in retreat and the landlord offered me a little mud hut out in the paddy fields, typical of the very basic shelter farm labourers used from time to time when tending the crops. There was no glass or shutters for the windows, no running water or electricity and of course no loo. When the wind blew too hard, I had to get down low and cover myself with a blanket. Whenever I was not needed at the nunnery, I spent days or even weeks at a time in retreat there. I never had any difficulty spending ten to twelve hours a day meditating, sitting cross-legged. Most Westerners do, but for some reason I didn't. I was rarely bored or restless. Tibetans said this was because I had been practising in past lives. I couldn't think of a better explanation.

After one of my retreats I met up with Karma Thinley Rinpoche in Delhi. Rinpoche greeted me with, 'How wonderful that you have finished your retreat. What signs of success have you had?' I thought you were not supposed to look for signs of success, so I took this to be a trick question. I told him, 'None.' 'What?' he said, in astonishment. 'No signs of success? No more faith coming? No more compassion?' I was shaken. If I was not gaining in faith and compassion, then what was I doing? I realised that my pretending to have gone beyond hope of success and fear of failure was an affectation. There had to be *some* signs of success even if it was just continuing to have the inspiration and determination to keep going on the path. All that was definitely increasing.

In my retreats I was getting occasional momentary glimpses of a deeper understanding in much the same way as I had always done even as a child. I was looking for the truth and I just tried to be as simple as possible as I looked into the nature of my direct experience. I was never disheartened however elusive the truth seemed to be. My conviction that what I was doing would eventually enable me to truly help others sustained me.

Four

New-found Independence

Mike had been keeping in regular contact, sending letters to me at the nunnery. 'I can tell from your letters that you are happy in your new life,' he wrote, after I had been away for about six months. 'If you intend to continue living as a nun then you can't be proud and independent. I have decided to start sending you money monthly by money order. How much do you need?' What incredible generosity and faith both in Dharma and in me. Gratefully, I asked him for £5 a month. This was a sizeable portion of his monthly salary as a post-office engineer, but it meant that I was no longer tied to the nunnery as a volunteer. I would be free to travel, study elsewhere, go on pilgrimage or whatever. 'Well Sue,' he used to say, 'there is one thing I have always noticed about you. You always do what you say you will do.' I was determined not to let him down.

The next letter from Wongmo informed me that her permit for Sonada had run out and she had to leave and so she had decided to enrol at the Sanskrit University in Varanasi in or-der to learn Tibetan. I decided to go and enrol there too. So, newly independent, I set off for Varanasi. Karma Thinley Rinpoche happened to be there when I arrived and encour-aged me to go to the burning ghats to contemplate death and impermanence. It was a sobering experience to stand by the smouldering bodies, watching human remains being tossed into the Ganges as hungry dogs were beaten off with sticks. Face to face with death in the raw shatters one's body image. We know it is all blood and gore on the inside but until you see it sizzling and popping in the fire like this it's hard to really take it in. It served to impress on me the power of my mind to create a deluded view of reality. In a strange way I enjoyed the experience because it shocked me into waking up.

I moved into a shared room with Wongmo at the Sanskrit University. Next door was a young Indian girl studying Vedanta and very devoted to the Goddess Shakti. We got into long conversations and I spent many hours in the library reading up on Vedanta. It all sounded like Mahayana Buddhism to me.

After a month or so I decided to move to Sarnath, which was a half-hour bus ride out of Varanasi. It is a sacred pilgrimage site for Buddhists because it was there, in a deer park, that the Buddha gave his first teaching on the cause and cure of all suffering. In those days it was a quiet little country village built alongside a lovely public park and gardens within which is a great ancient stupa, a round tower-like structure about 100 feet high containing the relics of the Buddha. Around it were the ruins of the old Buddhist monasteries, some of them dating back to the early centuries BC, and a deer park in memory of the original one. Many Tibetan monastics who were studying at the Sanskrit University in Varanasi lived in Sarnath. The nuns at Tilokpur told me that among them was a young nun from their nunnery called Karma Ozer, who was expected to eventually become the abbess of the Tilokpur nunnery. I had letters of introduction and gifts for her from the nuns at Tilokpur.

She was sitting in her room quietly meditating – as I was always to find her – and yet as I entered she sprang forward from her bed with an eagerness and warmth that I found almost embarrassing. She took my hands gently in hers, smiling happily, her expression innocent and simple but very intelligent. She was a paragon of grace and beauty. She offered me tea and as we talked of how everyone was in Tilokpur she giggled girlishly and a mischievous humour broke through. For her a guest was a rare occurrence. Her life here was somewhat lonely since the only other nun, her colleague, had dropped out of the course the year before. She now mostly confined herself to her room – not even going out for walks. She thought it would look bad for her, as a young woman and nun, to wander about the streets and park alone. So she sat indoors quietly, studying and meditating.

I asked her about her daily routine and she told me that she rose each morning at 3.00 am, like all her fellow students. After washing and dressing and doing her morning prayers, she had a simple breakfast before catching the bus into Varanasi for classes. Usually she would come back for lunch and then just study alone through the afternoon and evening – but now that I had come she could take a walk in the afternoons with me! We chatted and discussed all this and decided to go out straight away. I found it hard to believe that she didn't go out alone. It was certainly not forbidden. She looked delighted to be stepping out of her dimly lit room into the warm afternoon sunshine. Strolling around the stupa and the paths surrounding it, talking about our lives and the Dharma, we both felt like we had known each other forever.

I spent the winter months in Sarnath, living in a bare concrete room with a single light bulb sticking out from the wall and a thin mattress laid along the wall beneath it. The window, as was mostly the case in India, had no glass – just bars and shutters on the outside. I had to be careful not to leave anything too near the window lest passers-by reached in to fish it out with hooks or their long thin arms. My suitcase doubled as a table for my books and papers. I cooked on a small kerosene wick stove and kept food in the suitcase, out of reach of the mice and rats.

It was the simple life that I always loved. I rose every day at 5.00 am and made a long excursion into the fields where I would find a clear patch of ground on which to relieve myself. What a pleasure it was to squat under the clear blue sky, with the Indian plains stretching out so flat and vast in all directions. I often gazed up through the trees dripping with the morning dew, the ground mist beginning to lift as the sun's rays gained in intensity, and simply luxuriated in feeling completely free. Daily tasks could not be hurried. Even to fetch water from the well took fifteen minutes, as I waited my turn and then wound a bucket slowly down and up on a rope.

Since Tibetan classes were only once a week, I spent most days in the fine, modern temple in the park. An endless stream of pilgrims came to worship here throughout the day, gazing at its beautiful murals recounting the life of the Buddha. The whole place was bright, airy and very pleasant to sit in. I would find a spot against a wall and set myself up with my prayer book and cushion, meditating there for hours at a time, interspersed with periods of doing a few prostrations and circumambulating the stupa. At lunch time, I walked back through the tiny bazaar, taking in the sights, sounds and smells of the market stalls: the rickshaw bells, rasping crows, the children and dogs, snotty-nosed babies with their eyes made to look bigger and brighter with black eyeliner, and old Tibetans with their oiled grey hair in plaits, tied with coloured skeins of silk, wearing thick black dresses and striped coloured aprons. Elegant Indian ladies passed by in colourful saris with plastic bangles clicking on their wrists and tiny bells on their ankles. I loved it all.

I would carry my prayer beads in my hand, reciting mantras to myself a little ostentatiously as is the Tibetan custom. Tibetans passing me in the street bowed their heads in respect and said thank you again and again. They were happy to see me, so young and foreign, yet wise enough to have given up everything for the sake of the Dharma. Seeing me living like this gave them hope for the future and for me it was a joy to be living in a culture that had such a deep respect for the renunciate path.

Back in my room I cooked the same delicious meal of rice, dhal and vegetables every day. Sitting in my doorway to eat it meant contending with the hungry dogs, who sat with their hopeful eyes trained on me. It was very distressing, yet if I gave food away, I'd be hungry later myself. I wrestled with this, because I knew full well that if I gave in and fed them today, tomorrow they would be joined by others. I said mantras for them and prayed that they would have better lives next time. By not eating after mid-day, I had a long, uninterrupted stretch of time from lunch till bedtime during which I could study Tibetan and meditate. That time always passed very quickly.

'My sister Karma Yangzom is a *real* meditator' Karma Ozer told me proudly, explaining that she was in a three-year retreat with five other nuns at Kalu Rinpoche's monastery in Sonada. 'I just study,' she added wistfully as if wishing herself in her sister's shoes. I was used to such remarks from Tibetans. Meditation is seen as the real work of life. Everything else is just distraction unless you are already Enlightened. That is not to say that Tibetans think everything else in life is useless or meaningless even in Dharma terms. However, what Karma Ozer had in mind was that in order to fully realise the nature of mind as pointed out to us by our teachers, we have to meditate on it for years on end. Even great highly realised yogins have to devote themselves to meditating on it for many years to stabilise it and develop its qualities, let alone ordinary people like ourselves. It's probably going to take us lifetimes.

My weekly trip to Varanasi by bus for my Tibetan class was a long, hot, noisy ride and there wasn't always a class when I arrived because of strikes, public holiday, the teacher off sick and so on. By the time the term ended we had only had three or four lessons. Nobody raised an eyebrow, as that was simply the pattern of life in India. Everyone was making plans for spending the summer somewhere cooler than the plains of India. The obvious choice for me was Sonada as Kalu Rinpoche was teaching Westerners there, Karma Ozer would be there soon and her sister Karma Yangzom was willing to help me with my Tibetan. I left and never returned to Varanasi.

Sonada was within the restricted area of Darjeeling, near the border with Sikkim and China, so foreigners had to have a permit to stay there. I had to travel by train to Calcutta (now Kolkata) to apply for and collect my permit. From there I boarded the train up to Siliguri, and on arrival found the pint-size Darjeeling train waiting there in the dark. I boarded the so-called 'Toy Train' and fell asleep immediately. After about six hours I awoke to find myself zigzagging up the steep sides of a Himalayan valley with a narrow road running alongside.

The mist was so thick I didn't have much sense of where I was. Suddenly fruit sellers were offering me their wares through the open window from stalls that came right up to the side of the train. Someone announced that this was Sonada, so I grabbed my possessions and stepped down onto the road, totally disorientated.

With my rucksack on my back and suitcase in one hand and bucket and stove in the other I wended my way through the mist to Kalu Rinpoche's monastery – a ten-minute walk through lush countryside on the road running alongside the railway. Eventually the monastery emerged above me on the right-hand side. I climbed up a steep path to its entrance, then passed by a small one-storey concrete temple into a courtyard with a masonry house in front of me where Kalu Rinpoche and his few attendants lived.

The mist prevented my taking much more than this in, so I made my way to what looked like the main building. A monk emerged from it and said in what sounded like perfect English, 'Can I help you?' Unfortunately, that turned out to be the full extent of his English. Having established that I had come to stay for a while, he helped me find accommodation to rent a little way up the road. All I could see was mist, so I was totally astonished a day or two later when I woke up to discover I had a magnificent view down the deep valley over hundreds of little fields and scattered housing.

Rinpoche's room was lined with windows with the same sort of view. He always sat on his specially carved wooden bed and received people all day as they came with their various requests and problems. We Westerners gathered every afternoon for teachings even though the only translator knew very little English. Rinpoche explained about the hell realms of which there are eight hot and eight cold. He spared us no detail of how the beings suffered there and what wrong action they had engaged in to experience this. Between each gap while he waited for the translation to happen, he would play with the white cat sitting perfectly still beside him on the bed, painting its cheeks red and balancing a white scarf on its head like a big hat. He gently pointed out that although the cat was in the right place and right time, it was incapable of learning Dharma, this being yet another indication of how lucky we all were. Tibetans would come in from time to time asking him to do divinations about what medicine they should take and so on. The carpenter would pop in to discuss Rinpoche's drawings for the new house to hold a giant prayer wheel; newly arrived refugees from Tibet would ask him for blessings for those who had died on the way. He would do rituals for them and then give us the next teaching about the hells and what karmic actions result in us being born there.

I wanted to find myself a secluded retreat place further up the mountain, away from the road and the monastery. Kalu Rinpoche told me he would make a divination for me and tell me the result. The next day he announced that it would not be safe for me to move to a secluded place and that I should stay in the monastery in the retreat place where a group of five nuns were staying. I didn't realise that foreigners were not usually allowed to stay at the monastery and I happily went along with the plan. I don't know why he made an exception for me, maybe it was because I was living as a nun and had made it clear I only wanted to meditate. It meant the nuns had to clear their woodstore to make room for me. The wood was piled up outside my window and covered with polythene. I was very touched by the enthusiasm with which they did this for me. It was a simple room in a building made of thin wooden planks and a stamped earthen floor. I had a bed like a wooden table with a thin mattress I'd brought with me. I kept more or less to the same basic routine as the other nuns and they seemed to accept me as one of them right away. However, whenever I offered to help with the cooking, fetching water and so on, they would say, 'No, you just keep meditating. Meditation is our work and you are doing it for us.' So modest!

Theirs was not a closed retreat in the way the monks' retreat was. They came and went to shop in the bazaar, were expected to join in building projects with the other monks when needed, went into Rinpoche's house to receive teachings, and joined the rest of the monks for special events in the temple. They had been selected by Ani Kechog Palmo to do this retreat in order to form a core of trained nuns for Tilokpur nunnery. The five of them were all very strong characters in their own right and seemed unaware of Ani Kechog Palmo's intention for them. They none of them went back to Tilokpur after the three years. One of the nuns, Ani Tsewang Choden was from the north-west Indian province of Kunu and was a disciple of the great female lama Shukseb Jetsunma and of the famous Kunu lama Tenzin Gyamtso. Listening to her talking about them brought them very alive for me – she had so many wonderful tales! She was in her fifties and had had a son, Tenpa Gyaltsen, before becoming a nun. He now supported her by teaching English in the Indian army. I would meet Tenpa when he visited in the summer holidays, and he became a close friend of mine.

The nuns' meditation sessions started at 4.00am and went on till 8.30pm, with hour-long breaks for breakfast, lunch and tea. This kind of routine is standard for Tibetans in retreat. Each session of practice is called a *'toon'* and the standard is to do four two-and-a-half-hour *toons* a day plus a few other shorter sessions of prayer. The retreatants meditated alone in their rooms. Karma Yangzom told me that they often fell asleep and I didn't find that surprising given their poor health and lack of nourishment. She acknowledged that ideally retreatants would have sharp faculties and keep awake and focused so that insight into the true nature of reality could arise. That was the real point of retreat. She paused and then added cheerfully that nevertheless if you couldn't live up to this ideal, you could still accumulate good karma (or *punya*) simply from your good intentions and best effort. I never managed to get up at four. I rose at five. Beyond that I didn't find it a punishing regime.

It seemed that even before I arrived it had been decided that I was Karma Yangzom's friend. I suppose as I was Karma Ozer's friend that made sense. She immediately adopted me and took it upon herself to take care of me. She insisted that she cook and shop for me. She informed me that if she shopped for me the shopkeepers would charge less, as there was one price for those perceived as being rich, like Westerners and another for those perceived as being poor, like Tibetans. I thought this a very civilised arrangement!

My room was small, maybe eight by six feet but Karma Yangzom's room was even smaller. She could not lie down with her legs stretched out. She had a window with a spacious view though. My window faced the muddy mountain side just a few feet away, so I often joined Karma Yangzom for my *toons,* sitting next to her on her bed from where I could look out of her window to relax my mind from time to time. Her one luxury was a small paraffin stove beside her for making tea. Above the head of her bed was her shrine – an open-sided wooden box fixed to the wall, with a row of shining offering bowls full of water and a butter lamp constantly burning before pictures of the Buddha and various lamas.

On the top of the box were her Buddhist texts, carefully wrapped in cloth.

As she got to know me, she confided in me more and more. 'I worry a lot these days,' she confessed. 'In Tibet I didn't worry because I never wanted for anything. Since I always had more than I needed, I was known for my kindness and generosity, constantly giving stuff away. But now I am a refugee, I find I'm not the sort of person I thought I was at all – I worry all the time about not having enough of anything. I just get the very poor supply of food we are given by the monastery. We are supposed to supplement it ourselves, but how can I? I borrow money from the monks, but then I worry about not being able to pay it back. I get very weak and hungry. Last winter I was frightened that I'd die.' Karma Yangzom's next comment took me by surprise. 'It's not that I mind dying, but to die here in retreat of hunger while I'm under the care and protection of Kalu Rinpoche – well, it would reflect badly on *him* and it's really not his fault. He's responsible for so many people, how can I expect him to give me more? He has already been so kind to me.' I decided there and then to share whatever extra money I had with her.

There was only one other foreigner whom Rinpoche allowed to stay in the monastery at that time and she was an English lady who I made friends with, called Ruth Tarling. She had been a close student of Rinpoche's for many years already, so he always made an exception for her. She only stayed a few weeks each year because she was working in London. I told her about Mike and she offered to take him a small gift from me. This turned out to be fortuitous.

She told him in conversation that she wouldn't be able to live in India on the amount of money he was sending me. That was because she was eating the kind of food we are used to in the West, which is expensive in India. Anyway, without further ado he quadrupled what he sent me each month from then on. I told him I didn't need so much money, and so was using it to make offerings to my lamas and to help my monastic colleagues, especially Karma Yang-zom. At the end of his next letter he simply wrote, 'Look after yourself and your friends.' What an extraordinary person! He seemed naturally to have a Tibetan attitude towards Dharma practice. There were absolutely no strings attached – even if I wrote to him or sent him small gifts, he would write back saying that I was under no obligation to do so as I was practising the Dharma on his behalf.

At any one time there were a dozen or so Westerners from various countries coming to the monastery each day. None of them could stay very long in the area because of the permit situation. Having a British passport had got me three months without any problem, but others were not so lucky. Kalu Rinpoche would stress to us each day how difficult it was to be born human. Human beings are few compared with those in the other five realms of samsara, most beings by far being in hell. But even as a human few have the opportunity to practise Dharma. We used to joke saying if you wanted to practise Dharma, it wasn't enough to be born human these days – you also needed to have a British passport!

Rinpoche continued his stories day after day with more and more details about the sufferings in the six realms of samsara. He told us about weird monsters living in lakes in Tibet who as humans in past lives had done something bad like lying or stealing. I didn't believe any of it. If ever there was a Tibetan present when he told these stories they would listen enthralled like children. When it came to the particularly gruesome bits about the hells they would gasp and grab their prayer beads, desperately reciting mantras under their breath from what I took to be a combination of compassion, fear and faith all at once. Could it be that they were getting the same sort of thrill out of these stories as some people do from horror stories?

Many, if not most, of the Westerners had come via the hippy trail and found these stories credible and scary because of the sorts of trips they had been having. They are particularly scary if you don't have the faith that the Buddha, Dharma and Sangha can save you. Typically Tibetans have faith and just as typically Westerners do not. Being reminded of these stories, Tibetans repent their faults and feel joyfully freed of them and their evil consequences; their faith in Dharma therefore increases. Without faith in the redeeming power of the Dharma, however, remembering your faults and evil deeds leaves you with feelings of guilt, low self-worth, self-hatred and depression. Stories about karma and its results compound the problem by leaving you in a state of abject fear and despair. It must be hard for people from cultures where faith is strong to imagine what it's like to be so profoundly without it as many Westerners are.

I was still struggling to open up to the kind of world view that Kalu Rinpoche's teachings implied. There were many pieces of the jigsaw missing, subtleties left to be discovered and many false assumptions on my part that were getting in the way. Kalu Rinpoche, for his part, was learning on the job how to teach Westerners. He had had no preparation for this. These foreign people who seemed to know nothing, like children, were not like any children he was used to. I was there right at the beginning of his learning curve. To help myself take his teachings to heart I would write up my notes and illustrate them with little drawings to somehow bring them to life for myself. When other Westerners saw my notebook they wanted to copy it out, and I am told it was hand copied a number of times over the years.

One important message that I did pick up on was that even when one devotes oneself to meditation there are traps. You can think you have reached an elevated state, a divine state, but actually the ego is still clinging to existence in a way that will not allow Enlightenment to happen. I took on board the fact that you can make subtle mistakes in meditation that could have serious consequences, although I wasn't really clear about how to avoid them in my own meditation.

Whenever Rinpoche started talking about the true nature of mind and of reality I perked up, and as time went on Rinpoche talked about it more and more. He would sit there before us holding up something like a piece of fruit or a Buddha image or anything he had to hand and cover it with the corner of his blanket or a cloth of some kind as he explained one simple principle over and over again. This is that we all have Buddha Nature. He would use the example of a lump of gold covered in dirt. The gold is there under the dirt, but you cannot see it and it doesn't shine. If you clean and polish it to remove all the impurities, then it shines like gold. Like that, if we remove the dirt of our negative mental states from our mind then the Buddha qualities will shine forth in all their glory. They have always been there. If we didn't have Buddha qualities from the beginning then there would be no use in trying to produce them by removing impurities from our minds – just as a lump of coal would only ever be coal, however much you polished it.

It reminded me of the Vedanta teachings I had talked about with my Indian friend in Varanasi so I asked Rinpoche what he thought of Vedanta. He asked me about it and I said that as far as I could see it matched Mahayana Buddhism on every point. 'Every point?' he asked. 'Yes,' I said boldly, even though I wasn't sure. 'So, what are you asking?' He was clearly not interested in making a distinction if there wasn't one. Fair enough, I thought.

I understood that Buddha Nature was the mind, but what did it mean to say the mind was like gold? I could understand that my mind was misunderstanding reality, but I couldn't really understand the concept of its being covered over or obscured by anything. It has literally taken decades for the significance of these profound teachings to really have much impact on me.

Indeed, as I was to learn as the years went by, what Rinpoche was saying was highly controversial within the Buddhist tradition. Much of the Buddha's teaching is about impermanence, suffering and not-self, stressing the illusion and dream-like quality of conditioned phenomena. Many Buddhists both past and present believe that this is all there is: that everything is conditioned, including the wisdom and compassion of the Buddha. I thought that for a long time and never questioned it. I was vaguely aware that nirvana was supposed to be unconditioned, and that in Buddhism, unconditioned means unchanging, but I didn't think much about what that meant. It didn't occur to me that this is what Kalu Rinpoche was talking about. Much later I discovered there are different views in the Buddhist tradition about what the unconditioned could possibly be or mean. In Kalu Rinpoche's image, it is the piece of gold obscured by wrong ways of thinking.

I had always assumed 'mind' simply meant thinking and thoughts. As I started to let go of thoughts in meditation, I was gaining familiarity with a certain sense of the space they played in, as when we say 'a thought came into my mind'. Beyond that I didn't yet have any sense of anything permanent and unchanging. I had already made a start in approaching my own thoughts differently with my investigations under Trungpa Rinpoche before I came to India, and Karma Thinley Rinpoche's skilful undermining of my habitual ways of thinking had helped me open up my perceptions further. Now Kalu Rinpoche was telling me about a whole different way to understand the mind itself. I still had a long way to go before I would really see what he was getting at, however.

Part of the problem was that this perspective relied on the concept of emptiness, which is unfamiliar to anyone steeped in western thought, and has radical implications. Kalu Rinpoche would sometimes hold up a glass of water and say, 'To us it's a glass of water, to a being in hell it's a cauldron of molten metal, to a hungry ghost it is a vat of inedible pus, to a fish it's a place to swim in and to a god it's a vase of nectar.' I could understand the human and the fish part of the simile, but the rest was lost on me. Over the years I puzzled about what kind of universe it is where the same thing can be all these different things to different beings depending on their perception. What was that saying about the nature of the universe? It is a very telling example – revolutionary in the extreme and very hard to understand. You have to understand the Buddhist idea of emptiness and you find emptiness by realising the true nature of mind. I was a long way off from understanding any of that.

Shortly after I had settled into my new life in Sonada, excitement started to build up because the monks' three-year retreat was coming to an end. Family and friends were preparing for the feasting and celebrations. A young lama called Bokar Rinpoche had been in the retreat with them. He was about five years older than I was and had been recognised back in Tibet as the reincarnation of the previous head of Bokar monastery in western Tibet, hence his title. Karma Yangzom said, 'They say he is a *great* meditator – but not proud – he is so simple and approachable you can even ask him questions!' For Tibetans in general but for nuns in particular it takes a lot of courage to ask questions. I have even heard them discouraging each other from doing so as if somehow it were presumptuous for a nun to do so because women should be meek and humble. It is an example of how sometimes social customs in Buddhist countries can masquerade as Dharma when in fact they are quite the contrary. I don't know how I would ever have learnt anything if I had not felt able to ask questions.

On the day the retreat ended we nuns all trooped into his tiny room one behind the other to offer our traditional white scarves (*katags*) as a way of making a connection. I didn't get much of an impression of him that first day. His face was long and solemn and he didn't have much to say. Some days later he was circumambulating the temple on his own, hands behind his back and feet at an angle – an odd and distinctive gait. I wondered if he was rather aloof since he always seemed to walk alone. Then an old woman ran up to him with her head bowed in respect. As she stopped in front of him she looked up at him with a huge grin and his face broke into a beautiful, open, welcoming smile. That was it. If he could smile like that for her, then why not for me? I decided that next time our paths crossed, I would smile first and not allow myself to be awed into shyness.

I'll never forget that first smile. I was standing by the spring, washing some pots, and as I looked up I saw him stepping solemnly down the stone steps towards me. Without waiting for him to acknowledge me, I smiled my warmest smile and there it was – his face lit up for me as it had done for her. He laughed lightly and happily like a child, and tried to talk to me. I don't remember what we said to each other, but shortly after that I began my lessons with him.

We agreed that I would teach him English and he would teach me Tibetan, but after the first few lessons he said to me, slowly but accurately, 'When... will... you... be... able... to... start... the... preliminary practices?' 'You've been learning English before,' I said. 'A little,' he replied. That was his last formal English lesson with me. After that we worked each day for two or three hours on translating texts that I needed for my practice. I was very lucky to be there when Bokar Rinpoche had just come out of his three-year retreat, because it meant he didn't have much of a programme, so had plenty of time for me. In the decades to come he would build his own monastery and attract hundreds of Western students. But back then, I pretty much had him to myself!

He was very circumspect in the sense that he always insisted that Karma Yangzom accompany me to our sessions together and if neither she nor another person was in the room with us he would call out of the window for someone to come, so everyone knew that nothing was going on be-hind closed doors between himself and this young western nun!

For some reason known only to himself, a wealthy young American started to tell the rest of us Westerners that Bokar Rinpoche was so rich it was useless to give him the kind of little things that we gave to other lamas. They would just mean nothing to him. I believed that for a while, until Karma Yangzom told me she had overheard Bokar Rinpoche (through the thin partition wall between his room and hers) saying to his attendant, 'Gosh, someone has given us five ru-pees. That is going to be useful.' Hardly the talk of a rich man! Amazingly Karma Yangzom had enough courage to ask him what his financial situation was and discovered that far from being rich he was in debt. His so-called riches were all the treasures of his monastery that he held in safe keeping. It wasn't his wealth at all. Once I knew that, I made it known to the other Westerners, with the result that a young man named Ken Mcleod took it upon himself to make a danger-ous three day journey into the wilds of east Nepal to find the rather shady money lender whom Bokar Rinpoche had used and pay back his debt for him.

The preliminary practices that Bokar Rinpoche was asking me about start with doing 100,000 prostrations. Previously in Tilokpur Karma Thinley Rinpoche had suggested I do one hundred prostrations before breakfast. I had seen people doing full length prostrations on the floor and had had a go at it. It was rather a pleasant experience lying there feeling you had surrendered your all to the Buddha. The next two or three prostrations were not quite the same as the novelty wore off. After ten of them I was already struggling and de-cided that he must have been having me on.

'You were joking, weren't you?' I had said when I saw Karma Thinley Rinpoche later that day. 'One hundred is too many. Ten is enough isn't it? After that it all gets too uncomforta-ble and distracting. You can't meditate properly doing that.'

'I not joking,' he replied. 'Some people doing 3,000 a day.' I thought that excessive, but I had started doing a few each day because I liked doing them. However, Bokar Rinpoche was prompting me to undertake the full set of 100,000. In conversations with other Westerners I heard that an English nun in Tilokpur had done the full 100,000 prostrations and I thought, 'If she can, then I can too.' Several years later I discovered she hadn't finished them at all – nonetheless her reputation had spurred me on!

These preliminary practices are standard for all the different schools and lineages in Tibetan Buddhism. There are four parts to the practices: as well as prostrations they include ritual offerings, prayers and mantras. Although they are called preliminary practices, on closer examination one finds they are full-on actual practices, rather than merely preliminaries. Each has a liturgy that has to be recited 100,000 times. I would need to translate these liturgies before I could start the four sets of 100,000.

I was well up for spending one to three hours a day translating texts, sitting at Bokar Rinpoche's feet head to head poring over the texts, learning Tibetan as I went. I would look up all the words beforehand in my dictionary and discuss what I was learning with Karma Yangzom as a further exercise in learning Tibetan. Bokar Rinpoche and I spent weeks and months like this on and off for the next four years. What a rare opportunity and an amazing privilege! I wanted it to go on forever.

I was learning from him all the time on all sorts of levels. On one level we were both learning from each other about the differences in the assumptions he and I were bringing to our discussions. I would ask a question and he would answer it, but if he could see by the look on my face that I was not totally convinced by his answer (even if I assented to it), he would lean back laughing and say, 'You are not satisfied.' He would think in silence for a while and then come back with another answer and sometimes repeat this process a few times till I would change my expression and say 'Ah!' as when the penny drops. He would laugh even more then and say, 'Now she gets it! Ah! Ah!' Then he would become serious again and ask me what I had been thinking for it to have taken me so long to get the point. I would tell him and he would sit back and consider my point of view for a while. Sometimes he would say, 'I agree with that. I think what you were thinking was right.' He had a very open and flexible mind that made him a brilliant teacher.

Bokar Rinpoche and Kalu Rinpoche took a somewhat different approach to teaching. Once I started to study with Bokar Rinpoche, Kalu Rinpoche would always direct me back to him if I asked him a question. At his afternoon teachings Kalu Rinpoche would often mention prostrations in connection with the idea of removing obscurations and veils. I found the language unappealing, so it was a relief to be able to discuss it with Bokar Rinpoche as we worked on the same kind of language in the texts.

'What *are* these obscurations and veils then really?' I'd ask and a discussion about the nature of mind would ensue. It was all shorthand for subtle truths that he could point out to me one to one and which I could then pursue in the context of meditation practice. 'Removing veils and obscurations' is a clumsy phrase in English compared with the term *tibjang* in Tibetan. Tibetans use *tibjang* almost synonymously with Dharma practice. What else is 'practice' other than removing veils? The true nature of mind is already gold. It is not something you create through your own effort.

I could just about get my head around that, at least intellectually. I had more difficulty with the idea of *punya* (Tib. *sonam*) translated variously as merit or luck depending on context. Kalu Rinpoche would carefully explain that *punya* was the happy result or fruition of positive karmic action. Misery was the fruition of negative karmic action (Skt. *papa*, Tib. *digpa*). In our innocence we accepted the then current translations of *punya* and *papa* (*sonam* and *digpa*) as 'merit' and 'sin' respectively. Prostrations we were told generated merit or luck (*punya*) and purified sin (*papa*). 'Sins finishing!' my Tibetan friends would exclaim in satisfaction when they encountered difficulties in life. 'You great lucky (*sonam*),' they would say respectfully when observing me engaged in Dharma practice. It was how they talked all the time in their daily life. 'Westerners are expert in vitamins – they know what is good for the body,' observed Karma Yangzom thoughtfully. 'We Tibetans are experts in *sonam* and *digpa*. We know what causes good and bad effects in future lives.' She was latching on to the huge gulf between the way we Westerners thought and how they as Tibetans thought. It might all be concepts but it made all the difference when it came to how you lived your life.

Kalu Rinpoche made little bendy movements with his long thin trembling fingers, saying, 'Just doing prostrations mechanically without faith and devotion is like a worm wriggling along on its belly like this.' I wondered if I had faith and devotion but supposed I must have because I was still there practising and eager to learn more. 'But why do 100,000 prostrations?' we would ask. 'It is like soldiers square-bashing in the army,' said Kalu Rinpoche. 'It builds up your stamina and prepares you, body and mind, to be a good spiritual practitioner.' I wondered if this didn't contradict what Karma Thinley Rinpoche had taught me about relaxing the mind. Kalu Rinpoche assured us, 'Your mind relaxes naturally when you are totally exhausted physically.' Still I took some convincing that hours and hours of prostrating didn't take precious time and energy away from meditation.

Thinking that you have to try something in order to judge it, I let it be known that I was going to do one hundred prostrations a day in the temple. It seems the word spread rapidly around the whole monastery and there was great excitement that for the first time, a Westerner was taking up prostration practice so seriously. I cried in the temple the first time I tried to do a hundred prostrations. I had committed to doing it, but I didn't understand what I was doing. What did it mean to say this exercise was purifying sins and accumulating *punya*? What is a Buddha *really*?

I was still struggling to understand the liturgy I had just translated. It was full of all sorts of strange terms and concepts. I was supposed to be taking Refuge in the Buddha, Dharma and Sangha with every prostration, while visualising them in the sky before me. I couldn't even visualise the sky in the poorly lit temple crammed with sacred images and paintings, so forget about Buddhas. Then I was supposed to be able to see the Guru, the yidams, dakinis and Dharma protectors. It was all just words to me. It would have helped if I had known what they were before I took Refuge and the empowerments all those months ago in Dalhousie, but nobody had told me much at all. Nobody seemed to care about my ignorance.

I asked Kalu Rinpoche what was actually meant by Buddha. I had assumed he was a historical person who had died and not like a god you prayed to. His simple answer was, 'The Buddha is the same as the Guru.' Did he mean himself? Was I prostrating to him as the Buddha? Actually, that just raised more questions than it answered. It didn't tell me anything about what a Buddha was.

Kalu Rinpoche was quite famous and well known so many people came to see him. Bokar Rinpoche being younger and less well known tended to get ignored, which is why I had him more or less to myself. I would join the other Westerners when Kalu Rinpoche was giving a teaching, but I didn't realise how out of touch I was with the others until one day they all came to Bokar Rinpoche for a teaching. It turned out that the way I asked questions in class annoyed some of them as it seemed to them that I held up the teachings. They sent one of their number to speak to me nicely about it afterwards and request that I desist from asking questions in class. So the next time we were in a teaching with Bokar

Rinpoche I was very careful not to say anything. Ironically enough the class finished early because the others wanted to go to watch a football match in Darjeeling on television. After they had left Bokar Rinpoche turned to me and said, 'If you have questions then you must ask.' I was so relieved. I never stopped asking questions after that.

Kalu Rinpoche asked Bokar Rinpoche to teach us all about the Buddha qualities. He seemed a bit surprised to be asked to do this, but started teaching them from a text. It all sounded pretty absurd. The Buddha was supposed to be 20 feet tall, with long ears and webbed fingers. When it came to his arms reaching down to his knees someone from the back of the class piped up, 'Good heavens!' and we all burst out laughing.

Since none of it seemed to relate to the nature of mind, I just ignored it all and was none the wiser about why or how to prostrate to the Buddha with faith and devotion. Nonetheless, I kept going with the practice and told Kalu Rinpoche each day how many I had done and each day he suggested I doubled the number the next day. I went from 100 to 200, 200 to 400, 400 to 800 in a matter of days; 1,600 was too big a leap though. Having done 800 in the morning I told Karma Yangzom I was going to take the afternoon off because I felt so exhausted, dizzy and weak. 'No, no, you must go back after lunch. This is a sign your body is changing – you will find this afternoon it will go very easily.' I didn't believe her so to prove her wrong I went back expecting to feel worse and worse as the day wore on. I was wrong. By the evening I had completed another 800 as if I were flying. It was exhilarating! Since then I have found out that prostration practice is supposed to straighten the subtle energy channels and currents in the body to make the mind and body free-flowing and flexible as a preparation for deep meditation practice. If only I had known that in advance!

From the beginning when setting out for India I had had the sense that this was forever, I didn't intend to return to the

West until I was Enlightened and since there was no guarantee I would reach Enlightenment in this life I had no plans for returning. Even though I first encountered the Dharma in the West, I didn't believe you could seriously practise it there. You had to have the good fortune to be able to stay here in the East to plumb its depths at the feet of great lamas such as Kalu Rinpoche in the company of committed practitioners such as the monks and nuns I was living with. I didn't believe that a brief exposure to the teachings derived from just a few months in the company of a lama was enough. It had to be a lifetime commitment both to understanding the language and culture as well as to deepening and stabilising one's practice. To my mind these were far too early days to be thinking of committed Dharma practice in the West. I knew Karma Thinley Rinpoche was thinking of joining Trungpa Rinpoche in Scotland but at that point Dharma being taught in the West was not an idea that I took seriously.

Imagine my horror and indignation therefore when I woke up one morning to a tremendous hullaballoo as the news spread rapidly around the monastery that Kalu Rinpoche had gone off to the USA with a rich American student with no indication that he intended to return. Monks and nuns were weeping in despair as if he had died, saying, 'It is like the sun has disappeared from the sky.' For us Westerners it seemed outrageous. Part of the whole mystique was that people had to come here to the East to absorb the atmosphere. We were the ones who had made the great effort to come here to learn at the feet of our guru and now he had just disappeared into the West. Although we felt let down and distraught, all we could do was keep going with our daily routine and wait to see what would happen. I continued with my prostrations and working with Bokar Rinpoche on translating the text for the preliminary practices.

After some months, to everyone's huge relief and joy, Kalu Rinpoche returned and took up residence again in the monastery. Normal life resumed and Kalu Rinpoche regaled us with his experiences in the West. 'In the West people told me desire is good and they didn't believe in making people monks and nuns,' he said and then mischievously looked across at an American monk and myself saying, 'Oh dear. What have we done to you!'

It was not just our little community in Sonada that sighed with relief to have Rinpoche back among us. I heard that the Dalai Lama had remarked how pleased he was that Kalu Rinpoche had returned: 'So often lamas going West is like losing needles in a haystack,' he said. 'You never see them again.'

Bokar Rinpoche started teaching me about the preliminary practice which consists of mandala offerings. This entails offering up the whole world to the Buddhas in the form of a flat metal mandala plate of rice grains representing the whole universe. The text described the universe as if it were a flat world and I wondered how I was supposed to take this. I asked him why the texts taught the world to be flat. He thought carefully for a while and then said, 'Because it is flat.' That was a revelation to me: I hadn't imagined he actually believed it was flat! I told him it wasn't, and he was surprised. I told him that contrary to what it said in the texts, there was no big mountain in the middle of the world either. At that he jumped up and hurried out of the room to check with Kalu Rinpoche, who had presumably seen the central mountain on his trip to the States. When he came back with the information that the world was not flat, nor did it have a central mountain, he was clearly puzzled and amused, but he didn't seem very bothered that his whole world view had just been shattered. I asked him again why he thought the Buddhist texts taught that the world was flat when it wasn't, and he said, 'Maybe things have changed since the time of the Buddha.' I said things couldn't have changed that much, and he thought about my reply before remarking, 'Well, the Buddha taught different things about the nature of the world according to who he was talking to at the time. Different texts give completely different accounts. Some say it's round.' Then he added, 'It is important to check out things that the Buddha said in our own experience. We Tibetans are so bad about that. The Buddha told us not to believe things just because he said them, but I have always believed the world was flat without checking it out.' After a while he laughed happily as he concluded, 'Well, the Buddha taught that the world was like a dream and an illusion, so it isn't all that important anyway.'

Over the next five years I came and went to Sonada depending on the permit situation. I had to leave when my permit ran out and would go to Tilokpur, Nepal or other Buddhist pilgrimage places to practise and do retreat. It took me about a year, often practising ten hours a day, to finish my 100,000 prostrations and the other three sets of 100,000 preliminary practices. In this I was a trail blazer. Following my lead, other Westerners around Kalu Rinpoche started to do the same. It caught on as the thing to do if you were a serious practitioner. Just for good measure I eventually did the whole set of preliminaries three times over. This delighted my Tibetan colleagues, even though it is not unusual for even lay Tibetans do them far more times than that.

I am not sure whether the preliminary practices increased my faith or not. It helped build trust between me and my Tibetan teachers, showing that we Westerners were open to instruction and ready to practise the Dharma seriously. It was a time of big change in the way Westerners were relating to Buddhism. We were no longer just scholars writing books about it or groupies hanging out with lamas, enthralled by the exoticism of it all. We were now really engaging in it. I came to learn that this was happening simultaneously all over India and other Buddhist countries and even in the West.

If the preliminary practices were not increasing my faith, what did I have faith in and what was holding me there? It was the lamas themselves who inspired confidence in me by the way they were and through the conversations I was able to have with them. Applying all I learnt from them to my practice, especially to my meditation, was changing my whole world view and the way I conceived of reality. This is how my understanding and faith gradually deepened. This kind of interaction creates an environment and atmosphere and is what is meant by sangha. Was *this* what Trungpa Rinpoche had meant by having faith in the qualities of the sangha rather than specific personalities. Is it what he meant later by 'absorbing the vibes'? Studying texts helped in the sense that they structured the teachings, but they were brought alive through discussions with my teachers and colleagues.

Doing the prostrations definitely reinforced my determination to leave worldly life behind me and to give myself completely to the path leading to Enlightenment which is awakening to Truth. The physicality of having to throw myself down on the floor fully outstretched again and again chanting prayers as I did so, helped align body, speech, heart and mind with my deepest heart wish. It was a powerful practice of training in renunciation and self-discipline. I was buoyed up by the sense that doing this particular practice was pleasing my teachers, so I was not tempted to give up when the going got difficult. This made my life simple and straightforward. Bringing my mind back again and again to my motivation for practising turned each prostration into a kind of meditation. I was letting go of meaningless mental chatter and concentrating my mind on opening myself up to the Truth beyond all concepts. I was chanting words in praise of the Buddha, Dharma and Sangha but in fact I was only dimly aware of what any of that meant. Now I look back on those days I am surprised how much inspiration I found in doing the practice even though I knew so little compared with what I know now.

Five

Learning from Bokar Rinpoche

Each year Karma Ozer came to visit her sister Karma Yang-zom in Sonada during the long holidays between her University terms. When the three of us were there together, we spent many happy hours between meditation sessions talking and joking over endless cups of tea. Both the sisters had been nuns since childhood and told me stories about their experiences in Tibet, their escape from the Chinese and about being refugees in India. Especially they told me about Khenpo Tsultrim Gyamtso Rinpoche, who had been their main teacher in Tibet. 'Khenpo' is an academic title, more or less equivalent to Doctor or Professor. What made Khenpo Rinpoche very special was that he was also well known for his realisation as a yogin – like an Enlightened professor. Karma Yangzom told me that Khenpo Rinpoche and Bokar Rinpoche were alike in the sense that both were very clear and approachable. You could ask them questions.

A tiny black and white photo of Khenpo Rinpoche sat on Karma Yangzom's shrine and I often found my attention inexplicably drawn to it. I developed a strong wish to meet him someday. They told me he was living as a wandering yogin in Bhutan practising in charnel grounds. Karma Yang-zom first met him when she was very young. He had been living in a charnel ground near their nunnery and some of the nuns asked him to be their teacher. He must have been quite young himself then and in order to keep to the monastic rule to not be alone in a room with a woman, he taught her through the door. She had been so curious to see what he looked like that she had peeped through the keyhole.

She ducked away quickly when she saw him looking straight back at her!

In 1959, as the situation with the Chinese in Tibet was rapidly worsening, the nuns were wondering what to do, and they asked Khenpo Rinpoche's advice. He said he would lead them to India and that they had to leave immediately. Despite great reluctance, they did – a band of about twenty nuns, ages ranging from very old to mere children, led by a young yogin without a guide. From then on he was always referred to as the 'nuns' khenpo', which is no high-sounding title, since in traditional Tibetan circles nuns are of low status compared with monks. Years later the nuns heard that the Chinese had invaded their area the very night they left. On arriving at an abandoned monastery the next night, they wanted to stay because they were all so tired, but Khenpo Rinpoche wouldn't let them. At the time, they thought he must be mad but later they found out that the Chinese had again taken it over as soon as they had left. Karma Yangzom was sixteen and her sister was eight years old at the time. As they said good-bye to their mother, she was crying and so was little Karma Ozer. Karma Yangzom knew that she must not cry too or all would be lost. She held back her tears, but years later, she still regularly woke up to find her pillow wet with crying for her mother.

Karma Ozer was always either studying or meditating whenever I saw her and mostly meditating as far as I could see. However, whereas she was calm, her older sister who was supposed to be the great meditator was always fussing about and anxious. In Tibetan Buddhism there is a kind of tension between those who study the classic philosophical texts and commentaries and those who simply focus on meditation and other devotional and ritual practices. 'To meditate without studying is like trying to scale a cliff blindfolded. To study without meditating is like trying to scale a cliff with no legs,' I was told many times by different teachers. I thought of all I was learning from the practice texts I was translating with Bokar Rinpoche as studying, but later on I realised that what Tibetans tend to mean by study is scholastic studies such as Karma Ozer was doing in Varanasi. Since many great yogins gain realisation through relying on the oral instructions of their yogin teachers and since some can't even read very well, scholastic learning is clearly not essential and can even just be a source of pride. I often heard it said that many a great scholar has died a bad death, implying that scholars are not necessarily good practitioners.

With this in mind Karma Yangzom was worried about her sister and wanted Bokar Rinpoche to speak to her about the importance of meditation practice. She came back from seeing him shame-faced. 'I feel so embarrassed,' she confided. 'I told Rinpoche how worried I was about Karma Ozer and asked him to speak to her because she won't listen to me.' 'What did he say?' I asked. 'He told me the story about the frog in the well. I'm not sure what he meant by it, but I think he was pointing out my faults – my pride perhaps.' 'What is the story of the frog in the well?' I asked. 'There is a frog in the bottom of the well who calls to his friend on the surface outside of the well: "Hey, you should come down here and see the sky above me – it is amazing, so bright and blue, so high and huge." He keeps calling to his friend like this, but his friend never comes. Eventually his friend says, "Why don't you come and see my sky, then?" The first frog finally decides to go and see. He climbs up to the top of the well and jumps out. As he does so, he looks up and sees the full extent of the sky in all its vastness and brightness. He is so totally overwhelmed that his head bursts with the shock.' Karma Yangzom felt she shouldn't ask Bokar Rinpoche about this matter again. She needn't have worried, as Karma Ozer subsequently spent most of the rest of her life in meditation retreat.

Another special friend of mine in Sonada was a monk named Tenpa Gyamtso, who was just a few years older than I was.

He was very open-hearted, with a warm and happy smile. Other Tibetans saw him as a good practitioner and half in admiration and half in fun would often tease him. Unlike so many of the other monks who sought out wealthy Westerners as potential sponsors, he made a habit of befriending poor Westerners who looked in need of help. The others would joke, 'He is so poor himself, you would think he would learn, but no. He always does the same thing!' One time when I was leaving Sonada and my monthly money order hadn't arrived, he was concerned about me and gave me all the little money he had. I was reluctant to accept this but he reassured me, saying, 'You need it more than me because you're travelling. I'm ok as I can eat scraps off the other monks' plates.' He and I became good friends and talked deeply about Dharma, chatting happily in Tibetan with each other for hours on end.

Throughout my days in Sonada I took every opportunity to learn Tibetan from the people around me. It helped that hardly anyone knew English. I took to learning like a child does. I would watch people doing things such as washing something up and ask them, in Tibetan, what they were doing. Then I would try to repeat their answers, substituting different words to find out which were the nouns and verbs. Like a child, I ended up saying some ridiculous things, like 'I am saucepanning the wash', but I learnt very quickly. Within six months I was able to hold my own in conversation – though that is not to say I spoke well! It was a fun way to learn spoken Tibetan.

With Bokar Rinpoche I learned classical Tibetan, which is used for talking about Dharma. Tibetans use the same language for talking about Dharma as was used a thousand years ago. It's a bit like people speaking English as Chaucer did. It really brings the ancient texts alive when you can hear them still spoken as written so long ago. The few translations that existed of the texts I needed were full of faults, and this spurred me on to try to make my own translations of everything I needed, even if it was a laborious and time-consuming endeavour. I enjoyed translation work immensely and it helped me grapple with the teachings. How to translate any term became a study in what the term actually meant in practice.

For quite a few of the key terms there were no equivalents in English. One such word was *sem* (Skt. *chitta*) which was commonly translated as 'mind'. Kalu Rinpoche sometimes looked at us fondly and smiled, tapping his forehead and saying, 'You Westerners think your *sem* is here, don't you?' Then, tapping his breast bone, he would say, 'We Tibetans have our *sem* here.' He was obviously very amused by this. We were just baffled. To our way of thinking, of course the mind was in the head; indeed for many people, head and mind are synonymous. From the scientific point of view, we still have a lot to learn about the heart, but even now generally speaking we don't associate the mind with the heart.

At the time I would just laugh too because I didn't realise how serious this issue was. I had always considered Buddhism and the teachings on reality to be about the nature of mind in the sense that we Westerners mean it. That was what I was interested in, and by always translating *sem* as 'mind' I did not realise that not only was I restricting my own understanding but also helping perpetuate this notion that *sem* was in the head, not the heart. No wonder I did not understand what Kalu Rinpoche had been teaching us about Buddha Nature, faith and devotion. What place did they have in a Buddhism based in the head? We don't talk about purifying our heads, do we? We talk about purifying our hearts. It is maybe an old-fashioned way of talking, but a 'pure heart' still carries meaning.

Sem wasn't the only word I was having trouble with. The problem of how to translate *punya* (Tib. *sonam*) kept coming up. The usual translation of 'merit' just didn't capture the meaning, since for Tibetans *punya* is a cosmic principle, associated with all the goodness arising from positive karmic action. It is more important than food and money even, because a good supply of food and money is dependent on having a good supply of *punya*. That is why, typically, when you make a gift of even a little money to a poor Tibetan, hoping they will buy themselves food with it, they are likely to spend the first part of it on an offering to the Buddha, Dharma and Sangha in order to generate more *punya*. The second part they give to you the donor and only the third part of it they use for themselves for food. They are happy to give away most of what they are given because if they have used it to generate *punya* they feel rich and fortunate!

Time and again Kalu Rinpoche would remind us, 'Enlightenment requires a vast accumulation of *punya,* so never tire of doing good actions with your body, speech and mind.' There was no getting around it. I *had* to know what it meant. The closest I got at the time was that it was like sowing a huge amount of seeds that would ripen later as good conditions for practising Dharma and helping others, in this lifetime and in future ones.

I was beginning to think in terms of future lives by this stage. It was just the way everyone around me thought and talked. 'Is it true that Westerners don't believe in past and future lives?' asked Karma Yangzom. I told her it was. 'But they all seem to be so well behaved. They don't kill, lie and steal – they are quite honest and trustworthy.' 'Why wouldn't they be?' I ask. 'We wouldn't be if we didn't believe in karmic cause and effect. It is what makes us behave ourselves. What makes Westerners behave themselves?' That is when I realised just how much of the Tibetan culture I had absorbed simply from being around them all the time. I couldn't remember how I used to think. 'They are just taught not to be selfish and to be kind to others and so that is what they try to do,' I said. 'That is hard,' said Karma Yangzom. 'How wonderful that they try. They must be Bodhisattvas who have been Buddhist in past lives,' she concluded. Even though I found these ideas of karma quite familiar at this stage, I was dubious about how seeds planted in this life could ripen in a future life.

Nevertheless, I really liked the idea that you could accumulate *punya* from rejoicing in the good deeds of others. This is a brilliant practice because if someone is doing more good than you are, you can gain the same *punya* as they are by simply rejoicing at what they are doing. You don't have to do anything else. It is so much more wholesome than feeling competitive or thinking their doing so well means you are failing in some way. It is a great antidote to jealousy! Kalu Rinpoche told us the story of a beggar woman who made vast *punya* by rejoicing at the good done by a rich man who threw a feast for the Buddha. The Buddha announced that this woman had accumulated more *punya* by her simple act of rejoicing than the rich man whose bounty they were all enjoying, because she was humble and he was proud. The rich man became enraged and this created so much bad karma that he lost lots of *punya* that day instead of gaining it. The story had a sad ending though, at least for the old woman. The rich man threw another feast at which her mind was so full of thoughts of greed for the food she lost *punya* and this time the rich man could surpass her.

Keeping the five most basic Buddhist precepts against killing, stealing, lying, sexual misconduct and intoxication helps accumulate *punya* so it is perhaps surprising that Tibetans typically are big meat-eaters. They are the first to admit this goes against the precept to not kill and the Bodhisattva vow to care for all beings, but their excuse is that in Tibet it is difficult to grow vegetables and so they have got in the habit of eating meat. They agree it is not a good excuse but there you are. Many of us Westerners had difficulty with this, because compassion for all beings seems to imply not eating meat. When I was in India I only knew two Tibetans who didn't eat meat – the great yogin Chatral Rinpoche and Ani Tsewang Choden. She and I would make cheese and onion dumplings sometimes that were so good all the meat eaters wanted to eat them too. We hoped this would convert them to giving up meat but there seemed little chance of that. One day I happened to be in the monks' kitchen chatting to the cook – a big man with a greasy black apron and huge ladle with which he poured himself some of the meat stock to taste it. He saw me eyeing what he was doing and asked, as a joke, if I also wanted some, knowing full well I was vegetarian. Since I wasn't feeling too good that day and thought it might be because I wasn't getting enough protein, I said 'yes', which rather shocked him. 'But you've taken a vow not to eat meat,' he said. 'You can't just eat meat when you feel like it.'

I told him I didn't have a vow and he was even more astonished. 'What is the point of not eating meat if you don't have a vow? If you take a vow that will vastly increase the *punya*. Go and take a vow with Bokar Rinpoche and then make sure you never eat meat.' I asked him why, if he believed this, did he eat meat. With disarming honesty he replied off-handedly that he was used to it and that he was not strong-minded enough to change his ways. He was happy to just rejoice in my *punya*. Bokar Rinpoche was delighted when I told him I wanted to take a vow. 'You will be protecting all animals forever instead of just a few that you simply happen not to eat,' he explained. 'A cat too lazy to catch mice doesn't make bad karma as long as it doesn't kill but doesn't make much *punya* because it doesn't have the good intention to not kill. If you have a vow against eating meat, all the time you do not eat meat you are accumulating *punya* because you are fulfilling your intention.' So I made a promise in front of Bokar Rinpoche not to eat meat, out of compassion for all beings. He was very pleased and said, 'Now you are truly a protector for all beings.' At that time Bokar Rinpoche was not vegetarian, even though he told me he wanted to be. He didn't want to put the cook to any extra trouble or to look like he was up-staging Kalu Rinpoche, who ate meat. Later, when he built his own monastery, Bokar Rinpoche made his whole monastery give up meat.

One of the things that makes it difficult to translate *punya* is the idea that it can be dedicated for particular purposes as if it were a commodity that you could give away. One of the few Westerners I spent any significant time with during my years in India was Ani Pema, an English nun just a few years older than I was. We both spent time in Sonada learning from Kalu Rinpoche and Bokar Rinpoche and ended up travelling and staying in retreat with each other sometimes. She had come overland to India on the hippy trail and had very little money. One day Pema was going on a rare trip from Sonada to Darjeeling, a few miles away, to do a bit of shopping for several monks and nuns in the monastery who needed medicine. She found the very little money she had was not enough for all the medicines needed. She gave up the idea of doing her own shopping, which included a new pair of flip flops, in order to buy just that little bit more medicine. Walking home to Sonada her old flip flops gave out and she ended up barefoot and arrived back with feet sore and bleeding. This turned into a huge opportunity for everyone at the monastery to rejoice in her *punya*. 'How kindhearted – just like a Bodhisattva!' they exclaimed admiringly. 'We pray all the time for the happiness of all beings, but we would never do that would we? How wonderful!' They raised their eyes heavenward, soaking in the goodness – rejoicing in her *punya* and thereby generating the same amount of *punya* themselves.

There is a sequel to the story. After a while it came out that one of the people who'd requested medicine from her was a rich monk (strange though it sounds, some monks were known to be rich!). Indignation mounted against this man, who did not need her charity, but it quickly subsided again when it transpired that he hadn't asked for medicine for himself. He had asked for it on behalf of a local layman. So why had he not bought him the medicine himself? His thinking was that he would let Pema make the *punya* from buying medicine, because as a Westerner she would be happy to do that, and meanwhile he would use his money to make offerings in the temple of butter lamps and food for the monks. As a Tibetan, he knew there was more *punya* in offering to the Buddha, Dharma and Sangha than to a simple layman and that Pema as a Westerner would not realise that. So he could dedicate the *punya* he was making by his offerings in the temple for her benefit. On hearing his thinking, the Tibetans were more than satisfied that he had been trying to maximise the amount of *punya* being generated and that it was not his fault he didn't know Pema had so little money. In this way the whole incident generated loads of *punya* that everyone could rejoice in and dedicate to the Enlightenment of all beings!

After a year or two in India I got hold of one or two books by Trungpa Rinpoche, who was now teaching in America. I found his whole approach to teaching Dharma amazing and quite different from what I was learning at the feet of my masters in India. He explained the six realms of samsara as psychological states and didn't seem to mention *punya* at all. I found this reassuring and it was how I wanted to be taught so I went to Bokar Rinpoche to tell him this. He handled Trungpa Rinpoche's books lovingly. 'Tell me what he says in them,' he asked. I read a few paragraphs to him and then paused to ask if he understood the English. 'No,' he said, 'but it sounds so sweet to my ears. I am making a wish that I will be able to teach like that one day.'

He was obviously very much in awe of Trungpa Rinpoche, as if he knew him personally, though in fact he only knew him by reputation. Trungpa Rinpoche has always been held in high regard by all the lamas I have known, even though in some circles he is regarded as a controversial figure. We heard strange stories about what he was doing in the USA which sounded quite outrageous: he had given up being a monk and was drinking, smoking and had lots of girlfriends. Tibetans are very quick to condemn such behaviour in ordinary lamas, many of whom have been seen to go off the rails, but Trungpa Rinpoche was regarded as a highly realised lama whose conduct could not be judged by ordinary standards. In the tradition there are plenty of stories of highly realised lamas or yogins behaving in ways that for ordinary beings would be regarded as wrong or even mad. The point of such stories is that such lamas have supernormal powers that enable them to cut through concepts and benefit beings in ways the rest of us cannot hope to understand.

'But why doesn't he talk about *punya*?' I asked. 'I don't know,' said Bokar Rinpoche. 'All I can tell you is that it is important and you really need to believe that.' Possibly Trungpa Rinpoche didn't mention *punya* in his writing because we have no word for it in English. He might also have felt that accumulating *punya* is not the best motivation for following the path. As he told us in Reading when I first met him, 'We Easterners can learn something from the West about a social conscience.' He was tapping into what really motivated Westerners without complicating things with words and ideas stemming from a completely different culture and world view.

In Dalhousie I had been told over and over again that the empowerments were all about *Adhishtana* (Tib. *chinlab*), which is usually translated into English as 'blessing'. However much I asked, I never got a satisfactory answer to what was meant by this word in the context of Buddhism. Like *punya* it is a very difficult word to translate, and in fact I feel it's better to stick with the original Sanskrit terms rather than trying to transpose their meaning onto English words that carry a totally different history.

The term blessing is very general in English. Once Bokar Rinpoche, as a friendly gesture, wrote a letter to my mother enclosing in the envelope some protection cords to put around the neck, some mantras and a leaf from the Bodhi Tree in Bodhgaya. I wrote the letter for him and explained that Rinpoche was sending her his blessing. She wrote back thanking him and sending him a packet of little mementos of her own, telling him this was her blessing for him. Bokar Rinpoche was quite touched although a little surprised. His intention had been to make a connection (Skt. *nidana,* Tib. *tendrel*) for her that would link her to the blessing (*adhishtana*) of the Buddha, Dharma and Sangha and help her escape the sufferings of samsara. The blessings she sent him didn't have any power like that.

From his point of view, however, the fact that she had sent her gifts strengthened the connection or *tendrel* with him. Often *tendrel* is translated as auspicious connection or link. I keep to the Tibetan rather than the Sanskrit word here because there are so many contexts when talking to Tibetans where the word *tendrel* comes up naturally in conversation. I am not sure the Sanskrit equivalent, *nidana*, has all the same connotations. Tibetans will use the term *tendrel* to indicate that things are coming together in an auspicious manner, which means the right conditions have been set in motion in the past and are set to continue in the future. You can actively do things to make sure things will come together in a positive way such as making the effort to meet holy people or seeing a friend off in a special way. Such actions create *tendrel* which one might translate as auspiciousness. Signs and portents indicate that something auspicious is about to happen. This is a result of *tendrel* established in the past. In English, we tend to say someone is lucky when things work well and we do things 'for luck'. In Tibetan they use *tendrel* in such situations. However, good *tendrel* is not the result of lucky chance. It is a sign of having made good connections in the past and of them continuing into the future.

Sometimes the way the term *tendrel* is used sounds like what we might call a superstition. For example, it is thought of as bad *tendrel* to give an empty container to anyone. It is a sign of poverty both for the giver and the receiver. So Tibetans will tend to make sure there is something in a box or bag they are giving you or returning to you. One time in

Nepal I was walking down the steps from the stupa as a Tibetan family passed me on their way up. I heard them cry out with delight because I, a nun, was carrying two buckets full of clean water towards them. I heard them uttering over and over to each other 'What good *tendrel*!' which would translate as 'How auspicious!' It was obvious to me that they were going to the stupa that day to pray for blessing, perhaps for someone who was sick. I passed them several times that morning and they were obviously still excited about the *tendrel* of that first meeting.

Making good connections is a major preoccupation for Tibetans since it is an important element in generating *punya*. This explains why, traditionally, a first priority for a Buddhist practitioner is to make offerings to the Three Jewels, the Buddha, Dharma and Sangha. They are believed to have great blessing power (*adhishtana*), so making a strong connection with them gives power to one's hopes and aspirations. This is what offerings, prostrations, taking Refuge, pilgrimage and all the other Buddhist rituals and customs are about. All this activity generates *punya* through linking into sources of *adhishtana*. Even if a Tibetan doesn't understand much Dharma he will join in ritual actions at holy places. The understanding is that all one needs to do in order to participate effectively is to make a skilful vow, prayer or aspiration (Skt. *pranidhana*, Tib. *monlam*) and all will be well. It might be little more than a Westerner making a wish at a wishing well, but for Buddhists it is not just wishful thinking. It is for real. Buddha images, shrines, stupas, texts, places, holy persons and their relics, are all believed to be sources of blessing power.

Another Tibetan term we Westerners had trouble translating was *de pa* (Skt. *shraddha*), usually translated as faith. The trouble with 'faith' is that for many Westerners, especially those interested in Buddhism, the term is too strongly associated with blind belief which is not what is meant. The term confidence has better associations perhaps but for me lacks the sense of open-hearted self-surrender that *shrad-dha* has. Kalu Rinpoche explained on many occasions, that faith was like an iron ring, and the blessing of the Buddhas was like a hook, demonstrating this by hooking with the forefinger of one hand a loop made with his forefinger and thumb on the other. Our job was to create the ring so that the Buddhas could easily hook us out of samsara. It was a graphic image but still didn't tell me what the hook of *adhishtana* was or how to make the ring of faith strong.

One day a Danish man came in for a blessing from Bokar Rinpoche. This was Ole Nydahl, who would later become Lama Ole and be instrumental in drawing thousands of Westerners into Buddhism. He was a very physical kind of person and somehow Rinpoche understood this. He took his head in both his hands and pushed it around this way and that as he recited some kind of blessing. Ole was totally overwhelmed and staggered out of the room clearly well satisfied with his feeling of being thoroughly blessed. Rinpoche laughed happily. Another Western student who had witnessed all this was a young French man called Denys (later to become Lama Denys Teundroup). He looked puzzled and said, 'When we come and ask you questions and try to understand the finer points of the teaching, you encourage us as if that is the right approach. When other people come in and all they want is to feel they have had a strong blessing, you seem to encourage that. Can you explain which of these is the right approach?' Rinpoche told us, 'It is excellent to ask questions and try to understand the teachings. It is also excellent to have a lot of faith and seek blessing. Best is to have both keen intelligence and strong faith, but if you are going to have just one of them, then it's best to have faith.'

On a very basic level faith, even blind faith, helps us create connections (*tendrel*) with people, places and things that have the power of blessing (*adhishtana*) – but I was still struggling with what blessing meant. In Buddhist cultures, all these concepts are taken as given and are so much part of the language, customs and whole way of thinking that it doesn't occur to the people there to try to explain them. As a Westerner all I had to go on were misleadingly simplistic translations. It was only by living with Tibetans and hearing what they talked about and how, that I learnt how these various big ideas formed the conceptual framework that drove their every action. I was right to be asking what blessing was when I first arrived in Dalhousie, but it is no wonder I didn't get a decent reply. It was too early in the process of transmission of Buddhism to Westerners. Nobody had the language skills to plumb the depths of what was being said or to explore what we understood by the words we were using.

Furthermore, in a Buddhist country, Buddhist technical terms are often used in a loose way in everyday talk with the understanding that their meaning goes deep and can only really be understood by an experienced yogin. We Western converts who do not have the same conceptual framework built into our way of thinking and talking from a very early age are not going to respond psychologically to teachings in the same way as those who do. We might adopt the words and the customs, but even so, we are not rooted in them. We and our language are rooted in another culture and world view. Our journey is bound to be different. It is a wonder then that I managed to keep going at all.

Mostly I avoided attending events in the temple. Unlike many of the other Westerners around at the time, I didn't like the imagery or the sound of the musical instruments. The images and paintings of the Buddhist so-called deities, though beautifully crafted, didn't speak to my heart. Who were they all? What did they have to do with me? Then again, to my undiscerning ears, the temple music of horns, drums and cymbals sounded like droning vacuum cleaners and crashing dustbin or saucepan lids. Nevertheless, I occasionally made exceptions such as the annual celebration at the end of the rainy season retreat. This retreat period dated from the time of the Buddha when, to prevent monks trampling the crops, they stayed indoors for the duration of the rains.

At the end of the retreat all the monks gathered in the temple listening to first one monk and then another who had been chosen to stand before the assembly and give a discourse on the Dharma. Each held forth in muted tones and at a brisk pace, perhaps out of nervousness. It was all very formal and hard to follow, so I was not paying much attention, when suddenly I became aware of a ripple of excitement passing through the crowded room. All the nuns near me were giggling, trying to hide the fact by covering their mouths with the corner of their upper robes. The person speaking at the time was Lama Geleg, who was ranting raucously at the assembly, his voice rising in pitch by the moment. Lama Geleg was a garrulous old monk with few but protruding teeth. He always spoke loudly and forcefully, which seemed to amuse people rather than annoy them. Now he sounded like a speaker on a soap box at Hyde Park Corner, exhorting and abusing those around him. Every now and then the whole assembly would burst out laughing, but mostly the monks were silent, clearly listening hard (which is more than they had been doing for the rest of the speakers). Kalu Rinpoche, sitting high above on his throne, gave little away, though as always a wry smile played around his lips and his gentle eyes twinkled. Bokar Rinpoche, sitting at the foot of Kalu Rinpoche's throne, was laughing uninhibitedly, and striking his lap with big measured slaps. Karma Yangzom was laughing far too much to explain what was happening. All I got was, 'Oh, it's good what he's saying, it's really true.'

When he had finished haranguing us, Lama Geleg sat down looking like a man who had got a lot off his chest. It wasn't until later that I found out what he'd been saying. Apparently, he had stood up and started speaking in a conventional enough way by giving a discourse on loving-kindness and compassion for all beings. Then suddenly, he had started accusing the assembled company of hypocrisy, ill will and greed. 'You sit there mouthing sacred texts and prayers like "May all beings be happy" from morning to night, and yet and yet, what are you thinking? Eh? What's in your heart? It's ill will, that's what it is. Love on your lips and ill will in your hearts. If you can get what you want for yourself, what do you care about anyone else? Call yourselves Maha-yanists? Call yourselves Bodhisattvas? Making a few rupees by selling this or that – that's what your meditation is about. Greed and ill will. If someone says something you don't like, you can meditate on that alright. You keep that in your heart and worship it. That's what your hearts are like. "May all beings be happy," indeed. That's the last thing you're thinking about!' He continued in this vein for about half an hour.

Afterwards I heard the nuns muttering things like 'Who is he to tell us that?' and 'Is he so pure himself?' and 'He will just make bad karma talking to the assembly like that.' Karma Yangzom agreed with them but couldn't help laughing and admitting that what he had said was all true.

Lama Geleg lived in a tiny wooden cubicle on the corner of the retreat centre. Karma Yangzom and I went to visit him there one day. The room was criss-crossed with strings hung with small strips of drying meat. It was quite revolting. He offered us a seat on his bed – which was piled high with blan-kets, jackets, texts and boxes – and handed us bits of hard cheese to chew, while pouring us Tibetan tea from his ther-mos flask. He asked with his customary directness how my meditation was going. 'Okay,' I told him, 'but I'd like to find some really isolated retreat place, maybe in the mountains somewhere.' He wanted to know why. I explained that I wanted fewer disturbances and distractions, but he was scornful: 'What's meditation without distractions?' he asked. I was taken aback. He was questioning a fundamen-tal assumption of mine that solitary retreat in the mountains was a good thing. Surely only worldly attachment or sheer misfortune prevents any self-respecting Tibetan Buddhist from taking to the mountain fastnesses! This is what the great 12th century poet and yogin Milarepa was so famous for. But Lama Geleg was glaring at me with a challenging eye.

I knew he was an experienced yogin, so he was not dismissing meditation. I told him I thought the silence would be helpful, and he wagged his finger at me threateningly. 'What's the point of meditation that only works in silence, eh? Is it silent here? Is it silent in the bazaar? Are the birds and the wind silent? Is your mind silent? Eh? Eh?' It was a compelling point. 'And what about when you die? Do you think it's going to be silent then, eh? Do you think the elements of your body are going to break down and dissolve into each other silently? Do you think you'll hear no claps of thunder, no roaring wind, or fire or rumbling and quaking, or shouting and shrieking, no fierce disturbing manifestations? You think it's all going to be peace and light, do you? Is that what you think? Eh? Eh?' I think there must have been an expression of dismay on my face because he eventually dropped his voice and continued in a kindly and earnest tone. 'No, my dear, you've got to learn to meditate anywhere. Meditation is for developing equanimity, not for clinging to outer forms. It is for facing the shock of the true nature of mind appearing vividly as the clear light experience at the time of death and for finding your way between this life and the next. That is not a peaceful experience so you have to prepare for it. You need stability and equanimity at that time. Forget about peace and quiet – that is for babies and sleepers.'

I took what he said seriously and realised I was becoming attached to a particular idea of what meditation should be like. 'You take it from me my dear, it is the true nature of mind that you have got to learn to recognise. You make sure you get that from an experienced and realised yogin like

Kalu Rinpoche or Bokar Rinpoche. Then keep that in your mind for all your life and you will be alright my dear. Peace and quiet indeed, bah, idle talk, idle talk!'

I wondered how much equanimity I had. I was finding it easy to be patient while I was in India, and my Tibetan friends remarked on it. I suspected that it was easy because I had few worries and responsibilities, plenty of time and mostly everyone I met was very kind to me! In other words, I had little cause for impatience. By contrast, my friend Tenpa Gyamtso had plenty of cause for it and yet showed remarkable equanimity. He had been the runner for the monks in three-year retreat and it was his job to buy them anything they needed, but he was so forgetful that the monks were always getting angry with him. He never got angry back. People would say admiringly, 'He is a *real* practitioner! Always the same – always happy, kind and relaxed.' I once saw one of the cooks yelling at him angrily for something he'd done or not done. There was something so gracious about the way he was standing there in receipt of it all – not ignoring it and yet not flinching.

Apart from those times when I was working on translations with Bokar Rinpoche, I was spending most of every day in meditation. I was still struggling with how to balance the vigilance and constant effort needed to resist habitual thought patterns with the relaxation of mind that Karma Thinley Rinpoche had spoken about. I kept asking Bokar Rinpoche how to get the right touch: 'When I try to relax I fall into distraction, but when I try to be vigilant I tend to get obsessive. How do I do it?' He acknowledged that it was difficult. At the same time, all my teachers demonstrated relaxation very simply in their own way of being.

They *demonstrated* relaxation yet they seemed to actively encourage obsessiveness! For example Kalu Rinpoche loved to tell stories such as the one about a monk who had a bramble growing by the door of his retreat hut. Every time he passed it, it ripped his robe, but he never stopped to repair the robe because he was always thinking that death might strike at any time, and so he wanted to spend every moment of his time in meditation. What did it matter to him if he ended up naked? My Tibetan friends were so full of admiration for dedication like this that I expected them to be that way themselves, but mostly they weren't. They seemed to have a very relaxed attitude to life – as if there were always plenty of time for everything. 'Kali kali,' they would say when I was anxiously wanting to get on with things. 'Kali' means gently or slowly. 'Kali kali – one step at a time,' they would say re-assuringly, while at the same time cautioning me again and again against wasting precious time. I took this so much to heart that it didn't cross my mind to just spend time in town hanging out with friends or even just to go out for a walk.

When my young Indian friend from Varanasi wanted to make a special trip to Darjeeling with her father in the hopes of seeing me again, I was so fixated on the preciousness of every moment of my time that I told her I had next to no time to spend with her. That seems very mean to me now but at the time I really agonised over it. If I gave time to her just to hang out, then where would it all end? I just wanted to focus on meditation and study.

For all those years in India and Nepal I had no radio, phone or media of any kind to distract me. I wasn't doing any of the things we usually think of as relaxing yet I felt relaxed. Nevertheless, I was finding it hard to *completely* relax in meditation. If I wasn't actually doing something I classed as practice I felt uneasy. I had trained myself to feel this way.

From the moment I woke up in the morning until my last thoughts before going to sleep at night I would be reciting the Refuge and Bodhisattva vows, aspiration prayers and mantras, or doing visualisation practices and meditating. Even in my breaks I would tend to be studying and learning things by heart. With all of this plus the emphasis on impermanence and the need to accumulate *punya* for the good of all sentient beings, I began to forget the way that Karma Thinley Rinpoche had been teaching me, in his very laid-back style. It didn't stop me enjoying the ordinary things in life, but it was as if they had no value in their own right. I could let them go but still the meaning of *complete* relaxation in my meditation practice eluded me.

My English nun friend Pema had much the same attitude and problem. The difference was that she was in ill-health. Like me, she deprived herself of all the luxuries of life but because of her health she was suffering. She started to notice how much desire she felt – even for comfort, well-being and small pleasures – and became determined by sheer force of will to eradicate it. But the more she denied herself, the more she became obsessed with desire so that it even permeated her dreams.

Then the pineapple arrived. It was a gift from a friend: a ripe, sweet-smelling pineapple. She put it on her shrine and sat with it in front of her for two days – tortured by it. The next time she went to the monastery for a teaching, she took the pineapple as an offering to the lama. She set it on the low table in front of Kalu Rinpoche and after the teaching, she moved forward to speak to him, telling him how much trouble she was having with desire. 'The more I try to give it up, the stronger it gets,' she told him. Kalu Rinpoche was sympathetic. He paused. Then to her astonishment, as if reading her mind, he said, 'Take this pineapple, for example. It's like a dream or an illusion. As long as you take it to be real, it causes desire and suffering. You have to let go of the mind that grasps at self as real and then at objects as real. Letting go of the pineapple by itself won't do anything.' Here is the clue to *real* relaxation – it is in the mind that can truly distinguish the real from the unreal. It is not in what we are doing or not doing.

This relates to mindfulness which was what first attracted me to Buddhism. I thought I had understood what it meant, but there was more to it than I thought. When I first got involved in Buddhism, I thought that it meant paying attention to the present moment. I had hoped it would improve my memory, make me less forgetful and prevent me losing things all the time. However, when I asked Bokar Rinpoche about mindfulness he said, 'It doesn't matter if you forget mundane things like that as long as you remember the Dharma.' He explained that our present life was a precious opportunity that is soon lost, if not through distractions then in death. Mindfulness is about making skilful use of every day, every moment, so that it is conducive to happiness now and in the future, for ourselves and all beings. 'Just paying attention to the present moment doesn't help,' Rinpoche explained. 'A cat is practising mindfulness when it focuses on a mouse, but karmically this is not wholesome behaviour. It is only going to lead to the cat being reborn in the lower realms of samsara!'

He and Kalu Rinpoche both reminded us constantly that the mindfulness that truly helps is remembering that samsara though vast and deep, an endless series of births and deaths driven by karma, is also an illusion. Giving up attachment and aversion allows us to seek the truth, which means awakening from the illusion. This is the true wisdom that leads beyond birth and death. I asked Bokar Rinpoche specifically, 'Isn't mindfulness about focusing on the here and now, in our direct experience, moment by moment?' He said it was, but that did not mean becoming absorbed in all kinds of experiences. He said that when I had the right view, I should rest in that, whatever I was doing. I wanted to know what he meant by 'right view'. 'Is it seeing the true nature of mind?' I asked. 'Yes,' he replied. 'Look! Look again and again at the mind to see its true nature.'

It was conversations like this with my teachers and colleagues that gave me confidence that I was on the right track. Seeing the true nature of mind was what I was trying to do, and I needed to cultivate it through mindfulness. For some people, seeing the true nature of mind is a powerful experience of everything dropping away for a while, leaving them in a vast and even scary space of emptiness. For me it was just momentary glimpses of another way of knowing beyond the thinking process – intriguing yet fleeting. These glimpses were enough to keep me constantly inspired.

At home with my parents, brothers and Mangel-wurzel the cat.

Below left: **Trungpa Rinpoche** (front) at Samye Ling Monastery with **Akong Rinpoche** (right), Sherab Palden Beru (left). Printed with kind permission of Samye Ling.

Below right: **Karma Thinley Rinpoche** 1971.

Kalu Rinpoche, teaching in the three-year retreat centre where Bokar Rinpoche did his retreat, Sonada 1968.

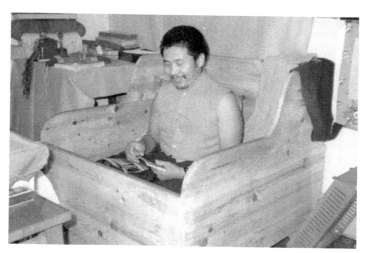

Tenpa Gyamtso in his meditation box, possibly at Kagyu Ling in France in the early 80s.

The **16th Karmapa** in his room at Rumtek with **Shamar Rinpoche**, **Situ Rinpoche** and **Jamgon Kongtrul** next to him. Around the time of my ordination in the room I was ordained in 1973.

Front to back left side: **Bokar Rinpoche**, Pawo Rinpoche, **Gyaltsab Rinpoche**, **Shamar Rinpoche**. Centre: **Kalu Rinpoche** in front of the **16th Karmapa**. Front to back right side – Beru Khyentse, **Jamgon Kongtrul**, **Situ Rinpoche**. 1972 at the consecration of the stupa at Sonada. I was present at this occasion.

Six

Pilgrimage, Ordination and Retreat

One day, out of the blue, Bokar Rinpoche said, 'You should go on a pilgrimage.' I had little understanding of why a pilgrimage was important, and it seemed a bit of a distraction at the time, but Bokar Rinpoche had told me to do it, and I was always one for adventure. Since my permit for staying in Sonada had once more run out, it was a good time to go, so Bokar Rinpoche gave me a list of all the sacred places connected to the life of the Buddha that one should visit including Buddha's birthplace at Lumbini, the spot at Bodhgaya where he gained Enlightenment, the location of his first sermon at Sarnath and the place where he passed away in Kushinagar. I set off, all by myself, for about six weeks, travelling by train and taking all my worldly possessions with me.

I had my bedding, clothes and books on my back in a rucksack, my saucepan and wick stove in my bucket at the end of one arm and a suitcase in the other arm. To save money, I spent my nights in the ladies' waiting rooms in the railway stations. Indian husbands stand on guard all night outside the ladies' waiting rooms, so I felt very safe there. I travelled mainly in the states of Uttar Pradesh and Bihar, visiting Bodhgaya, Kushinagar, Rajgir – where Buddha taught the Heart Sutra, Shravasti where he demonstrated miracles, Kapilavastu – the place where he grew up, and Pataliputra – where Emperor Ashoka convened the Third Buddhist Council in 250 years BC, and then I travelled up to Lumbini in Nepal. Places like Bodhgaya and Lumbini have become quite built-up now, and these days are full of tourists and pilgrims, with many temples and monasteries established by followers of Buddhist traditions from all over the world.

When I was there, it was much quieter. Each of the sites was just a few simple buildings in a sea of fields. They were remote places that took days to get to on country buses or cycle rickshaws, without much choice in terms of places to stay and eat. At Shravasti, for example, there was just a crossroads and a tiny building where an old monk told me he had lived for decades trying to raise enough funds to create a place for pilgrims to stay.

The furthest south I went on my pilgrimage was to Ajanta, which is famous for its thirty or so cave temples. It lies on the Deccan plateau to the north-east of Bombay (now Mumbai). As I arrived the sun was just coming up and I looked out along the long rocky expanse of a cliff curving round a river bend, with trees and bushes above and below. The caves carved into the cliff face each had a grand entrance supported by pillars. The scale of it took me by surprise. I entered one of the caves, and it was like entering a cathedral with a high fluted ceiling. There was a Buddha image at least five metres high at the end where a church altar would have been. There were side chambers and stone benches cut into the rock here and there, and the morning light was flooding in through the high window above the doorway. I was awestruck. I sat down to recite some prayers. Because of the acoustics my voice resonated like a whole monastic assembly rather than a single person. It felt wonderful.

I chanted for half an hour or so, until suddenly I became aware that I was being watched by an Indian caretaker in his white cotton loin cloth (*dhoti*) and shirt. '*Bas,*' he shouted. I ignored him. '*Bas*' means 'enough': I was determined not to be stopped by some kind of officialdom. This was a Buddhist temple and I was reciting Buddhist prayers. Why should I stop? He squatted down in front of me, staring at me intently. I kept on chanting. Another loud '*Bas*' echoed into the space. I kept going. He tried just once more. Finally, after another half an hour, I reached the end of my prayers and started to close and wrap up my text. 'Have you finished your prayers now then?' he enquired. 'Yes, thank you very much,' I replied rather curtly. 'What a shame,' he remarked. 'I tried to stop you before it was too late.' I was intrigued. 'There are another twenty-nine caves to visit and now you have finished all your prayers in just one of them.' I laughed: so that was his concern. I was touched. 'It's ok,' I said, 'I have all day and plenty of time to pray in all of them.' He nodded happily, putting his hands together and bowing to me. '*Acha hey*!' he said, meaning 'Very good!'

Rajgir is a spa town in Bihar on the plains of India. It is a pilgrimage place where yogins of all different religious persuasions have meditated for millennia. There is a cave in the hills near Rajgir where the Buddha's disciples gathered to compile a record of his teachings after his passing. I arrived there in a bus from Bodhgaya bursting with people and as I was stepping down, a kind Indian man approached me. He'd worked out from my attire that I was a Buddhist and asked me if I had anywhere to stay. Since I didn't, he led me to a Buddhist temple. 'Here are Buddhists,' he said authoritatively, and then with a bit of doubt, 'I think they are Buddhist. They are Japanese.' I started to hesitate, but he boldly approached the gate and gave it a hard knock. When nothing happened, he started throwing stones into the garden to attract attention. I felt quite embarrassed. Then the gate was opened by a bright young Japanese monk dressed in white shirt and trousers and a light-yellow monk's robe. My new friend announced that I was a Buddhist and they should give me a room. It was not how I would have put it. Nonetheless I was given a place to sleep in a dormitory, so I was very grateful for the man's initiative.

During the next few days I was made very welcome. The small group of Japanese monks and nuns living there told me their stories, often about how they had been travelling as hippies and then met their guru who had encouraged them to become monks and sometimes told them to go off alone to start a new religious community somewhere else.

Their main practice was to beat a single-skinned hand drum and recite the mantra 'Namu Myoho Renge Kyo' (meaning 'Hail to the Lotus Sutra') very loudly to a steady, forceful rhythm. I found the whole atmosphere and energy of the place very inspiring. I was especially impressed by their guru. He glowed with an inner peace and joy that was infectious. I wanted to stay and learn from him, but since I had teachers and a tradition already, it seemed inappropriate. You cannot give yourself to more than one teacher at a time – though you can, of course, receive teachings and blessings from as many teachers as you are so fortunate to meet. But as with any kind of learning, you need to accept the discipline of being trained by someone who has taken responsibility for you, otherwise who will correct and guide you according to your personal needs?

I really loved the drumming. Everyone was given one of the single-skinned hand drums that were said to deliver beings from falling into the lower realms of suffering, simply by dint of their hearing it being played. In Buddhism there are many magical things like that. On the one hand, we are told that there is a path and we have to do it all ourselves, purifying our bad karma, accumulating *punya*, doing lots of meditation and so on. On the other hand, we are told that if we say this mantra or touch this holy object we will never go to the lower realms again. This is blessing (*adhishtana*) and connection (*tendrel*) again. Personally, I just enjoyed banging the drums – especially the big drum, which was like a huge barrel – it was wonderfully energising, a bit like doing prostrations.

After a day or two, the monks told me that they were now going to fast for a week and asked if I wanted to join them. 'A week!' I thought, somewhat daunted, but didn't say anything other than to agree. 'Well, what is there to it except not eating?' I thought. The days rolled by – one, two, three – and I felt I must be purifying something, if only my own faintness of heart, when on the fourth morning I rose to the smell of cooking in the kitchen! I wondered who might be eating. When the morning session had ended and everyone disappeared, I went back to my room. After a few minutes a monk came to find me and asked whether I was coming to breakfast. It turns out they had been pulling my leg about it being a week. But plainly I'd proved my keenness as I was later invited up to the temple above Vulture Peak to drum the New Year in. I felt very honoured to be invited even though they told me there would be no evening meal. All evening we drummed and chanted ourselves hoarse, and then at midnight, we were summoned to the dining room for a sumptuous feast. On this occasion they explained why they had misled me. 'We have very few places and we couldn't invite everyone who wanted to come, but we wanted to invite you. So we told everyone that there was no food. We knew you would come, food or no food.' So that was my good karma, you might say! We all slept on the shrine room floor that night, and at dawn we were out round the stupa, banging our drums and chanting in the beautiful light of the rising sun.

Vulture Peak is a rocky outcrop from which the Buddha is reputed to have taught many Mahayana Scriptures, including the famous Heart Sutra, to a vast mystical gathering of Bodhisattvas from faraway universes. I went there alone one hot afternoon and climbed the steps up to the top, surveying the vast expanse of Indian plains stretching out to the horizon. I tried to link into the reality, mystery and power of this sacred place, and settled down to meditate. Individual moments may be fleeting, but time stood still in that place. I recited prayers of high aspiration in Tibetan with great love and yearning. I had repeated them so often that I knew them by heart.

From time to time, noisy Indian pilgrims and tourists wandered by. I did not worry about whether they were staring at me. I was used to looking eccentric, a Westerner with a shaven head in Tibetan robes. Indians often could not make out whether I was a man or a woman, but in a holy place I would usually pass without much comment.

After a while, I found that I had attracted the attention of a small Indian man, barefoot and simply dressed in the usual white *dhoti* under his long white cotton shirt. He addressed me loudly as the Lord God, knelt before me with a radiant smile, and bowed his head to my feet, again and again. 'The Lord Buddha,' he said, announcing this with conviction, using the titles interchangeably with the ease so typical of Indians. I felt a little uncomfortable as the recipient of his devotions; however, I had absorbed enough of the culture to know that they were his own business and brought their own reward. I did not have to take any of it personally. Then I thought that if he had such pure vision as to see me as a religious person in spite of all my faults, I should bow to him. So I did. He was delighted, and we both bowed to each other again.

He rolled back onto his haunches and sat looking at me intently for a while. I didn't know quite where to look. In broken English he told me, 'You Lord Buddha.' He paused. 'I have big worries and then come here to this holy place. I put my worries in God's hands and now I meet you praying here. Lord Buddha. Wonderful. I think I have good fortune now.' We both bowed to each other again, then he asked for my prayer beads. 'Give me that,' he said. I felt my prayer beads were something special to my practice and should not be given away lightly. On the other hand, it seemed inauspicious to refuse such a request in a holy place, so I handed them to him. 'Thank you,' he said. 'That is very fortunate for me.' He looked well-contented. I resumed my meditation, and he hung around making loud prayers from time to time, until at last he wandered off, leaving me to sit and contemplate emptiness in silence. Who could ever say for sure that he did not in fact meet God that day? Who is to say I didn't?

When I left the Japanese monastery after about ten days, they gave me one of the drums, since I had said that I would like to keep using it and chanting their mantra. I banged and chanted as I travelled on the bus from Rajgir to Patna, and by train from Patna to Siliguri – an odd sight indeed, as a Westerner in Tibetan nun's robes banging a Japanese drum. Indians are very open-minded when it comes to religion, and generally very tolerant of bizarre devotional behaviour. They nodded and smiled and seemed to appreciate my religious fervour, until late into the night on the train from Patna an Indian gentleman approached me and said tactfully that perhaps even the most dedicated devotee might sometimes need to stop to rest. Then he added politely that even if they did not, other people did, so would I kindly give them a bit of a break. I self-consciously put my drum away, feeling grateful to him for having told me so gently.

On arriving back at Sonada I showed Kalu Rinpoche my drum. He listened to me as I explained all about it and looked interested. After a while I ventured to say, 'I am wondering quite how banging this drum goes with my other practices in the Tibetan Buddhist tradition.' Kalu Rinpoche simply replied, 'Well, it is hard to sew with two needles.' I took his point and decided to put the drum aside.

I had met up with Karma Thinley Rinpoche in Bodhgaya while I was on pilgrimage. He seemed very pleased to see me and after asking me about how my Dharma practice was progressing, he took me by surprise. 'Are you one day marry?' I told him life was too short for that. After a pause he said, 'If you not want marry, you do be nun. Good be nun, take vows – much *punya*.' In effect, I had been living as a nun since I arrived in India without actually having taken ordination, and I wasn't convinced it was necessary to close my options by taking vows for life. I was reminded of the comment Trungpa Rinpoche had made in the letter he sent just after I arrived in India, in which he said it was good that I was living as a nun, even if I gave up later in life. If it wasn't certain I would be a nun all my life it would be better not to take nun's vows. Yet Karma Thinley Rinpoche's point about the *punya* generated by taking vows made so much sense to me, that when I arrived back in Sonada, I spoke to Bokar Rinpoche about it. He was very pleased and encouraging. Since I happened to be on my way to visit the Karmapa in his monastery at Rumtek in Sikkim, Bokar Rinpoche told me to ask for ordination from him.

I had been to Rumtek before. The journey there from Sonada was quite a trek, beginning with a bumpy six-hour ride along steep-sided, forested mountain valleys in a crowded jeep via Darjeeling to Gangtok, the capital of Sikkim. In Gangtok I used to stay with Tenpa, Ani Tsewang's son who made me most welcome. After a further one-and-a-half-hour jeep ride from Gangtok one arrived at the Karmapa's monastery in the small village of Rumtek. There was a rather basic guest house opposite the main gate where I used to stay.

I would spend my days in Rumtek visiting the impressive main temple and the various eminent lamas living around the site, including Shamar Rinpoche, Situ Rinpoche, Jamgon Kongtrul Rinpoche, Gyaltsab Rinpoche and Chokyi Nyima Rinpoche, all of whom were barely twenty at the time – and also one of their teachers, Thrangu Rinpoche. Kechog Palmo was often there, staying in a room nearby the Karmapa. This was amazing, as traditionally women would not be able to live in a monastery, let alone in such a privileged position so close to the Karmapa.

Each time I went I was able to have at least two personal interviews with the Karmapa as well as seeing him during rituals in the temple. In general he gave off a radiance and charm that seemed to fill the whole room, but whenever I entered into his presence it felt as if he just switched all that off so that suddenly everything felt very ordinary and homely. He might start busying himself with whatever was at hand, as if to give me time to accustom myself to being in his presence, before turning to me with some query or comment. It put me at ease. In retrospect, I realise how wary of his kind of charisma I am. It was as if the Karmapa was picking up on this and responding by switching it off so that I could feel directly what was underneath it. It felt like openness and trust, and so of course I trusted in return. In fact, I felt so relaxed and at home around him that I had to keep reminding myself that this was the Karmapa and that he didn't really know me. Yet it felt as if he did and as intimately as all my other teachers did.

Similarly, Shamar Rinpoche, the most senior of the Karmapa's four main disciples living in Rumtek, always received me in a relaxed way, as if I were a family member he saw frequently and knew very well. We would chat about this and that. One time he asked me if I liked flowers, and said that he loved them, adding, 'I don't know why I love them so especially.' Then as if musing to himself about his three colleagues mentioned above he said, 'Situ Rinpoche likes kites very much... Jamgon Kongtrul likes sweets... Gyaltsab likes, erm... what does he like? Let's see... well actually what he likes is meditation.' Another time he beckoned me to the window, saying, 'Look! You can see His Holiness watching the Dharma opera being performed over there. Can you see?' I stood alongside of him peering out of the window as if with an old friend.

On this visit I was going to ask the Karmapa for ordination, so I wanted to do everything properly. I wanted to make a special offering, but I had very little to give him by way of money. I had, however, hit on the idea of offering him the precious drum that had been given to me in Rajgir. At my first interview with him, I knelt before him as I offered it and watched him draw it carefully out of its cotton bag. His eyes lit up and to my surprise he shamelessly asked me how much it cost! I told him how I had come by it and he smiled and asked his attendant to bring him a drumstick – something more elegant than the plain wooden stick I had been using.

He listened to the instrument's distinctive tone and was obviously pleased with it. That evening I thought I could hear the sound of it emanating from his quarters when he was doing his evening prayers. I hardly dared hope it was really my drum he was playing. What an honour that would be! Several years later when the Karmapa was on tour in the West, I noticed he had with him an unusual single-skinned hand drum with Tibetan style dragons painted on it. It grabbed my attention of course and when I looked closely, I could discern here and there, where the paint had worn thin, the Japanese calligraphy underneath. My drum that liberated upon hearing had been taken right round the world by the Karmapa, no less!

I had assumed that to be ordained by the Karmapa was an everyday occurrence, so I was not at all surprised when he immediately agreed to ordain me, no questions asked. It was as if he already knew all he needed to know about me and had confidence that I would be able to live up to the vows. I had to wait around in the ante-room to his chambers hour after hour for several days, being told all the time that the Karmapa would be with me shortly. Every so often I would be told to go away and come back a little later and then again wait hour after hour for days on end. It was a bit unnerving but a good test of my resolve. Eventually, I was summoned into his presence in the upper shrine room. After all the waiting it was all going to happen there and then, without any warning or preparation. I was suddenly informed I should have had my new nun's robes all ready to put on after the ceremony, but I hadn't had any made. Seeing this, a kindly monk said, 'Well, anyway you had better strip down to your vest and underskirt for the first part of the ceremony.' So there I was on the balcony at the top of the monastery, stripping down to my vest and underskirt, surrounded by a milling crowd of monks preparing to officiate at the ordination ritual. As if this wasn't disconcerting enough, I was then asked what I had brought as an offering and I hadn't brought anything more than the drum I'd already given. I later discovered that in Tibet to be ordained by the Karmapa was considered such an honour you would be expected to offer herds of yaks and sheep or something! To save the day, someone kindly pushed a big bag of sweets into my hands as an offering so that I didn't enter the room empty-handed. That would have been considered very in-auspicious (bad *tendrel*).

Shamar Rinpoche and some other lamas were sitting with their backs to the window in a row alongside the Karmapa. I had to kneel in front of him, feeling rather flustered as I strained to understand what he was saying and what I was supposed to be doing. I was unfamiliar with the words of the ordination ritual, but one of the monks was prompting me and somehow we got through the whole thing and I was successfully ordained. It wasn't quite what you might ex-pect an ordination ritual to be like, but it was a miracle that it happened at all in the sense that with all his other respon-sibilities one wonders how the Karmapa had found the time to arrange a one-off ordination like that. He usually gave ordination to whole batches of monks at a time. I felt highly honoured and pleased with the special connection with the Karmapa that this had forged.

He kindly saw me again the next day and I asked him what my name was now that I was a nun. He asked me what the Refuge name was that Kalu Rinpoche had given me. When I said 'Karma Sonam Lhakyi', he told me it was a good name and to keep it. Then he paused, looked at me for a moment and said, 'No, that won't satisfy you,' and asked his at-tendant for a pen and paper. He carefully wrote the name Karma Tsultrim Zangmo on the paper and handed it to me. The name means 'good (or pure) lady of moral discipline'. There were other nuns around at the time with that name and so to avoid confusion I never used it. I kept to my origi-nal Refuge name, since anyway the Karmapa had indicated that I should. Curiously, the short form of my new name was pronounced Tsulzang, which sounds very much like Susan – my name at birth.

Arriving back in Sonada from Rumtek as an ordained nun I was greeted with a clamour of excitement. Everyone was so pleased and grateful that I had taken this step. As an affirmation of my commitment it gave them hope for the future of the Dharma. There were congratulations all round and I was showered with small gifts and invited to celebratory cups of tea. For my part however, having lived like a nun for so long already, taking the vows didn't really mean a big shift for me spiritually. Nonetheless, at twenty-five committing myself to being a nun for the rest of my life was a big decision that I took very seriously. It meant I had to let go of a few lingering fantasies. For example, I still harboured the idea that there might be a perfect partner for me out there somewhere, with whom I could live a life dedicated to Dharma. I knew teachers sometimes told their disciples to marry, but I wasn't counting on that. Above all, I wanted to show others it was possible to live happily without a partner.

During that period when I was coming and going between Tilokpur and Sonada, a new temple and living quarters were being built in Tilokpur for the nuns. When I returned there shortly after having been ordained, they were consecrating Kechog Palmo's new retreat house that had just been completed. The nunnery now consisted of a number of brick and concrete buildings constructed on a small, levelled knoll, up on the plateau above the valley. The reddish clay that dropped away down towards the river was scattered with boulders and bushes. In the centre of the knoll was the temple itself, a simple building with one side open, looking out across the undulating plateau on the far side of the valley.

As I entered the house that was being consecrated that day, Karma Thinley Rinpoche, sitting on his low throne at the far end of the crowded room, gave me such a benign and overwhelmingly warm smile that I hesitated on the threshold, afraid he'd mistaken me for someone else. But he was looking straight at me, with an expression of pure delight. I was deeply moved, but felt a little shy suddenly.

The nuns, who were sitting facing each other in rows, chanting to the rhythmic sound of the drum and cymbals, at first beckoned to me to take a seat. But seeing I had no tea mug with me, and tea was about to be served right then, they sent me off to get one. A young nun, standing by the open door, cautioned me to mind my step as there were ants crossing in front of the threshold. In the blackened kitchen where an old nun was tending the fire beneath a great vat of Tibetan tea, I equipped myself with a standard pint enamel army mug. Back at the new house, Karma Thinley Rinpoche was now squatting by the door post, talking intently to the young nun who was still sitting by the threshold reminding the nuns as they passed in and out to mind the ants. He looked up at me and said it was time I took over from her as she had already done the job for long enough. 'You mustee protect them. The Buddha protect us and we protect everyone. They are our mothers. They all very kind to us before, but we forgotten. We everything very big forget. But we Buddhists now and mustee help them.' I protested. 'There are millions of ants in the world. I can't be everywhere protecting them and all the other creatures there are to protect.' I desperately wanted to believe that somehow those ants were not my responsibility. He didn't sympathise with me at all. 'You mustee do something,' he insisted. 'They very small and can't protect themselves. They don't know they are in dangerous place. They very big ignorance. They work very hard all day, but in very dangerous place. You mustee help.'

So I watched over the ants, although most of the nuns were being careful anyway. Mentally I was busy trying to rationalise my way out of this seemingly endless and futile task. I loved the Bodhisattva ideal of dedicating myself to bringing all beings to Enlightenment, but surely that didn't mean spending my days shepherding ants? After a while,

Rinpoche wandered off, only to return a few moments later with a plank of wood discarded by the builders. He leaned it up onto the doorstep as a ramp for the nuns, which allowed the ants to scurry back and forth under it. 'There,' he said with a smile of satisfaction. 'Now they safe.' 'Very clever,' I laughed. He smiled. 'You see – I big Bodhisattva now. I save many creatures like that. Now everyone happy. You mustee be big Bodhisattva too. Save all beings. They very big ignorance, not knowing about how to protect themselves. Like me, you mustee help.' Clearly I wasn't learning very fast. As on previous occasions, I had not made the effort to think carefully about how I could help. I was still too busy making excuses all the time instead of letting the natural power of love and compassion work through me.

Something was about to happen that would change the lives of Karma Thinley Rinpoche, the nuns and myself. Ever since I first met Karma Thinley Rinpoche, he had been agonising about whether he should accept an invitation from Trungpa Rinpoche to join him at Samye Ling in Scotland, or another invitation he had received to go to Toronto in Canada. He had tried to decide by means of divination, his own and others', but in every case the divinations had told him that it was equally good to go to either place. Now I discovered that the Karmapa had finally sent him a telegram saying, 'You may proceed to Canada,' and so that is what he was going to do. He asked me whether 'you may proceed' indicated it was the best option but I couldn't say it did really.

I felt such a special connection with Karma Thinley Rinpoche as my teacher that I wondered if it was appropriate to ask him for an empowerment, even though I still didn't really understand what an empowerment was. I had had so many from Kalu Rinpoche, but none from Karma Thinley Rinpoche, even though he was such an important guru to me. Whenever I asked for an empowerment Karma Thinley Rinpoche would say that he would give me one, but then he didn't, so I had resigned myself to thinking it would never happen.

Then suddenly, shortly before he left for Canada, he told me that he would give me an empowerment that day and that I should prepare for it in my mud hut in the paddy fields where I did solitary retreats. He came across the fields to my hut on his own without an attendant, bringing with him various ritual objects and proceeded to set up a makeshift shrine with a minimum of fuss. I particularly noticed Rinpoche's eyes as he gave the empowerment. In hindsight I think he was using some of the special gazes from the Dzogchen teachings. I was impressed by the whole ritual and felt very honoured and grateful for the connection he was making with me and the trust he had in me. I wanted to live up to that. It was one of the very last things Rinpoche did with me before leaving for the West and it felt very significant.

'You do meditate on emptiness,' instructed Karma Thinley Rinpoche when I told him I was planning to do a year-long solitary retreat in Tilokpur. 'Emptiness very important. It your Enlightenment mind.' I didn't ask how exactly I was to meditate on emptiness. Trungpa Rinpoche had told me to meditate on the spaciousness outside and Karma Thinley Rinpoche had pointed me in the direction of the mind not being anywhere or anything. I had read references to emptiness in the Songs of Milarepa – a copy of which I had with me. Kalu Rinpoche had talked about not clinging to self because all that we cling to is not real, like a dream or an illusion. I had also talked to Bokar Rinpoche about the nature of mind as something beyond thought, which seemed to suggest emptiness. Other than that I just had my meditation, which consisted mainly of noticing thoughts as they arose and then not getting caught up in them and not trying to stop them. That in itself was challenging enough and I always got the sense that was leading somewhere even if it was just fleeting glimpses of something that one could perhaps call emptiness. I wasn't sure but I was keen to spend more time just looking.

I set myself up in retreat in my usual mud hut in the fields. During that whole retreat I was never bored or at a loss about what I was doing. I felt relaxed and happy and found that my thoughts became more and more transparent as time went by. I began to have an inkling of what might lie beyond words and concepts, and that told me there was something significant happening. It was not dramatic but somehow I had faith and confidence in what I was doing and what I was discovering.

An Indian woman from the village brought me a pot of water every few days, which she carried on her head across the fields from the village spring, and that was all I had for my cooking, washing up and bathing. It was such a simple way of living and yet it didn't feel like any hardship. A nun called Ngawang came once a week from the nunnery with any post or provisions I needed and might chat for a bit. Other than that I remained in silence.

Under the corrugated iron roof of my hut, just above head height, was a loft with a floor of split canes. It was so flimsy that you could see the light through the canes. My only furniture was my wooden bed, constructed like a low table. One night I was about to fall asleep when I heard the canes above my head creaking as if some large animal were moving about. Not sure what to do, I decided to relight my candle. I thought perhaps, since it was fire, it might frighten an animal away. I placed it at the head of my bed and prepared to go to sleep. The heavy creaking started up again and was just about overhead when I found myself doused with water and the candle spluttered out. That was a very clever move, I thought: something has wee-ed on me to put out the candle. I wondered if monkeys might be intelligent enough to do something like that and whether there were monkeys around in Tilokpur. But anyway whatever it was up there seemed much too big to be a monkey. As I desperately set about re-lighting my wet candle with the now damp matches, the creaking increased in volume, and then to my dismay a heavily calloused foot appeared between the canes in the ceiling just a few feet from my bed. It was a human being!

Grasping the re-lit candle, I ran out into the middle of the paddy field crying 'Karmapa Khyeno' at the top of my voice. It is the mantra calling on Karmapa to help. Since I was under a vow of silence, I was not allowed to speak, but I was allowed to recite mantras and I vaguely hoped that by shouting it loudly it would also act as a more general call for help. Someone might hear and come to my rescue. This was highly unlikely since I was a long way from any other dwelling. I stood for some minutes yelling the mantra until it occurred to me that it might be better to hide than to make myself such an obvious target. I found some bushes to hide behind and settled down to wait and see what would happen next. I was so terrified that I found I wanted to defecate, so I did.

I don't know how long I waited. All I remember is that after a while I heard a thump as the thief dropped down from the loft onto the soft ground. Then I didn't hear anything more. Eventually the sky began to lighten and the sun rose. I went back into the hut. Strangely, almost nothing had been disturbed. Someone had carefully moved the loose leaves of my Tibetan text, still resting on their cloth cover, onto the straw mat in order to open the small metal trunk underneath. My purse (which was in fact empty) lay exposed among a few other items. Nothing in the trunk had been disturbed or taken. The only thing that was gone was the tartan cloth that had lain over the metal trunk. I cannot think why. My sleeping bag, coat and kitchenware were all still there. I can only presume that the thief, being an Indian, had been spooked by my simply reciting prayers in response to being burgled – and perhaps also by how few possessions I had. He must have decided that he had disturbed a genuine holy person in their devotions and had perhaps taken the cloth as a souvenir or a blessing.

As dusk fell on the following evenings I felt a strange sense of foreboding, which was an unusual change in mood for me. It took me a while to realise that it was connected with the experience of being burgled. It wore off after a while and by the time Ngawang's weekly visit came around I had got over it. She told me there had been a thief around the village recently and that was probably who it had been. Apart from this one incident, I found the whole experience of that long retreat very satisfying, even though in a way nothing much seemed to happen. Often people tell me that they go through many different experiences in retreat, with lots of ups and downs, and things coming up for them, but that has never been my experience. For me each day followed on from the next in more or less exactly the same pattern. I was very, very happy living that way.

Once during one of Ngawang's visits, she told me that my Canadian friend Elizabeth had gone deeper into the jungle and was going to be in retreat for three years and not speak to anyone at all during that time – not even the person supplying her with provisions. I said I was pleased, but a few hours later I noticed that I felt uncharacteristically downhearted, as if something had upset me. As I thought about it I realised that I had not liked hearing about my friend's retreat. I was shocked. There I was, trying to meditate and become Enlightened in order to help all beings, and yet when I heard about someone else doing the same thing but even better, I didn't like it. I realised it must be jealousy, plain and simple. How embarrassing! I had somehow taken her retreat to be putting mine in the shadow, making it less impressive, and I didn't like that.

It was very uncomfortable to have to admit that there was a part of me so obviously trying to use the spiritual path as a way of preening itself. Secretly it was harbouring the hope that she would not be able to pull it off and that something would stop her achieving her objective. Would that then make me better than her? This is clearly ego-clinging, the very thing Karma Thinley Rinpoche had been pointing out to me over and over again since I arrived in India. I had tried to convince myself it was a small fault. Yet how could such a poisonous mind live alongside all my genuine hopes and aspirations for the welfare of all beings? I think there was a part of myself that wanted Enlightenment in order to be beyond criticism, including my own self-criticism.

I didn't torment myself with self-criticism as perhaps I might have done as a child. I had given that up quite quickly once I ran into Buddhism. I no longer saw it as a virtue to feel bad about myself. That is just another kind of self-clinging. I simply noticed my unskilful mind state and the suffering it immediately caused me. The feeling of embarrassment I was left with by contrast felt honest and wholesome.

That first long retreat had the least amount of structure to it of any I ever undertook but was perhaps the most spiritually productive. Towards the end I would just sit outside on the rocks in the dry river bed near my hut for hours and hours, totally engaged in letting go into a kind of spaciousness that was opening up for me and that felt immensely significant. I was trying to maintain awareness of some kind of essence of my being, or essence of experience itself, that seemed to open out into some other dimension. To say it was a timeless dimension sounds almost too grand, yet perhaps that is the best way to describe it.

After less than six months my Indian landlord sent me a message saying he needed the hut for his workers so please would I move to another hut of his that happened to be a lean-to right next to the school playground. If only he hadn't promised me I could stay there a year – I could have looked for some other place. I complained bitterly to Ngawang as she helped me move all my things, saying, 'I am having such a big obstacle to my practice.' She quickly put me in my place by saying, 'Tcha – you don't know what obstacles mean! Losing your country is an obstacle. What you are suffering is nothing.' When a month or so later the landlord wanted to move me again I decided to give up and, since Karma Thinley Rinpoche had already left Tilokpur for Canada, I went back to Sonada.

Seven

What is the Nature of Mind?

I spent the next three years mostly in retreat in either Sonada, Tilokpur or Nepal. For Sonada and Nepal I needed a government permit or a visa and getting one was not always straightforward, especially just after my six-month retreat in Tilokpur because at this time in 1971 the war with Bangladesh was at its height. Several Westerners told me that even after giving handsome bribes they were not getting a permit, even for a very short stay. I wondered what to do when I remembered that soon after arriving in India when staying with Mrs Jerrat, one of her Indian friends had told me, 'Every Indian feels it is their duty to help a holy person. If you are a sincere religious practitioner, they will feel obliged to help you. To get round this they will try to provoke you and if you show signs of pride or anger they will feel relieved of that duty because clearly you are not a genuine holy person.' Now was the time to test this out.

I boldly told the officer in charge of granting permits that it was his religious duty to give me a year's permit because I had to spend time training with my guru. He questioned me about who this guru was and insinuated that I was lying or was deceiving myself by just pretending to be a religious person out of pride and conceit. Maybe I was sexually frustrated and was doing it from anger and so on. I ignored it all and just kept repeating my original statement calmly but firmly. As my informant had predicted, the strategy worked. I had to wait a couple of weeks but then lo and behold I was handed a permit for six months which was far longer than I had expected. For several months I was the only Westerner around in Sonada! Once back there I was again in the remarkable position of receiving one-to-one teaching from Bokar Rinpoche on a daily basis for month after month, which meant I could ask him questions relating to my experience of the nature of mind; questions I had been investigating since childhood and was pursuing with ever deepening clarity. The daily conversations with Bokar Rinpoche took things to a whole new level of depth and precision. It was exciting because I had the time to meditate and so to experience the significance of what I was discovering ever more directly and completely. What sort of questions do I mean? Things like: how it is possible to know anything at all? How is it there seems to be a mind that knows things that aren't mind and then how, when we look more closely, we realise we can never know anything that isn't mind? What do we really mean when we say mind and not mind? What is the mind without thoughts? What is it when there are? Above all what does it mean to rest in the *true* nature of mind?

Basically, I wanted a theory of everything. I felt I kind of knew the answers lay in a reality beyond the grasp of concepts, so I would have to realise it in my experience in meditation. That is why I was only interested in meditation and found it difficult to take an interest in traditional Buddhist concepts. When I thought about them, I was always trying to make sense of them as if I should be able to understand everything right away. I didn't want to start accepting a whole new belief system. I wanted to *know.* I wanted to know the secret of everything. Traditionally, Tibetan lamas teach their students by moving them along step by step, teaching from texts or according to standard formulae. Students do not expect to understand the deepest teachings until they have gone through all the preliminary stages, done all the right practices to purify themselves and remove obstacles and accumulate enough *punya.* As a Westerner, however, I just bombarded Rinpoche with questions at all levels at once. I think he enjoyed it because my questions would take him by surprise. They were not the kind of questions he usually got asked. For example I might ask, 'What is a Buddha really?' or 'Why is there anything at all?' and 'What is the universe out there that science is exploring?' He was always game to have a shot at an answer and then discuss with me what had made me ask the question in the first place.

Once Bokar Rinpoche was explaining something to me from a text about the nature of mind and I asked him what it meant. He gave me a few explanations and definitions, which I wrote down and then said, 'But what does all this mean *in practice*?' He looked at me quizzically. Hadn't he just explained it? Then he suddenly changed tack and asked, 'You mean *really*?' Not knowing what else to say, I said 'yes'. At that he began to wrap up the text in its cloth binding. 'Well, if you want to know what it *really* means ...' he said, putting the text to one side and sitting up straight, 'You have to look into your own mind.' He then looked at me intently and started asking me questions that forced me to focus more and more precisely on what exactly I was experiencing when I meditated on the nature of mind.

One time he said, 'The mind is like a worm in an apple, isn't it?' I couldn't agree, so he told me to reflect on it for a day or two. When I came back, I still couldn't agree with him. I didn't believe the mind was stuck in a ball of matter like a worm in an apple. It sounded silly but actually isn't that how we think of the mind in the body? As I argued with him, he was clearly taking note of how I was thinking and tailoring his questions accordingly. Suddenly he stopped arguing with me and said I was quite right. How can the mind be like a worm in an apple? But what are the implications of that? If it is not in the body then where is it? He was now willing to help me move to a deeper level of exploration and understanding. He wasn't letting me rush ahead of myself with just a superficial level of understanding. It would have been a mistake to think that just because I *thought* I understood something, that I actually did.

Not all teachers allow their students to argue with them like this. It can sound quite disrespectful. With me though it was a sign of my deep respect that I persisted with my questions. I never dismissed what Rinpoche said as irrelevant or wrong. I was just puzzled and determined to keep coming back with questions until I was satisfied, and in the end I always was.

I came away from this kind of teaching with a feeling of excitement at a sense of a direction that was opening up. What had been pointed out was a fleeting glimpse of something that I knew I wanted to pursue, and that I could really work on within myself from then on. As the years have gone by those fleeting glimpses have opened up further and become more stable. With that comes an increasing sense of their significance and a new perspective on the nature of reality, which in turn allows me to catch further glimpses of what still lies beyond me. It is always tantalising and deeply satisfying at the same time. One never needs to look beyond what one is experiencing right now, this moment, in order to discover something profoundly important. If, on the other hand, one is not interested in looking at one's experience, questions such as how big is your mind or where are your thoughts and so on sound nonsensical.

This is what happened to a Tibetan nun friend of mine who came to live with Karma Yangzom and myself in a simple, one-roomed stone house on the hill above the monastery. She was known as Bokar Ani because she was from Bokar in Tibet. She was short, with remarkably rosy cheeks and a bright, disarmingly innocent smile. Although she insisted she was Bokar Rinpoche's sister this was untrue; she had only ever been the milkmaid in his monastery. He very kindly never denied that she was his sister yet nonetheless she was constantly complaining at his unkindness to her to the point that she just sounded stupid. 'He wouldn't even speak to me today,' she told me indignantly. 'Well, he is in silent retreat, isn't he?' I said. 'Yes,' she said, shaking her head in disapproval. She just wasn't making any sense.

One day she took Karma Yangzom and me by surprise by announcing that she was going to ask Bokar Rinpoche for teachings on the nature of mind. She had obviously been listening to Karma Yangzom and me discussing such teachings and she didn't want to feel left out. Dressed in her best, she proudly trotted off down the hill in eager anticipation of these special teachings. On her return in the evening, she looked crestfallen. We asked her what had happened. 'That Rinpoche never is nice to me,' she said, dropping her head sadly. 'He just insulted me.' 'What did he say?' we asked in disbelief. With a martyred air she said, 'He told me I didn't have a mind.' The next day, we asked Rinpoche what had transpired. 'Oh yes,' he said with a fond and slightly amused smile. 'She asked me for teachings on the nature of mind, so I asked her where her mind was.' He paused. 'She just got up and left without telling me why.' When we told him what she had said about it to us, he simply smiled. What can one do? He had tried to get her to look at her direct experience and she had completely got the wrong end of the stick.

The deepest level of understanding of the nature of mind is called Mahamudra or Dzogchen and so all the teachings and help with investigating the nature of mind that I had from Bokar Rinpoche and my other teachers were part of the process of being taught Mahamudra or Dzogchen. It was affirming to find that all my teachers seemed to recognise what level of understanding I had reached and could always point me further.

With the teacher's help one starts off with an initial glimpse of the nature of mind as the basis and then the path consists of stabilising and deepening that glimpse, so it becomes full realisation, also called Enlightenment or the Heart of Awakening. Sometimes a teacher can trigger a dramatically strong experience of the nature of mind in the student – almost like Enlightenment itself or the whole world disappearing. Even so the experience usually fades away quite quickly and for everyone, whether their first glimpse is dramatic or not, the most difficult task of all is to persevere with the practice without getting distracted until reaching Enlightenment.

Among the various practice texts that Bokar Rinpoche and I translated together was the famous 'Mahamudra Prayer' by Rangjung Dorje, the third Karmapa, who lived in 13th–14th century Tibet. I was incredibly fortunate to have it transmitted to me verse by verse over a period of several months. After he taught each verse, I would spend forty-eight hours meditating on it before going back to tell him what I had understood. He would test my understanding and then give me the next verse.

I was completely bowled over by the genuineness of Rinpoche's whole approach – an approach that took nothing for granted. It meant I had to be as absolutely honest as I could. That is not easy. I would sit for hours and hours just looking at my mind and now and then experience glimpses of something profoundly significant, but there was no way I could make the glimpses happen. They happened by themselves. There was no way I could hang on to them either. I just had to let those moments go and trust that they would happen again. Bokar Rinpoche assured me that gradually, through persistent practice, the glimpses would become stronger and the habitual tendencies that obstructed them would get weaker. 'It is like a strong man wrestling with a weaker man,' he said, demonstrating with his arms quite graphically. 'Eventually the strong man gets weak and the weak man strong. Then it is easy.'

I understood my glimpses to be intuitive leaps into another way of knowing that has nothing to do with the logical, analytical mind that is always trying to make sense of our world. Rinpoche explained, 'Meditation instructions are like a finger pointing at the moon. It is no good keeping your eye on the fingertip, even though the fingertip is pointing in the right direction. You have to make an intuitive leap to transfer the attention from the finger to the moon.' This was something that I had to discover how to do for myself over the decades to come – always trying to get the right touch and checking back with my teachers from time to time to make sure I was on the right track.

Bokar Rinpoche took me as far as he could, given the limitations of my understanding at that time. One of my sticking points was the role of the guru, which I had already tried to engage with during the preliminary practices. As well as prostrations and mantras, another of the elements of the preliminary practices involves praying to the guru, in the form of the Karmapa, and asking for his blessing (*adhishtana*). This connection with a genuine guru is said to be crucial in Mahamudra, but I had difficulty understanding what 'guru' meant in this context. It seemed to mean more than just to receive teaching and guidance from someone.

Even though Bokar Rinpoche had given me so much instruction he still wanted me to ask the Karmapa for pointing-out instruction on the nature of mind, presumably in order to receive the *adhishtana* of such an important connection with him. I had no objection to this, so the next time I was in Rumtek I requested instruction from the Karmapa. As is customary I was sitting on the floor in front of him and he was staring down at me about two feet from my face with his eyes wide open saying, 'Where is your mind?' I tried to remain as open as possible, but I couldn't help thinking, 'He knows already!' After a few moments the Karmapa told me gently that my teachers would explain it to me over time. I was happy with that.

As my mind opened up, I gradually found myself thinking more and more in terms of past and future lives. Buddhist ideas about karma, rebirth and what happens at death that I would previously have considered entirely foreign had started to make sense, because I had started letting go of many of the preconceived ideas that had previously blocked my understanding. It had become obvious to me, for example, that the mind was not of the nature of something that dies. My conversations with various Tibetans and Indians on a daily basis were subtly influencing my thinking and opening me up to a whole different world view. I now thought in terms of samsara meaning the state of being trapped in the suffering of endless rebirths due to misapprehending the true nature of mind. Death was the opportunity to make sure our next birth would enable us to continue on the path to Awakening. In other words, what happens at the time of death is of vital importance.

There was a woman called Jayang who lived at the monastery. She had married an ex-monk and had had many children by him in Nepal, but most of them had died. Now she, her husband and her sole surviving son lived in Sonada. One day her husband came back from a business trip saying that he felt unwell. Jayang asked Kalu Rinpoche what medicine he should take, but while they were waiting for the reply, her husband complained of cold feet, and half an hour later he was dead. Everyone was very shocked. In fact, when we heard the news, Karma Yangzom was sure there had been a mistake. 'I saw him only half an hour ago and he was fine,' she said.

She and I hurried down to Jayang's room. A crowd of monks and lay people who were gathered silently outside let us through and we joined her at her husband's bedside. Her twelve-year-old son Tashi was sitting cross-legged, staring at his prayer book open in front of him as his mother urged him to pray to help his father on his way to the Pure Lands. 'Don't cry,' she urged him. 'It will disturb his mind and make obstacles for him.' Yet she was crying herself. A couple of nuns sat beside her as another one made tea. 'Don't cry, Jayang,' they soothed. 'Remember what the Buddha said: remember impermanence. We always forget because we are like madmen clinging to dreams and illusions. You have meditated all your life on impermanence so remember your meditation now and don't grieve.' They put her prayer beads into her hand and urged her to recite mantras on it as they did the same on theirs. *'Om Mani Padme Hum,'* they murmured, until the whole room was buzzing with the sound. Jayang became calmer as she held her prayer beads to her heart and moved her lips, silently reciting the mantra, with tears still flowing down her cheeks.

I was very struck by the way everyone's understanding of the Buddha's teachings was put into practice at the moment of death. The nuns reminded Jayang that death comes without warning, and that ultimately only the Buddha, Dharma and Sangha are trustworthy. 'All else fails us, so pray for their blessing,' they said. 'We never know when our karma will ripen and death will be upon us, so pray to them without distraction. Don't waste time while you are alive.'

Witnessing this death scene in Sonada showed me how the way we think at the time of death can make a huge difference to how much we suffer. I couldn't help contrasting Jayang's experience with that of my Indian friend Mrs Jerrat whose way of thinking left her in total confusion when faced with the sudden death of her son. On one of the last times I arrived at her house, I found her *very* changed. I noticed that she had drawn a sheet all around her shrine and was refusing to go near it. She was angry with God because her son, a promising astronaut in America, had been killed outright in a car crash. She couldn't understand how God had let that happen. 'I have prayed daily all my life for the protection of my family,' she said in anguished indignation. 'Nobody could have prayed harder and more sincerely than I did. So why has this happened? I am not going to pray to God again until I get an explanation.'

My heart went out to her and I wanted to help her somehow. Since Bokar Rinpoche happened to be in Delhi at the time I brought him to see her. He told her that karma sometimes takes a long time to ripen and a small deed done millennia ago can ripen as a big event out of all proportion to the initial cause. He gave the example of King Trisong Detsen's daughter, Pema Tsal, who died young because in a past life the king had accidentally killed a butterfly that had landed on his shoulder and he had never repented the act. That butterfly was his daughter who had now died young because of the bad karma of that act. I don't think Mrs Jerrat derived much comfort from this, but it did at least address her question. She had been of the view that if you led a good life, unless you did something bad in this lifetime then things could only get progressively better. Bokar Rinpoche explained to her that in the Buddhist view karma from countless past lives ripens haphazardly like dreams in our sleep. We cannot predict what karma will ripen for us next, just as we have no idea what kind of dream we are going to have next. This means that misfortune that ripens to us in this life is not necessarily a reflection of our present character or deeds. This was where Mrs Jerrat's view of karma differed from the Buddhist one. Rinpoche encouraged her to pray to the Buddha, telling her that the Buddha protects us even though he cannot always avert a disaster completely if the time for a karmic action to ripen has come.

I don't remember the moment I finally decided that I believed in karma and rebirth. Nevertheless, I seemed to have absorbed that world view by osmosis. Once when I was in Tilokpur, Ngawang was musing about how Westerners thought. I had told her that mostly they don't believe in past and future lives and so she was curious about how they coped with the fact that even people who live a good life often have to suffer a lot. 'When that happens to us, we comfort ourselves by thinking it is our bad karma finishing. Then it doesn't feel so bad,' she explained. 'How do Westerners think about it?' All I could say in return was that Westerners tend to think it's unfair, but there is no easy way of saying that in Tibetan. She was right to wonder though. For us Westerners it is often desperately hard to make sense of the sufferings in life even for those who have some religious faith. 'If they don't believe in past and future lives, what do they think happens at death?' she asked, obviously very puzzled by this foreign mind-set. 'They think they just end,' I said. 'What, they think their mind ends?' she asked in wide-eyed astonishment. 'That doesn't make any sense!' 'Well they think the mind dies when the brain dies,' I told her. She looked puzzled. 'But the mind is not the brain. It isn't anywhere. You cannot find it. How can you say it ends at death?'

She continued thoughtfully, 'Westerners seem so intelligent and reasonable and then sometimes I think they don't understand *anything*. For example, they think beings with small bodies like insects have smaller minds than beings with big bodies like cats and dogs.' I admitted that that was true, and added, 'Many of them think beings with small bodies don't have minds at all and so don't feel pain.' For her, this didn't make sense either. 'But the mind doesn't have a size. For the insect's mind, its body is its body just like our body is for us. *Of course* it suffers just like we do if it gets crushed or hungry or anything.' I couldn't think of anything to say in defence of the western materialist point of view. We have no alternative explanation for the mind, what happens at death, or the meaning of life at all.

I found it hard to remember the way I had previously understood things. The common sense, down-to-earth, materialistic, one-life theory that seems so rational to us in the West, now seemed weird and irrational. What evidence was it based on? What definition of mind or of what we are as beings was it based on? It now seemed hardly a theory at all but something that is used as a substitute for thought, rather than as the end-point of a deep philosophical investigation. 'Westerners just don't think of future lives. Their main concern is this one and how to enjoy it,' I said. My nun friend shook her head sadly. 'That way you can never get enough motivation to reach liberation from samsara. You will just keep being born again and again.'

At this point I realised that I had developed what in Buddhism is called renunciation. I really believed that as long as we do not realise the true nature of mind, we will keep taking rebirth again and again and be subject to every kind of suffering. I was now motivated by a wish to escape the suffering of endless rebirths, samsara. This longer-term view of what my life was about had changed the way I thought about everything. I lost all interest in anything else except practising Dharma. Nothing else mattered. Even if I didn't reach liberation and Enlightenment in this life, the important thing was to remember the Buddha, Dharma and Sangha as much as I could so that when I died, I would take birth somewhere I could continue practising until I finally reached Awakening. Realising the true nature of mind meant escaping the endless cycle of birth and death by awakening from this present state of ignorance, delusion and forgetfulness. Samsara was like a nightmare and I just wanted to wake up from it.

One of the handful of other nuns living in Sonada, Sherab Drolma, told me that she hoped to die in the presence of Kalu Rinpoche. 'Then I wouldn't mind dying today,' she said laughing happily. I am sure she meant it – she had a much more natural relationship to the idea of the guru than I did. Karma Yangzom agreed but said, 'I worry about what to do when I die. I have thought about doing *powa*, the practice where you send your consciousness out through the crown of the head, but I am worried I won't get the timing right. If you do it too soon before your time to die has come, it is like suicide and you make bad karma. It is best to just pray to the guru or even better for the guru to be there when you die.'

Guru is a Sanskrit word that Tibetans also use. The Tibetan translation of the term is lama. In India there is a tendency to call all Tibetan monks lamas so the term had a somewhat different connotation for me than guru. It was the idea of Guru that I was having trouble with. It wasn't that I didn't believe a guru was necessary or that gurus might have supernormal powers. My difficulty was with the idea of union with the guru, Guru Yoga. Once when Tenpa Gyamtso had told me that all one needed was complete faith in the guru I realised I didn't understand what he meant. Was this about believing one's guru had supernormal powers?

I knew that certain lamas had supernormal powers and I think my life was once saved by one. The Karmapa had told me to spend time in retreat by the two great stupas in Nepal, one due east and the other due west of Kathmandu. Tibetan style stupas consist of a white dome with a square stepped base and a spire on top. The two great stupas I used to spend time in retreat by were steeped in ancient legend and considered powerfully sacred pilgrimage places. The Karmapa had given me letters of introduction to Dabzang Rinpoche, who lived by the stupa at Boudhanath in the east and Sabchu Rinpoche, who lived by the stupa at Swayambunath in the west. I was very fortunate to receive teachings from both these lamas who kept an eye on me when I was in retreat. In those days Boudhanath stupa was surrounded by a village of traditional Nepali style houses and beyond that fields as far as the eye could see. Now it is in the heart of bustling suburban Kathmandu. I had found an attic room of a large house where a few other Westerners were in retreat way out in the fields about a mile from the stupa. It was here on the first evening of a solitary three-month retreat that I nearly met my end.

As I sat to meditate I felt a shooting pain in my backside and the next thing I knew I was feeling dizzy and needing the loo. It felt like I was actually about to die and I clearly remember thinking, 'I really didn't expect it to happen today!' I hurled myself out of my room and down the wooden staircase, shouting out loudly that I was dying. I got to the loo more or less in time and by then the whole household was gathered by the door of the bathroom. I was lying there feeling as if my consciousness was leaving my body. I kept shouting because I was afraid nobody would hear me as I felt so far away. I could feel hot hands on my skin and voices saying, 'She is blue-black – she is dying.' 'Call a doctor!' I yelled. No response. Then, 'There is no doctor around here.' Someone suggested a lama. 'Yes, a lama,' I cried. 'Call Dabzang Rinpoche.'

As we waited for him to come, some Tibetans were trying to arrange a mattress for me with a seat for the lama at my head as one would do for a dying person. Then suddenly the whole dying process stopped and I knew I wasn't going to die. It must have been about the time the message reached Dabzang Rinpoche telling him what was happening. He came hurrying out across the fields to where I was, but by the time he arrived the panic was over. He put his head around the door and said straightaway, 'You are all right, aren't you?' and I said 'yes', feeling sure it was because of the power of his blessing. It turned out that I had sat on a hornet!

A third place I stayed in retreat in Nepal was in the Asura cave at Yanglesho, where Guru Rinpoche is said to have achieved the state of Mahamudra. These days it is in the midst of a busy complex of monastic buildings with crowds of pilgrims passing through all day. In those days it was surrounded by countryside and hardly anyone came there so I was able to stay a week in retreat in the cave undisturbed. Guru Rinpoche, also known as Padmasambhava, meaning the Lotus-Born, is the founding father of Tibetan Buddhism – or at least that is how the legend goes. He is a bit like the figure of Merlin in the court of King Arthur – a wise man, yogin, sorcerer and remover of obstacles. He is thought of as a second Buddha but is not so clearly an actual historical figure in the way the Buddha is. The legend is that he never died. Many yogins have encountered him in person, in visions and dreams, and still do.

People said that the cave itself had been created by Guru Rinpoche pushing up the ceiling with his hands, but I wasn't very convinced by that story. On the other hand there was a hand-print in the rock not far from the cave entrance that looked as if someone had just placed their hand on it, leaving even the lines on their palm clearly imprinted there. It's the most remarkable thing I have ever seen. I asked if it was Guru Rinpoche's hand-print and a passer-by said, 'No it's just a local yogin. There are loads of hand-prints like that all over the place near my village.' I didn't think to ask what village that was! These days there is a hand-print above the door of the cave that looks like a glove print in concrete that is said to be Guru Rinpoche's hand-print, but I don't remember it being there when I was staying in the cave.

The famous lama Chatral Sangye Dorje Rinpoche lived nearby and I went to pay him my respects. His presence inspired a natural faith and confidence in me even though we didn't say much to each other. He made a deep impression on me as he had done so deeply on the American theologian and scholar Thomas Merton in the 1960s.

I spent much of 1973 in retreat in Nepal, but in the autumn I returned to Sonada once again. Towards the end of my stay Bokar Rinpoche gravely announced, 'I am going to be spending the next three years in retreat. I want you to spend your time doing retreat as well. There is no need to ask Kalu Rinpoche or the Karmapa what you should do. Wait for me to come out of retreat and I will tell you.' I was happy enough to do as he told me.

I went back to Tilokpur, to my mud hut in the paddy fields – the nuns there were always very happy to help me. Then I was joined by my English nun friend Pema and together we travelled to another place sacred to Guru Rinpoche, a cave above the so-called Lotus Lake, at Tso Pema. Although a major pilgrimage site, Tso Pema, up in the mountains of Rewalsar, in Himachal Pradesh was still just a tiny village at that time, with several temples and some yogins staying in caves in the hills above. The story is that the king of Zahor tried to burn Guru Rinpoche there as a punishment for illegally entering his daughter's nunnery to teach her Dharma. Instead of being burnt by the fire, Guru Rinpoche transformed it into a lake. The lake was famous for the reed islands that floated in it which would move towards people who prayed to them in deep faith. I didn't understand why they showed faith and devotion to reed islands, but presumably they thought Guru Rinpoche was moving them and this was a sign of his compassion. My mind kept looking for more mundane causes of the movement such as methane gas from rotting vegetation. Why would Guru Rinpoche manifest as moving islands of all things? I was more impressed by all the yogins we met in the caves up on the mountain side. They had made them quite cosy with doors and windows and one of them even invited us in for tea. We had so little money we could barely offer him enough to cover the cost of it but he didn't seem to mind. I was particularly impressed with the largest cave that had a huge ten-foot-high image of Guru Rinpoche inside it.

Having spent a week or two there, paying our respects and practising, we went further north up the Kullu valley to the small town of Manali, famous for its hot springs and fruit orchards. We secured a place to stay in retreat near Apho Rinpoche's monastery, just above the town, in a green and rocky valley dominated by the sound of its torrential river gushing over great boulders below. Apho Rinpoche was a fairly young married Drukpa Kagyu lama from a very famous line of yogins.

We were effectively camping in the space between the stilts of a wooden chalet built against a steep slope – so the back wall and floor were bare earth. It wasn't too bad when we first arrived, but as the rainy season wore on it became exceedingly damp and mouldy. The space was boarded up with thin planks of wood with a partition down the middle separating Pema's room from mine. We made beds for ourselves by laying out bits of wooden planks on the earthen floor, with thin mattresses laid over the top. I curtained off most of my small window so there was very little light in the room. I undertook a very strict retreat, during which time I didn't go out of my room, even to the toilet. Pema took the small tin can I was using from outside my room and emptied it each day. I lived in these conditions for three months. I was lucky it did no lasting damage to my health. Pema was not so lucky. She lived next door and cooked my meals for me on a fire under a tree outside because kerosene was in short supply at the time. She was getting sicker on account of the conditions we were living in, but neither of us fully acknowledged this. We were both very determined to keep up our retreat discipline come what may.

Pema used to crouch over the fire under the fruit tree for hours each day cooking our simple meals which she left for me on my windowsill. As the days went by, and spring gave way to summer, the apricots on the tree above her ripened, and I began to long for them. But she never brought me any. They ripened more and more and began to fall all around her. Still she did not bring me any. My initial vague irritation gave way to obsession. 'How could she be so stupid? Apricots are good for us. How can she not think to pick them up and bring me at least one or two a day?' As much as I would put such thoughts aside, they would be there again the moment my mind started to wander. From the lofty heights of pure thoughts focused on Enlightenment, my mind descended regularly to that pettiness. Later, when I came out of retreat, Pema told me that the apricots had all been bad – every one of them. All my suffering had been in my thinking. I had believed they were juicy, ripe fruits and hankered after them, when in fact they were rotten, disease-infested rubbish. As Kalu Rinpoche had pointed out to Pema with the pineapple, my suffering had been all about nothing, like in a dream and an illusion.

One morning we were shocked to learn that Apho Rinpoche had passed away. We hadn't realised he was ill even. His wife and crowds of disciples were all in mourning and there were various rituals going on day and night for weeks on end. These were led by an eminent old lama called Thukse Rinpoche who had come from quite a distance for the purpose. For us it was a wonderful opportunity to meet him and receive his blessing. He asked me my name, and I told him it was Sonam Lhakyi. Then quite unexpectedly, and I have no idea why, he said, 'No it's not – it's Shenpen Zangmo.' 'Shenpen' means 'benefit others' and 'Zangmo' means 'good lady'. I liked the name very much and told him so. He said, 'Well, it is your name,' and carefully wrote it out for me on a piece of his own crested notepaper. As he passed it to me, I felt it was a great blessing, suggesting as it did that I would be of benefit to others. I have never known a lama to do such a thing as rename a person on the spot for no obvious reason and at first I didn't have any intention of using the name. Little did I suspect my life was about to change forever and how apt my new name would be for what was to come.

Eight

Keeping the Dalai Lama Waiting

At about the same time as I received my new name, a letter arrived for me that was to mark a major turning point in my life. Bizarrely, it was the reply to a request for a permit to visit Sikkim that I'd made a year earlier. I had completely forgotten that I had even applied for it. I took this letter as an auspicious sign that I should go to visit the Karmapa and duly set out for Sikkim. Although Bokar Rinpoche had told me not to ask the Karmapa what to do, he hadn't told me not to see him.

It happened that as I arrived at Rumtek monastery the Karmapa was preparing for his first ever visit to the West. As I entered his room, made my prostrations and sat down on the floor before him, he grandly announced in Tibetan, 'I am going on a teaching tour,' and pointed to a huge map of the world on the wall above him marked with little flags on all the places he was going to visit. Then again in Tibetan he said, '*chi tabu*'. I didn't understand, so he kept repeating it until finally, when I still didn't understand, he started to bark like a dog! I realised that he was saying 'like a dog'. I often could guess what someone was saying in Tibetan by the context; in this case I just hadn't expected him to be saying that! Even then I queried it, 'Like a dog?' Then he explained, 'I'll be there, but all I'll be able to do is bark at people like a dog and they will have to bark back, because I don't know their language and they don't know mine.'

I laughed at the image this conjured up and didn't think much more about it. However, at the end of that week, the Karmapa told me he wanted me to return to Europe to help spread the Dharma. I was horrified. For a start, I didn't know how I would be able to live in the West. Mike and other friends who supported me by covering my minimal living expenses in India and Nepal would never be able to support me in Britain. This meant that once I was in the West I would lose all the freedom I had in India. I had had no intention of asking the Karmapa what to do, but now he was telling me, I wondered what I should do.

Shamar Rinpoche sympathised with my position and told me to double-check with the Karmapa that he had understood the financial implications of my returning to the West. I did that, but the Karmapa told me not to worry, money wouldn't be a problem. He told me to meet him in Samye Ling and he would tell me what to do next. Sister Kechog Palmo was in Rumtek at the time and assured me that it was right for me to go back to the West. 'You should go there and teach the Dharma,' she insisted. I doubted I was qualified to teach since I was not Enlightened yet. She herself was fully engaged in teaching Dharma and had been for years. 'I need to keep practising in retreat,' I said. 'We none of us know how long we have to live so have to take advantage of the opportunity while we have it.' 'Nonsense,' she declared emphatically. 'You people all think life is short, but I tell you it is long!' That didn't sound very Buddhist to me. Sadly, and somewhat ironically, she died suddenly a few years later at the age of sixty-six. I had come to associate Dharma with giving up one's homeland and material comforts and living in a completely different cultural environment. I couldn't imagine a situation in the West where Dharma could be practised in such a full-on way as I was practising in the East.

On my way back from Sikkim to Tilokpur, I had to pass by Sonada, and while I was there, Denys and his partner Rosemarie invited me out to eat at a restaurant in the bazaar – something I had never done in all my years there. They sat me down and, in conspirational tones, told me that plans were afoot for setting up a three-year retreat centre for Westerners in the *West*! For me, this would turn the world on its head. There were so many obstacles and uncertainties involved in doing long retreats in India and Nepal, such as having to apply for visas and permits, being turned out of accommodation by landlords on a whim, unhygienic conditions and unreliable medical care. Maybe in future it would be better to live in the West as a nun staying in retreat most of the time like I was doing here in the East. It was wonderful news and I became quite optimistic.

I sent a message to Bokar Rinpoche in his retreat telling him what had happened and asking him what to do. I'm pretty sure if he had told me not to go I wouldn't have gone. However, he sent a note out saying that he had changed his mind and that I should do what the Karmapa said and go back to the West. I never found out whether he had really changed his mind or whether he just felt his hand had been forced. I didn't realise it at the time but that was to be the last instruction I was to receive from him as my main teacher. Had I realised I wouldn't be seeing him again for ten years I am sure I would have cried my eyes out. As it was I had no idea what was going to happen next and hardly registered that I was parting from him at all.

During the weeks I was preparing to leave, there were only two things I consciously regretted not having done. I am not sure why they were so prominently in my mind. One was that I wished I had met Khenpo Tsultrim Gyamtso Rinpoche and the other that I wished I had been to Milarepa's cave in Yolmo, Nepal. I thought it would be impossible to meet Khenpo Rinpoche because Karma Yangzom had said that he was still wandering the charnel grounds of Bhutan as he had done for years.

I had heard of Milarepa's cave from another Westerner who had said it was the most amazing place to meditate. For some reason that had made a deep impression on me so I always wanted to go there. Now it seemed I had left it too late, at least for now. Milarepa is one of the best loved of Tibetan yogins, famous for being a sinner turned saint in one lifetime, a singer of yogic songs of inspiration and for a life of extreme ascetism in mountain caves in Tibet and Nepal. At the time I was unaware of any connection between Khenpo Rinpoche and the Yolmo cave so I cannot explain how the two had become associated in my mind. Years later I discovered he had a retreat hut and nuns' retreat place near the cave.

Before leaving Sonada, I took a trip up to Darjeeling, especially to receive the blessing of Dudjom Rinpoche, renowned for the depths of his meditation experience and as the teacher of many great yogins. I was shown into a roomful of yogins, many in red and white robes with matted hair. The atmosphere was electric as if they were in the midst of some deep teaching or transmission that I was interrupting. Yet Dudjom Rinpoche beckoned me in and handed me a small picture of Guru Rinpoche and a blessing cord, speaking to me softly and tenderly as if from a different dimension of space. I walked out of the room awe-struck.

I then went back to Tilokpur to do one last retreat. As I was wondering what practice to do my mother wrote to tell me that my paternal grandfather had died. I wanted to do some special practice for him and remembered that on one of the last times I was in Sonada, Denys had told me that I should ask Kalu Rinpoche for instruction in a practice called *powa*, which was about the transference of consciousness at death. 'He is giving it to everyone these days so it would be good to ask him for it,' he said.

I happened to come across Kalu Rinpoche when he was up on the hill above the monastery supervising the construction of a new building. I should have realised it wasn't the best of moments. Nonetheless, after standing beside him for a few moments as he observed what was going on, I just came out with it and asked for the *powa* teachings. He immediately turned his back on me and walked away. Slow to take a hint, I followed after him and he did the same thing again. I was now really curious about what this meant so I tried again and this time he turned to me and said, 'There is no need to learn the *powa* practice. All you need is Mahamudra.' Since Mahamudra is the final realisation of the true nature of mind this advice was somewhat daunting. Would I be able to attain such a deep level of realisation before I died? I think he meant that it was sufficient to rest the mind in its own nature as best one could, but at the time I wasn't sure what he meant. A day or two later he seemed to relent and he gave me the instructions on *powa* anyway, maybe as a kind of belt and braces strategy or maybe so I could use it to help others. He told me to practise them for a week which I did during the course of my last few weeks of retreat in Tilokpur. I dedicated the *punya* from doing the retreat to my grandfather.

I then started preparing to leave for England, which didn't take long since I had so few possessions and I couldn't make any plans from Tilokpur anyway as there weren't even phones let alone online booking facilities! The nuns at Tilokpur told me I should try to speak to the Dalai Lama before leaving. They assured me that he liked Westerners and always found time to speak to them. I was doubtful, since I didn't have anything in particular to say to him, but they insisted: 'You have been a nun for five years and speak Tibetan. He is bound to be interested in you.' They told me it would be a great blessing and encouraged me to take the two-hour long bus-ride up to Dharamsala the next day.

So it was that in the misty cool of the early morning I walked down to the village below the nunnery to meet up with about eight nuns who were all excitedly huddled by the bus stop, smartly turned out in their best robes and shoulder bags. They were all determined to accompany me to see the Dalai Lama, but when we arrived in Dharamsala everyone split up to undertake errands first. I went with one of the nuns to see an old lama at his little monastery off the side of the bazaar. We were courteously served tea and Tibetan biscuits and in the course of the conversation I mentioned that my grandfather had recently died. 'It is good to make an offering to the Dalai Lama on his behalf,' said the lama. 'It will make an auspicious connection for him. You make the offering and ask His Holiness to pray for him. You should write a letter with his name in it and add a picture if you have one.' I explained that I had neither a picture nor much to give as an offering. 'Never mind, it does not have to be big,' he said kindly, as he took out a sheet of paper and then painstakingly wrote a letter to the Dalai Lama for me. He was transparently shocked at how little money I had to enclose with it – since I was a Westerner he had naturally thought that I was rich and would give more than the few paltry rupees typical of poor Tibetan refugees. We both felt embarrassed – it looked pretentious to accompany so small an offering with such a stylish letter. But what could I do? My nun companion vouched for my poverty, explaining that I meditated a lot and was very devout. The lama told me, 'It is the connection that matters. If that is all you can afford then there is no need to feel ashamed.' Nonetheless, he looked unimpressed, and I left his room feeling rather sheepish.

To my surprise my companion then took me to her mother's house and after tea and a meal I realised the plan was to stay there overnight. We chatted and prayed into the night, sitting on the same hard beds that we would later curl up on to sleep, wearing our long underskirts and using our folded robes as blankets. The next morning, I set off for the Potala, the Dalai Lama's palace, accompanied by the rest of the nuns. I paid no attention to the location of the house I'd been staying in or the route out of the bazaar and had no idea where the other nuns had been staying. The approach to the Potala is along a mountain road with a view across the plains of India and the river winding its way far below. I stopped to look at the view and caught sight of an American friend I'd not seen for months sitting on a bench nearby. She exclaimed warmly how fortuitous it was that we had met at that moment since she needed someone to translate the Tibetan in a letter she had just received. I told her I could not wait because the nuns were all accompanying me to the Dalai Lama's office to ask for an interview. 'Oh, that can wait; this can't,' she begged insistently. 'See you by the gate,' my nun friends called gaily as they continued on their way without me. It must have been at least half an hour later before I managed to disengage myself and hurry after them. When I arrived at the gate to the Dalai Lama's palace, they were nowhere to be seen.

I asked at the gate about how to get an interview. 'Is it important? The Dalai Lama is very busy and leaving tomorrow. He does not have much time, and there are lots of people with important business waiting to see him,' said the gatekeeper. I was not sure at all that I warranted his time. I was still feeling sheepish about the size of my poor offering, so I just handed it to him with the letter, asking for my grandfather's name to be put with others for special mention in the Dalai Lama's daily prayers. Then I turned away, disappointed but philosophical, and made my way to the bus stop. I could not go and find the nuns because I had not noticed the way we had come in to the palace, so I got on a bus and travelled back to the nunnery. It was not until that evening, when the rest of the nuns came home, that the enormity of my blunder was revealed to me. I heard excited talking and shrieking as they met up with the rest of the nuns in the kitchen. Then several of them burst into my room, exclaiming and asking where I'd been. 'We looked everywhere for you,' they said. 'We looked at the bus stop – we must have just missed you.' 'I didn't know where to find you,' I explained. 'But the Dalai Lama was waiting for you,' they said. 'First for half an hour and then an hour.' I couldn't believe what I was hearing. The Dalai Lama had been waiting for me.

Apparently, the nuns had requested an interview on my behalf, and when they were told that the Dalai Lama was busy, they had said it was important because I was a nun and a Westerner and was going back to England after five and a half years. Not wanting to be responsible for the choice, the gatekeeper had let them ask the Dalai Lama directly. 'So we sent a message to the Dalai Lama and waited. A message came back to say that, yes, he would see you in half an hour. So then we went to look for you, but we couldn't find you anywhere. So we went back and asked the Dalai Lama to wait and he said to come back in an hour. So we ran all over the bazaar – everyone went off in different directions looking for you. You were nowhere to be found. We had to go and explain to the Dalai Lama. We just stood there in front of him like dumb idiots. He was very kind to us. He always is, he seems to have a special love for us nuns. He asked after the nunnery, and so on. But we had nothing to say. We were too terrified to think of anything to say. He must have thought us so stupid. All that fuss to see him and then nothing to say. We felt so stupid.' I was distraught. I wailed and howled, inconsolably disappointed by these chance happenings, and such a cruel near miss.

For days after that I could not bear to hear the incident even mentioned. One of the older nuns comforted me, 'Never mind, you've made a strong connection now, so you are sure to meet him in the future. It is a very auspicious connection for you that the Dalai Lama was waiting for you all that time.' Though I believed it, I remained and remain unconsoled. I have not had a personal interview with the Dalai Lama even as I write this although I have been in his presence a good number of times. I certainly have a strong connection with him though. Not many can boast of having kept the Dalai Lama waiting!

A week later, as I was leaving Tilokpur the nuns all lined up to offer me a traditional white scarf and say good-bye. 'Make sure you stay a nun,' they said menacingly, 'or we will all come there in a bus and give you a good hiding!' It was said in good fun and it made me laugh so it was hard to feel sad at that moment. Prophetically, the last thing I heard as I hurried down the hill to catch my bus was Ngawang calling out after me, 'Make sure you contact my friend Pat May as soon as you get to England!'

After a night on the train I was once more in the heat, dust, traffic and hurly burly of Delhi, busy sorting out my trip back to England. I had lived for five and half years in India and Nepal without ever going back to the West once, and now I was suddenly getting ready for my return. I did not know what I would be going back to do, where to live, how to make a living, who would be willing to help me – nothing. It was going to be a challenge. I found this exciting, even though, left to my own devices it was not what I would have chosen to do. My choice would have been to stay on in India until I was Enlightened.

Nine

Return to the West

My arrival back in England was accompanied by a huge sense of anti-climax.

Nobody was expecting me when I arrived at Heathrow airport because I hadn't told anyone I was coming back. It was late on a wintry afternoon and except for a little money to tide me over a day or two and a few addresses of friends and family in my pocket I had nothing to speak of. I was just throwing myself on the mercy of the universe.

I hadn't been looking forward to returning and it didn't feel like a home-coming particularly, but I was curious and a little excited because it was a huge step into the unknown. I had hardly kept in touch with anyone other than my mother and occasionally Mike. Mike was married now, and I had no immediate plan to meet up with him. He had told me that he wouldn't be able to support me in the West. Life here was too expensive especially now he had a family to support.

While in India I had contacted Samye Ling telling them I was a nun and that the Karmapa had told me to meet him there. Their response was to tell me the place was fully booked while the Karmapa was there so I couldn't stay then, although I could come afterwards. This was a bit of a blow, to say the least. However, it left me with a couple of weeks to visit a few people and then make my way up to Samye Ling just for the day so I could get my orders from the Karmapa.

That is as far as it went in terms of a plan. I saw no sense in contacting my parents because they were bound to want to know what I intended to do and I didn't know. I would contact them after I had seen the Karmapa and he had told me what to do.

In the meantime where was I going to spend the night? I looked in my address book and found the names of two English Buddhist nuns living in London whom I had met up with in Bodhgaya. I hadn't used a phone in years and was getting quite flustered fumbling for the right change, when a passer-by stopped to help me and gave me the coins I needed for the call. I was very touched by this act of kindness from a complete stranger and felt it boded well for my future in the West. I got through to Tsultrim Zangmo and her mother and explained my situation. Being travellers and adventurers themselves they were not too shocked at my suddenly landing on them and very kindly offered to put me up for a few days.

I set off with all my luggage to the bus-stop outside the airport, then suddenly realised I wanted to relieve myself. After years of unselfconsciously peeing out in the open alongside everyone else, I briefly eyed up the low wall behind me. A vague memory stirred, that urinating in public was illegal in this country. This must be culture shock, I thought.

As I stood waiting for the bus I was struck by how empty of people and quiet everything felt. Gone was the busy street life that had surrounded me the day before. It had all disappeared, tidied away behind rows and rows of neat houses and gardens with closed gates and doors. The swift moving traffic on smooth roads whooshing by sounded eerie.

Tsultrim and her mother and I stayed up late laughing and regaling each other with reminiscences of our times in India. They could tell me about their experience of being western nuns in England. 'Some people are all right with it and some not,' they told me. 'Some young boys were throwing stones at our windows the other day. I told them off, saying we had lived here longer than they had. Do you know what they retorted? "We thought you was monks!" As if that justified it!' It was both funny and worrying at the same time. The two nuns were caring and supportive, wishing me well, but I soon realised that they were not in a position to offer me any help. I was on my own.

I decided to visit my maternal grandmother in Weeley, where I had spent so much time as a child. Everything felt so familiar and homely as the sounds and smells of my childhood came flooding back. My grandma and Auntie Mollie didn't seem to have changed at all. The morning after I arrived my grandma, who was always an early riser, was busying herself cooking breakfast. As I stood alongside her by the kitchen table in my robes with my shaven head, she looked up at me and stared at me hard: 'You are the same old Susan, aren't you?' she asked. 'Yes, grandma,' I said. 'Yeah, I'm just the same.' She nodded as if reaffirming to herself that our relationship had not changed. 'Go and lay the table then dear,' she said.

My grandmother felt obliged to tell my parents I was there. Before we knew it, they had sped down from Cheshire by car, to get me. They were understandably upset and angry, and insisted on whisking me away up to Warrington, as if I were a naughty little girl they were still responsible for. I was twenty-eight years old and had not lived at home since I was nineteen! As ever they showed no interest in how I might be feeling. My mother was absolutely seething and my father was as always totally focused on trying to manage her and her tempestuous emotionality. It was like suddenly being thrown back into the worst times of my childhood.

By the time we reached Warrington I was feeling completely disorientated. I had had every intention of contacting them when I was more settled and would be able to give them the attention they needed and deserved. As it was, everything I said or did made things worse between us. The only thing I could think of to save my sanity was to re-establish my daily routine of prayer and meditation. I tried to escape to my room upstairs to chant my evening rituals, accompanied by my little bell and hand drum. I was vaguely aware this might provoke my parents, but I also harboured the fond hope that the blessing of the practice might work like magic to help resolve the situation. As one might have guessed, it just wound them up to breaking point. It must have seemed like a deliberate attempt to alienate and annoy them.

Amidst all this, my father took me by surprise one evening with the depth of his insight and understanding. He asked me while I was cooking the supper, 'Are you sure you have got the humility to carry this thing through?' 'Oh, he knows me and sees what I am about!' I thought. It was the first time he ever let me know how well he understood me. I wasn't sure I had the necessary humility, but I was grateful for his asking me. My mother, on the other hand, couldn't relate to me at all and things with her just went from bad to worse. Eventually she was effectively going berserk. After only three nights, my father shoved a five pound note in my hand and said, 'Go, just go.'

I rang up Samye Ling to check exactly when the Karmapa would be there. The receptionist asked me whether I wanted to stay overnight, which surprised me. 'Well, I would like to stay, but I believe you are full. You wrote to me in India.' That rang a bell for her. 'Oh, are you that nun that wrote from India?' I said I was. 'Oh yes, you can't stay.' I never did find out why I'd been banned in that way.

Not knowing what to do, I grasped at a straw. Ngawang's last words to me as I left Tilokpur nunnery came back to me. She had given me the name of her sponsor in Britain, a lady named Pat May. I rang her and she was clearly delighted. 'Oh come, come,' she said. So I escaped to Birmingham, with a tremendous sense of relief.

Pat had a natural appreciation for what my life as a nun represented, so I immediately felt at home. Both she and her husband Brian made me feel very welcome. However, she was at pains to impress upon me that these were hard times in Britain, which worried me greatly since I had arrived with no money and didn't know how I was going to support myself. The last thing I wanted was to be a burden on anyone.

Yet compared with where I had just come from, we were living in luxury. 'What would you like to eat?' Pat asked as I gazed bemused at the shelves and shelves of goods and food laid out before me in the local supermarket. 'Rice, lentils and vegetables,' was all I could think of. 'What about cake? Biscuits? Cheese, eggs, yoghurt? Some ice-cream? Quiche?' Pat asked. These were all things I considered expensive luxuries and hadn't eaten for years. I wasn't going to ask for them if times were hard. Then we came to a book stand where there was a beautiful book with glossy pictures of Thai monks. 'Do you think Ngawang would like this?' she asked. That put me on the spot. Only a matter of weeks ago I had been with Ngawang at the nunnery, where she lived in a small room with her old mother and was trying to support as many of her extended family as she could on the money Pat was sending her. I remembered her mother whimpering from the bed in the corner of the room asking for butter, and Ngawang telling her they couldn't afford it. How could I explain all that to Pat, who clearly had no idea what conditions Ngawang was living in? I simply said, 'I think she would prefer the money.'

Pat belonged to a Buddhist group that had just bought a house in Edgbaston to convert into a Dharma centre. Sister Palmo had contacted them from Samye Ling saying they should invite the Karmapa to visit Birmingham to bless the place. I was invited to a meeting to discuss the idea. The older members were concerned they were too small a group to be able to do the thing properly. I agreed that it had to be done right, and I told them they would need quite a lot of money to cover costs and make offerings, and a big house to host the whole of the Karmapa's party. Among them was a lawyer called John Maxwell, who offered to provide all that was needed, so I encouraged them to go for it and they did. I was thrilled that the Karmapa was actually going to come to Birmingham – this solved all my problems! In the days running up to his visit the group wanted my advice about various things, but by and large the event seemed to organise itself, which was astonishing given there was almost no time to prepare.

Then came the big shock. The night before the Karmapa was due to arrive we were up late into the night watching the news about the pub bombings in the centre of Birmingham. It was hard to believe this was actually happening so close to home. For me it was particularly shocking, since I had hardly read a newspaper for almost six years, and I had no idea what the troubles in Ireland were about, or what the IRA was. Terrorist attacks on ordinary citizens had been unheard of in the Britain I had left behind. They had now become a regular occurrence.

Plans for the Karmapa's visit continued regardless and the event was made all the more powerful by this sickening tragedy. For a city in shock and mourning it was a relief and solace to be welcoming the compassionate and joyful presence of the Karmapa into its heart.

John's family with amazing generosity had moved out of their big house in Edgbaston, to let the Karmapa's party take the whole place over. I piled in with the rest of them, sharing a bedroom with Sister Kechog Palmo and Sister Pema Chödrön, who had just been ordained by the Karmapa. There we were, three western Buddhist nuns sharing our stories late into the night. It felt a privilege to spend this time with Kechog Palmo listening to her recounting incidents from her truly extraordinary life!

Many grand personages had joined up with the Karmapa's party along the way so we were hard pressed to find room for everyone. The Karmapa's dashing young Tibetan translator, Achi Tsepal, ended up having to sleep under the stairs and was joined there at the last minute by the young Sogyal Rinpoche because there was nowhere else for him to sleep.

The days leading up to the visit had been exciting but also nerve-wracking as we prepared to receive the Karmapa. I had never served the Karmapa before and naïvely thought that he would not want to sit in an ordinary chair. I had only ever seen him sitting on a throne. John and I tried to construct a makeshift throne from a bookcase laid face down on the floor with a cloth thrown over it. I made a shrine alongside it. Actually by that time the Karmapa was well used to sitting in chairs so I don't know what he made of our effort. As we waited for the Karmapa to arrive, I occupied myself drawing the customary chalk pathway with the eight auspicious symbols on it all over the courtyard in front of the house. The welcoming party lined up, each with a white scarf, as the Karmapa in his big car and the rest of the entourage in procession behind swept up to the front door.

As the person asked to accompany him into the building and to his room, I showed him to his 'throne'. He took his seat and I started chatting away in Tibetan. At one point, I found myself saying, 'You know people in the West don't understand about how ritual activities such as making offerings on a shrine can have any spiritual benefit and create *punya*.' I don't know why I was telling him this, but no sooner had I said it than he looked at the offering bowls on the shrine, and said, 'It's *punya* to fill the bowls with water.' To my embarrassment, in all the rush I had forgotten to turn the bowls up and fill them with water. A Tibetan would never have made a mistake like that because to do so would have struck them as being inauspicious. I sensed the Karmapa gently teasing me for my pretentious remarks about other Westerners.

That evening the Karmapa performed the famous Black Hat ceremony at the Catholic school hall where John's wife worked. The place was packed. The radiant presence of the Karmapa filled the hall with an atmosphere of inspiration, hope and majesty. The deep mysteriousness of the ceremony impacts on all the senses: the Karmapa's concentrated look as he holds the crown on his head as if it would fly off by itself if he let it go, the continuous droning of the horns and trumpets, the smell of incense and the hushed silence of a room full of people spellbound by the magic of the ritual. We found ourselves transported as if into another dimension.

I had seen the Black Hat ceremony quite a number of times by then. The hat or crown is said to be modelled on one the Emperor of China saw above the fifth Karmapa's head which had been woven from the hair of celestial beings. It is said to have the power to liberate on seeing; I imagine it appearing to me when I die, to guide me on my way. The Karmapa meditates on Avalokiteshvara as he shows the crown and recites his mantra on crystal prayer beads.

The next day, at last the moment came for the interview with the Karmapa that would determine the future direction of my life. What would he tell me to do? He was very kind and said I shouldn't worry about anything. His instruction was to, 'Go to the Dharma centre in Manchester and teach the young man running it all the Dharma you know.' The young man was a Manchester University student named Dave Stott (now Lama Jampa Thaye), who had come down to Birmingham to meet the Karmapa and ask advice for his centre. He had been in the Dharma for two or three years already and was a student of Karma Thinley Rinpoche so I immediately felt comfortable with the idea of working with him.

The Karmapa continued his tour down to another Dharma centre called Kham House in Essex, started by Chime Rinpoche a few years before. Dave and I headed off to join him there. I was told that although Dave could stay there I couldn't. Again, I never knew why. Nevertheless I was allowed to attend all the events there and had a chance to speak to the Karmapa again. I told him I was without a lama to guide me in the West and he told me that Chime Rinpoche would help me. I was a bit doubtful about that, given the ban against me. I had however observed another lama, Ato Rinpoche, who lived in Cambridge. I was impressed by his presence and something about the way he moved – the way he did such a simple thing as turn a door knob and open a door with such grace and attentiveness that it seemed to express the essence of what mindfulness meant. I told the Karmapa that I would rather be taught by Ato Rinpoche, at which he looked very pleased and had Ato Rinpoche summoned. He was given the dubious honour of having me put under his spiritual care. That same night I set off by car to Manchester with Dave and his girlfriend.

As Dave was a university student living on a grant in a rented flat, he couldn't really afford to keep another person. Dave put out a jam jar on the kitchen mantelpiece and asked the people who came for Dharma meetings – mostly other students – to donate money for me. After each meeting, he would openly count the money in the kitchen in front of me, expressing alarm about how little had been raised. It was excruciatingly embarrassing. I had got used to a culture where leading a renunciate life is admired and appreciated, and had felt very integrated into society. I realised how supportive these cultural norms and attitudes had been for me and just how much I was going to miss them.

I found myself feeling disorientated and without any guidance. How was I to go about teaching people living in such a different way to the one I had become used to? I had no training for my new job and scarcely any support – no colleagues to consult with, no guidelines. I had yet to have a proper meeting with Ato Rinpoche to seek his advice. It was all completely up to me and Dave. He was bolder than I was and quite confident that the thing to do was for us two to chant ritual practices in Tibetan in front of everyone as they sat and listened. Since he was already using a low throne to teach from, he supplied me, as his teacher, with a slightly higher one. This is proper Tibetan protocol but felt quite weird in the circumstances. He couldn't read Tibetan very fast at the time, so we had to chant painfully slowly. I couldn't imagine what it felt like for the rest of the participants. There had to be a better way of teaching Dharma in the West than this!

At the first opportunity I went down to Cambridge to talk to Ato Rinpoche. He received me by appointment at his home where he lived with his wife and we talked for about an hour. He gave me some general advice and answered a few questions and then took me completely by surprise. He told me to get out of my situation in Manchester as fast as I could and find myself a job. 'If you stay there you will find after a while resentment will build up against you. You need to be financially independent.' I think he was quite rightly concerned about how naïve and unrealistic I was being.

For my part I was now at a loss. This seemed directly contrary to what the Karmapa had told me. He had said not to worry, money wouldn't be a problem. It seemed now that it wasn't money that was the problem so much as autonomy, the very thing I had feared at the outset.

I knew I had enough resourcefulness to be able to make a career for myself if I wanted to, but was that really what I should be doing? That would require a major turn-around in all my thinking so far. Since being told by Trungpa Rinpoche to take teaching from Karma Thinley Rinpoche in India I had always tried to follow what my gurus told me to do. I now had one guru, the Karmapa, telling me to do one thing, but then putting me under the guidance of another guru who seemed to be telling me to do the opposite. I concluded that I had put myself under the direction of people who didn't know what they were doing, so it was up to me to work something out for myself. My own common sense told me that since I hadn't a clue how to teach Dharma in the West, I should go back to the East.

As I was discussing my situation with some Dharma friends in Cambridge, a call came through from my friend Denys in France. He wanted me to come and help him at the Dharma centre in Paris that Kalu Rinpoche had just established. It was under the charge of Lama Gyurme, a bright young Bhutanese lama whom I knew from my days in Sonada. The invitation coming at that exact moment, seemed like the universe was offering me my next step. I accepted without hesitation and with a great sense of relief took a night train to Paris as soon as I could. As on other occasions Denys had saved the day for me.

Early in the morning at Gare du Nord in Paris I was struggling to remember enough of my school French to find my way to the address of the centre I had in my pocket. I made it without much trouble and was warmly welcomed by Denys, Rosemarie, Lama Gyurme and a few other residents of the new Dharma centre. It was a smart four-storeyed terrace house, with a beautiful shrine room done up in Tibetan style. Amazingly I was given one of the best rooms in the house alongside that of Lama Gyurme. I accepted the honour gratefully, although I was a little puzzled about what my role was going to be, given that my French was so poor.

It turned out that nobody was clear about their role or what they were supposed to be doing, including Lama Gyurme and Denys. We had a meeting with the residents of the centre, all sitting on the floor around a low table discussing the question of what a Dharma centre was exactly. The whole concept had been newly created for the West by teachers like Kalu Rinpoche, trying to work out how best to help their Western disciples. It wasn't a monastery, but a place where people could come to find out about Dharma. Was it a community? Were people supposed to follow a programme of training? Was it just a nice place to hang out and meet a lama? Lama Gyurme was complaining. 'Talk, talk, talk – that is all you Westerners do. Tell me what it is I'm supposed to be doing.' Denys got really annoyed at this. 'We don't know,' he said. 'You tell us. You're the lama who has been sent here to start a centre. If you told us what to do, we wouldn't have to talk so much. How are we supposed to work it out without talking? If you can, then you do it!' It was all very symptomatic of the situation. Kalu Rinpoche had left them in Paris with only the faintest clue about what they were trying to achieve.

The routine at that time was to recite prayers together in the shrine room in Tibetan every morning and evening. Kalu Rinpoche wanted all his Western students to practise the Four-Armed Avalokiteshvara practice he had taught us in India. I was given the task of translating the practice texts into English then writing out the Tibetan with English phonetics under each word and the English translation under that. I did all this painstakingly by hand and then it went for printing and distributing to all Kalu Rinpoche's Dharma centres around the world. These texts travelled far and from time to time over the years I meet people who were charmed by them and used them for decades.

Apart from this work, there wasn't really a role for me in Paris even though it was fun being there making new friends and getting first hand experience of life in a Dharma centre community. After some months, I noticed that I was actually becoming a bit of a nuisance. It didn't help that I wasn't very diligent in improving my French and this limited how much I could contribute to the running of the centre. In the end my room was needed for other purposes and it was clearly time for me to move out. As if the Universe had again come to my rescue, at this point Denys informed me that the Karmapa had started a Dharma centre in the Dordogne and needed a translator for the lamas he had left there to set it up. Would I be interested in the job? I was more than happy to go somewhere where I would be of some use, so I cheerfully set off once more into the unknown.

Ten

Becoming a Translator

After a long journey by train I was met at Les Eyzies railway station and driven half an hour or so through stunning countryside to a simple farmhouse, my destination, Dhagpo Kagyu Ling. 'Where would you like to sleep?' Stace asked. He was the young, rather attractive Englishman managing the Dordogne centre. 'What about here in the pigsty?' I poked my head in. 'It hasn't got a floor!' I exclaimed – it was so derelict there was only uneven earth and stones to sleep on. 'How about the stable then?' he enquired, showing me the dark interior of the barn. It had a concrete floor. 'Or you could try the attic, but it has no windows.' I climbed the outside ladder into the attic and decided, given there were no beds on offer, that the wooden floor in there was by far my best option. It was a good job I had brought my own sleeping bag.

Stace explained that an English millionaire named Mr Benson had dedicated a whole swathe of country in the magnificent hills, woods and fields of the Dordogne valley to Dharma purposes by giving separate parcels of property from his estate to the Karmapa, Dilgo Khyentse Rinpoche and Kangyur Rinpoche. A month or so prior to my arrival, the Karmapa had visited with his whole entourage and consecrated the property given to him and then left his nephew Lama Jigme, and a couple of attendant monks to set up his main seat in Europe there. The Karmapa placed Lama Jigme's brother the Shamarpa in overall charge although he was not living there. So there was Lama Jigme and his attendants suddenly left by themselves in the middle of the French countryside being looked after by Stace with occasional visits from Mr Benson to see how they were getting on. Lama Jigme spoke good English but none of the Tibetans knew French or could drive which made them very dependent on Stace and his full range of skills and ingenuity. The farmhouse didn't even have a stove, so the monks had to cook over an open fire in the kitchen. It was very simple living indeed.

As members of the Karmapa's own household, they were used to being treated like royalty and Lama Jigme in particular was not used to fending for himself. Nevertheless, they didn't seem at all fazed by this sudden massive change in their situation. Stace, who was living with the lamas in the farmhouse, was a volunteer who had been roped in to get the centre off the ground. He had made a start at creating a vegetable garden to feed everyone and was planning to convert the hay loft in the barn into a shrine room.

He was a charismatic and multi-talented character, very devoted to the Karmapa and keen to understand and practise the Dharma. Once at the Black Hat ceremony Stace saw the Karmapa appearing in the form of Avalokiteshvara, white with four arms. Because he thought everyone had seen it, he didn't say anything at the time. Later he saw a picture of Avalokiteshvara in that form for the first time. 'Oh look!' he said, 'There's a picture of how the Karmapa looked when he was showing the crown.' Everyone was amazed because although it is said that the Karmapa takes on that form when he shows the Black Hat, hardly anyone actually sees it.

Stace was in his mid-twenties and wore golden earrings decades before they came into fashion. He spoke fluent French and had spent his life travelling around the world, getting involved in whatever projects took his fancy. A few weeks after I arrived his travelling companion Jim came to join us. He lived in their red lorry with its own wood burning stove and chimney pot.

The news about the new Dharma centre was spreading rapidly to all the places the Karmapa had visited in Europe and beyond. Throughout the summer people would just turn up and want to stay, sometimes indefinitely, in tents and barns wherever they could. This meant that there were always between twelve and twenty volunteers around at any one time. A makeshift kitchen was set up in the barn and people washed under an outside tap. Although there was a bathroom and toilet in the lamas' house, everyone else had to manage outside. It was like being in India again, a home from home.

That summer felt delightfully wild and free. The place was un-formed and we had to make things up as we went along. I thoroughly enjoyed learning about organic gardening and the herbs that grew wild everywhere about us and watching the volunteers dismantling the pigsty and turning it into a dwelling. There was singing and guitar playing in the evenings by firelight and children running about having the time of their lives. The lamas were not giving formal teachings but hung around for people to talk to which was in itself a novelty for all concerned. One of the rooms in the house was kept as a shrine room for morning and evening meditation sessions. I was happy because I was able to keep working on my Tibetan texts, translating when necessary for the lamas and meditating several hours each morning and evening.

Stace had a big problem because he had no clear direction or budget. His money supply was scarce and unpredictable. He could hardly charge anyone to stay there because the facilities were so poor, yet the people working to improve them had to eat. There must have been a little money from somewhere but everything, including basics like milk, was severely rationed to the point that the fridge had to be padlocked. We even tried grinding our own wheat into flour each day, using a little tiny coffee grinder. Now and then people would turn up thinking it was a fully functioning retreat centre with accommodation and so on. What a shock they got, having travelled all that way, to be told they were expected to work, not meditate. It wasn't funny really, but we couldn't help laughing at their look of dismay and indignation!

Many of the people who turned up and offered their services as volunteers knew very little about Buddhism and nothing about Tibetan culture and protocol. The Tibetans had been monastics all their lives in the strict disciplined environment of a medieval mono-culture and imagined that they were being asked to recreate this kind of situation in the West. However they found themselves in the midst of an international melee of mostly young people from different cultures and sub-cultures excitedly living their way through the newly found freedom and optimism of their times. Added to the inevitable clash of values between the Tibetans and themselves was the language problem. Not only the Tibetans but also many of the volunteers were struggling with having to communicate in English. Everyone took the situation in their stride with remarkable equanimity given the difficulties they were facing.

The oldest Tibetan monk was referred to as 'Omzay' because he had been the *omzay* (Tib. *umdze*), meaning the chant leader, at the Karmapa's monastery in Sikkim. I suppose he must have been in his mid-sixties. He saw his main role as looking after Lama Jigme, at least thirty years his junior. Omzay wanted to make sure he was treated as he should be, given his rank both as a lama and as the nephew of the Karmapa. We Westerners had no idea how seriously Omzay took his responsibilities and how far from the Tibetan cultural norms we were pushing his boundaries. We didn't even call Lama Jigme by the title Lama.

One day Omzay came up to me with a look of utmost alarm on his face. 'Come and look!' he said. 'This is shocking, really shocking! What is the world coming to?' I followed the direction of his gaze. Lama Jigme was trying to wash his clothes in a bucket of cold water by the outside tap, but he looked quite contented, so it didn't register with me at first what I should be shocked by. 'His Holiness's own nephew! Look! He is the same as His Holiness himself – his very heart! Reduced to washing his own clothes. Stop him!' At that, he himself ran up to stop Lama Jigme and take over the task from him. I tried to understand what Omzay was feeling. Why was he so shocked? None of us was used to this way of living. At least Lama Jigme had a bed and a proper room.

A few days later at the breakfast table Omzay announced, 'I have been invited to visit some relatives in Switzerland.' He paused and then added sadly, 'I can't go, though.' 'Why not?' I asked. 'There will be nobody to look after Lama Jigme.' 'We can do that,' I said cheerfully – but he was un-persuaded. 'You don't know how to take care of him. You will just leave him to look after himself. I know you people. You don't understand anything. I couldn't be responsible for leaving him like that with nobody serving him. I couldn't face His Holiness knowing I had left Lama Jigme to fend for himself like that.' I didn't want Omzay to miss out on seeing his relatives, so I said, 'I promise I will serve him just as you would do while you are away.' He took some persuading, but eventually left by car as Lama Jigme and I stood on the doorstep of the farmhouse waving him off.

As the car disappeared out of sight, without a moment's hesitation, Lama Jigme calmly walked to the woodshed and picked up the axe that was resting in the chopping block. He took a piece of wood and set about chopping it. I am sure he had never done anything like that in his life before. He must have been watching other people doing it and been dying to have a go. Later, when I went to make his supper for him, he had already begun trying to do it for himself. Un-used to this kind of task, he had spilled a whole carton of yogurt on the floor and was trying to work out how to clear it up. Eventually he allowed me to do it for him – I think more out of a sense of inadequacy than anything else. I said I would cook for him but he insisted that he wanted to do it for himself, so I left him to it. Sometime later I called in to see how he had got on. 'It's all right,' he said, laughing shyly, 'but I put too much salt in.' After that he did let me cook for him. What I took away from this incident was the graciousness of a person who could allow others to serve him because that was what they wanted him to do and not at all because it was what he wanted. It was a new kind of selflessness that I had not appreciated before.

'The Karmapa is sending Gendun Rinpoche to be the main teacher here,' announced Lama Jigme some months after I arrived. 'He is a *real* yogin who has spent most of his life in retreat,' he added proudly. We couldn't wait for his arrival. He was to be the Karmapa's main spiritual representative in Europe and had been given the Karmapa's very own ritual empowerment vase as a token of his authority. As he wasn't well known, having always been in retreat, the Karmapa had written a letter of authorisation for him. The Karmapa told Denys, who had been asked to accompany Gendun Rinpoche from Rumtek to Dhagpo Kagyu Ling, that the great lama should spend his time in retreat at Dhagpo Kagyu Ling and not accept invitations to travel around teaching. He believed this would draw his students to Dhagpo Kagyu Ling. I was really excited at the prospect of having a great meditation teacher on hand to talk to again.

Gendun Rinpoche came accompanied by his attendant Lama Phurtse. As soon as they arrived I introduced myself, and was rather taken aback when Lama Gendun said, 'I know who you are. You are my translator. The Karmapa has told me about you.' I hadn't been aware till that moment that the Karmapa knew I was there. I was delighted that within minutes of our meeting, Gendun Rinpoche was already talking about the nature of mind! His whole presence radiated Enlightenment.

He had a strong east Tibetan dialect that I was unfamiliar with and a bit of a speech impediment, so it was difficult to understand him. I had to guess his meaning a lot of the time, but I got used to him when he was talking about the Dharma because I could recognise from context what he was saying. When he went off into other topics, I often completely lost the thread. He had such an odd way of putting things in conversation that I sometimes couldn't work out whether he had just said one thing or its complete opposite. It didn't help that he could be a bit sarcastic. For example, he might say, 'Go and live a worldly life if that is what you want,' but in a tone that suggested he was reprimanding the student rather than giving him an instruction to be taken literally. But could I be sure? Should I say literally what he had said, or what I thought he meant? It was especially hard if I wasn't even sure I had understood his words correctly in the first place. In the end, after I had acted as Gendun Rinpoche's interpreter on and off for several years, I got to understand him quite well because he tended to repeat things.

When he first arrived, he had almost no experience of teaching Dharma, even to Tibetans. He kept saying to me that he was over sixty, so was an old man and not up to adapting to this new way of life. As a hermit he wasn't used to being surrounded by people all the time, especially not an unruly bunch of Westerners whose culture and language he didn't understand and who didn't understand his. On top of that he was expected to teach them Dharma. Where to begin teaching people with no Buddhist background at all in their upbringing? I hadn't known where to start when the Karmapa had sent me to Manchester where at least I understood the language and culture. How much more difficult must it have been for Gendun Rinpoche taking on the role of teacher for the first time in the circumstances he found himself in?

As for me, I was now faced with a challenging new role in life. As the official interpreter for Gendun Rinpoche I was expected to be constantly on duty translating for him whenever he needed it. Even though the Karmapa had instructed Gendun Rinpoche simply to stay put at Dhagpo Kagyu Ling, since there was no heating in Dhagpo, when the winter came it was too cold to stay there. He therefore started accepting invitations from Dharma centres across Europe. He, Lama Phurtse, Stace, Jim and myself set off in the red lorry that Stace and Jim drove and slept in while the lamas and I slept in the various Dharma centres we visited in the south of France, Italy and then Greece. Looking back it wasn't really a very dignified way to travel, but all the Dharma centres were struggling for money and I think they were quite grateful for the economy involved. We stuck to the warmer countries in the winter and then later on went to Belgium, Holland and England. There was much to enjoy on these trips. Gendun Rinpoche was playful, teasing people and tweaking their beards. Even though he often said things like, 'You don't get to Enlightenment by laughing and playing about! You don't get to Enlightenment by singing and dancing!' he himself was always laughing. He might have just as easily said, 'You don't get to Enlightenment by being uptight and taking yourself too seriously!'

The first time I accompanied Rinpoche on one of these trips I was quite shocked by how hard I was expected to work translating for him, sometimes for three hours at a time twice or three times a day as he gave teachings, and then in between to translate for a string of people seeking personal advice. Rinpoche was so inexperienced he tried to tell everyone everything, so that interviews were taking over half an hour each. I got so tired I didn't know what was happening to me. I had lost my freedom trapped in a situation where I had no money and nowhere to go. Nobody thought of paying me anything, yet I was expected to be on duty from morning to night and to be grateful that I was not being charged to stay at the Dharma centres.

Nonetheless, I enjoyed translating because it meant I spent a lot of time in the presence of the Lama receiving teachings and also I enjoyed listening to people's questions and having to find ways of expressing them to the Lama in a way that he could understand. For many people their interview with the Lama was a life-changing event and they often asked deep and important questions about their spiritual life. I did my best but often felt a bit of a cheat because I was never saying exactly what the Lama was saying. I couldn't, no matter how hard I tried, because quite often there are not equivalent words in English for what is being said in Tibetan. Similarly, students questioning the Lama often used concepts that do not exist as such in Tibetan. 'Lama, is emptiness the soul?' someone might ask. 'Soul' is very hard to translate into Tibetan, where the same concept does not exist. Of course, the Lama's answer would reflect the way I chose to translate the question. I felt the responsibility of that keenly and was uncomfortable making this kind of choice for people so would often spend time talking to them for a while until I was sure what exactly they meant by the words they were using. Only then would I translate their questions to the Lama.

Once at someone's private interview, I was trying to understand their way of thinking, asking him to explain further what he meant by his question, when with a look of disdain, he said, 'There is no need to try to understand the meaning. Just translate the words.' Little did he know how much power he was putting into my hands! Personally, I couldn't bear for my inner life, my deep pursuit for truth, to be handled by a translator as a middle person between me and the lama. That is why I had learnt Tibetan. Even if the translator is honestly doing their best and has an excellent grasp of the language, you are still limited by their understanding of Dharma, as well as by the limitations inherent in translation.

A French woman translated for Gendun Rinpoche on occasion, and I remember a particular rich patron saying how much he liked her translations. 'I feel such a rapport with the Lama when you are translating,' he said. 'I don't feel that with every translator. You are very special. You and I have a special connection.' But when I listened to her translate, I couldn't believe what was going on. Gendun Rinpoche would hold forth for five or ten minutes on karma and rebirth and the need to give up worldly activities in order to follow the path to Awakening. In those days Gendun Rinpoche was no great believer in the path of practice undertaken in the secular world – he considered being a monk or nun, and practising in retreat, as the only serious path. However, the translator was not even trying to convey this unpalatable message to the rich patron. Instead she spoke quite eloquently on how there was no need to give up one's ordinary lifestyle, claiming that one could practise perfectly well in the midst of a busy life, and made no mention of karma at all!

The rich patron was entranced, which Gendun Rinpoche took as a sign that he was absorbing his message fully. He continued with increased enthusiasm, which was in turn completely misunderstood by the patron, and a tremendous feeling of accord built up between the three of them, as the translator shamelessly exploited her position. Everyone was smiling and nodding, the lama and the student each hearing what they wanted to hear! I was both amused and distressed at seeing this. As a translator I considered it my duty to choose my words very carefully, and this was just a step too far for me!

Once I was translating for a French monk who was a disciple of Gendun Rinpoche. He asked about going into a three-year retreat. Gendun Rinpoche replied, 'He can't do a three-year retreat. He is too crazy.' He used a word that sounded quite harsh to my ears. The monk had had a mental breakdown some time previously but was stable at that particular moment. It would have been quite accurate for me to translate what he said as, 'Rinpoche thinks you are bonkers,' but that would have been unkind and although Rinpoche was straight-speaking, he didn't mean to be unkind. 'Can you give me another way of saying that?' I asked him, but Rinpoche just repeated his first remark. I still hesitated to translate it. Eventually, after I had pressed him several times, he said that the disciple needed to wait to make sure his mind was stable enough first. This I could translate and it was received in the way it was meant.

Gendun Rinpoche didn't always need a translator. He could be very intuitive about people. I remember one time an old woman came in looking grief stricken. 'My son,' she began, 'my son, he is in trouble again and wants me to send him money. He has done this all his life, again and again. He even gets put in prison and then as soon as he is out, he gets into trouble again, always asking me for money. I am so worried about him.' She said quite a lot, and I was trying to think of how to summarise it all, because generally speaking I don't find Tibetan lamas are particularly patient about listening to detailed personal stories. I had only managed to utter, 'Her son is in trouble and asking for money,' when the Lama cut in and said very quickly and forcefully, 'Don't worry about your son. He is old enough to look after himself. You are old now and should be concentrating on doing prayers and purifying your mind ready for your next life.' I was aghast, sure that this was not what she wanted to hear, but of course my job was to translate and so I did. To my amazement, as I said the words, it was as if ten years fell from the woman's face. She suddenly looked relaxed and happy, as if someone had released her from jail. It felt as if the Lama and the woman were communicating without any need for a translator at all.

It seems that a good practitioner can be in tune with things and be so receptive and spontaneous that their actions and words often seem to come from personal knowledge because the timing and synchronicity are so precise. Yet when you enquire, they assure you that they have no such knowledge. Once I was translating for Gendun Rinpoche when a young man came in asking to take Refuge vows with him. Gendun Rinpoche immediately began preparing himself to give Refuge when the lad turned to me and said, 'I have a problem. Could you ask the Lama something before we begin? I've taken Refuge twice before, the first time from a lama in Darjeeling and the next from a lama in Germany.' I told him it wasn't a problem, that Gendun Rinpoche was always happy to give people Refuge, however many times they had had it before. The young man explained that he was worrying about which name to use, because each time he took Refuge, he got a new Refuge name: he already had two and wasn't sure what he was going to do once he got a third one.

I turned to translate this for Gendun Rinpoche, but when I looked up he was all ready to begin the ceremony, and before I could open my mouth to put the question, he was talking rapidly and expecting me to translate. After the ceremony was over and the new name had been given, I asked the student whether he wanted me to put his question. 'No need,' he replied with a big beam. He pointed to the small piece of paper Rinpoche had given him. 'He's given me half of the first Refuge name I was given, and half of the second. So it combines them both.' I turned to Gendun Rinpoche and told him what he had just done. He asked to be told the other two names, and when he heard them, he began to laugh. He threw his head back on his pillow and flung his arms out, embracing the sky. 'Ha, ha, ha!' he laughed. 'Ha ha! It's one vast expanse of Wisdom. It's all happening spontaneously in the space of Wisdom. Ha, ha, ha!'

Other times as a translator I didn't want to be responsible for giving a student advice that I thought might harm them. I have talked to other translators about this and one of them told me that once when translating for Gendun Rinpoche someone came in with a badly infected finger asking Rinpoche's permission to go to the hospital to have it treated. Rinpoche told him there was no need, just recite mantras over it. The translator took the law into his own hands and told him Rinpoche had given him permission to go to the hospital. He told me afterwards that he hadn't wanted to be responsible for the student's not getting the right medical treatment even if in this case Rinpoche was speaking from some kind of prescience.

Similarly, a Tibetan who was a lama's attendant told me once that while lamas often seem to have supernormal knowledge and give extraordinarily prescient advice, at other times they seem to be lacking even as much common sense as an ordinary person. He told me the story of how his lama had gone to visit a village where the crops had been destroyed by hail late in the season. He told them just to plant the crop again. It made no sense at all – there was no time for a second crop to ripen.

Having said all this I have to admit that Gendun Rinpoche did seem to be able to work miracles. The summer of 1976 brought a huge drought across Europe which went on for many months. Christian bishops and priests were praying for rain and still it didn't rain. Gendun Rinpoche started to pray for rain too. One of his faithful French disciples who lived in a makeshift shelter in a field on a nearby hill was convinced that Gendun Rinpoche was about to conjure up a storm. 'Oh, my shelter! It will get blown away,' he cried. A few days later a storm started brewing. I was with Rinpoche in his room as the winds rose to gale force. The rain was crossing the window in horizontal blasts. Rinpoche was reciting mantras and holding a bowl over a piece of his bedspread repeating the words 'Sherab Dorje' from time to time. At last the storm abated and Rinpoche's faithful disciple put his head around the door. 'My shelter! It will have been blown away. Where shall I stay tonight?' 'It's fine, go home. Don't worry,' replied the Lama. Sure enough when he got back to his field his shelter was just as it had been. The only sign of the storm was his bucket that had been blown from one end of the field to the other.

Rinpoche later asked after 'Sherab Dorje', but I didn't know who he was talking about. 'Sherab Dorje,' he explained. 'My disciple who was worried about his shelter.' 'Oh you mean Daniel!' I said. Later I mentioned this to Daniel, who looked puzzled. 'That is my first lama's name,' he said. I realised that Rinpoche must at some point have asked for Daniel's name and been told the name of his lama instead. He had been protecting his shelter by covering a place representing it during the storm, repeating what he thought was the man's name to complete the connection. It doesn't seem to have mattered that he was repeating the wrong name because he was so convinced it was the right one. I was reminded of the story of the great Tibetan poet saint Milarepa. He had protected the field of an old lady from a storm he had conjured, by covering it with something, in a similar way to the way Rinpoche had done.

When I asked Gendun Rinpoche about supernormal powers, he told me that at one time in retreat he had found he was able to see through walls and various things like that. He said it in a simple way as if he had been astonished when it happened. He then went on to say that gradually as his meditation went deeper that kind of thing stopped happening. He assured me that things like that can get very distracting and are not the point of Dharma practice. It can be a good sign when they fade away. When full realisation arises all those kinds of powers manifest spontaneously so there is no need to cultivate them beforehand.

On a number of occasions I got so exhausted from travelling around translating for Gendun Rinpoche that I just couldn't go on any more. I would wake up in the morning dreading the sound of Rinpoche's voice endlessly talking about profound truths that I could barely understand, let alone remember and translate with my very limited Tibetan. It was all too much. However much I pleaded with him he wouldn't slow down or stop. Even at meals I was expected to be on duty to translate small talk. The whole experience was so distressing that I ended up thinking, 'I don't want to hear another word of the Dharma. I just want to get out of here.'

It wasn't just exhaustion I was suffering from. It was layer upon layer of inner conflict. Gendun Rinpoche assumed that I responded to and had faith in the images and cultural aspects of Buddhism that were hard for me as a Westerner to relate to, and the more he hammered on about them the more disengaged I became. I told him that he was making wrong assumptions about Westerners and that people were telling me it was all too much for them too. Even translating those aspects of Dharma that did inspire me had become uninspiring because I was too aware of the distorting process that was going on in the translation.

I wanted time to reflect more deeply, in order to get at the truth behind the words, and couldn't bear having to repeat the same possibly misleading things in the same old way day after day. The longer the situation continued the more it felt like water being poured onto fire. Every inspiration I had for Dharma was being extinguished. It didn't matter what I said though, Rinpoche would not listen. He once laughed and said quite sweetly, 'People have always said of me I have no ears. I just don't listen!' I had to smile at his frank confession but it didn't really help my situation. I had heard it is said that the teacher could be good, and the student could be good, but still the relationship might not work. I decided that was what was happening to me. I just wanted to leave and go back to Bokar Rinpoche. Trying to do what the Karmapa had asked me to do was not working out.

Time and again students would ask me to request Rinpoche to teach less and simply sit to meditate with them. If he talked for hours on end, they ended up feeling overloaded, overwhelmed, and unable to concentrate because of feeling dull or restless. People told me they had given up trying to listen to him (and me) and just sat and let it all wash over them, simply enjoying the sense of being in his presence. So much for all my hard work trying to translate! It says a lot however about the power of his blessing that this was already inspiring enough for them. When I put such requests to Rinpoche he would be completely baffled. Unlike the Japanese, Tibetans do not sit together for long sessions of silent meditation. They do that alone in their own room. In the USA Trungpa Rinpoche had introduced the idea of group sitting practice, having seen it being done in the Zen tradition, and it caught on so that it eventually became normal even in Tibetan centres in the West. But these were the early days and Gendun Rinpoche wasn't used to such a thing though he did sometimes agree to stop teaching and recite prayers and mantras instead. We were able then to just sit and listen, which gave me a little welcome respite.

When the Karmapa next visited the Dordogne I told him at a personal interview that I was having difficulty as Gendun Rinpoche's translator because he worked me so hard and showed so little understanding of my difficulties. I had hoped that the Karmapa would have a word in the ear of Gendun Rinpoche on my behalf. Later when I went to see Gendun Rinpoche he was very upset. He asked me why I had said that to the Karmapa because now he was the laughing stock of all the other lamas to whom he had been praising me in glowing colours. It hadn't occurred to me that he would have been praising me in any way; I was touched that he had been. It hadn't occurred to me either that anyone in attendance on the Karmapa would have been maliciously passing around comments regarding sensitive matters that they had happened to overhear.

In general wherever Gendun Rinpoche went, Lama Phurtse went too and that continued to the end of Gendun Rinpoche's life. The Karmapa had sent him to live with

Gendun Rinpoche when they first arrived in India from Tibet. The two had spent the last ten years or so in retreat together in Kalimpong so were well used to each other. I loved to be with them because they were both completely dedicated and unworldly practitioners. Yet they were very different characters. Much of the time Lama Phurtse was a silent observer of what was going on, but when he spoke up his timing was perfect and his message always to the point.

At dusk one evening during our first visit to the Dharma centre in Athens, I was sitting with Gendun Rinpoche and Lama Phurtse as they engaged in their evening devotions. A Greek lady came in quietly, knelt before Gendun Rinpoche and placed in his lap a large bouquet of beautiful flowers. Gendun Rinpoche smiled at her graciously and touched her head, quietly muttering words of blessing and protection. She withdrew and Gendun Rinpoche held up the bouquet admiringly. 'Do you know what the karmic result is of offering flowers to the Buddha?' I said I did not. 'One is born beautiful,' he said wistfully. He held the bouquet up before his bedside shrine and, with head bowed, recited some words in Tibetan which I knew transformed this one small offering into limitless offerings before limitless Buddhas. As I took the flowers to put them in water, Lama Phurtse stopped chanting, drew his brows together, and then in the manner of a simpleton asked, 'And what happens if you don't offer flowers to the Buddha?' Gendun Rinpoche replied, 'They are born looking like you,' and burst out laughing at his own joke. Lama Phurtse looked blankly into space for a moment or two, as if musing to himself. He then lowered his eyes and continued with his prayers.

The next afternoon the same lady wandered over to where I was sitting opposite Lama Phurtse who was quietly reciting mantras to himself. The Greek lady was rather lovely looking, middle-aged, with an impressive head of long, shiny black wavy hair, set off by an elegant long white dress. I had been told she had been a singer and had made a best-selling record at some point, but now, in the aftermath of some kind of breakdown, was suffering from strange delusions and emotional instability. Her present preoccupation was with Gendun Rinpoche. He would not look her in the eye in the way she felt a man of true sensitivity should. After all, he was a man of God, God is love and love was what she felt. 'I love God and I love men,' she announced with disquieting passion. 'Would you be my confessor?' she asked. I shrank into myself, and she saw it. 'You Buddhists are supposed to be compassionate, aren't you? Can you not spare a person just a little of your time?' I hesitated. Suddenly she turned and fixed her gaze on Lama Phurtse. 'Oh, how beautiful he is! Beautiful... like a flower.'

Lama Phurtse looked up, with a somewhat blank expression on his long brown face as he squinted into the sun. He opened his mouth to speak, revealing his one protruding front tooth. The spittle hissed and bubbled around it as he spoke. 'What's she saying?' he enquired. I hesitated. He had only been in the West a few months, after a lifetime in seclusion in the protected environment of hermitages and monasteries. How could he be expected to cope with this woman's advances? The Greek lady repeated her eulogy. 'So beautiful... dear God, how like a flower.' 'What's she saying?' the Lama insisted again. I came out with it rather awkwardly, 'She says you're beautiful, like a flower.' He paused and then turned to look her up and down before saying, 'Tell her she's beautiful too, with her long black hair and white dress. She's beautiful like the goddess Tara.' I was astonished, but translated his message faithfully. She raised her eyes heavenward – serene, satiated, sublime – then put her hands together as if in prayer, and said, 'Thank you, Lord. Thank you!' She left praising God, swirling her white dress around her with sedate dancing movements. Lama Phurtse surveyed her departure with a hint of satisfaction. Then he looked up at me. 'You remember that. All sentient beings have been our dear mothers in some lifetime or another. They've all been kind to us, like our own mothers. So always give them what they want. *Remember* that,' he said, wagging his finger in my face.

Lama Phurtse, though gentle, was rather coarse-mannered. His missing front teeth added to the general impression of an unsophisticated and somewhat awkward figure. While in Athens, Gendun Rinpoche, Lama Phurtse and I would eat together in Gendun Rinpoche's room. One morning Rinpoche was up on his bed and Lama Phurtse and I were sitting on the floor below him, either side of a breakfast tray laden with bowls of yoghurt, toast, rolls and butter, plus a teapot, cups and cream. Just as Lama Phurtse was about to pour me some tea, he suddenly sneezed – a loud spluttering sneeze all over the breakfast tray. He had made no attempt to turn his head or cover his nose and mouth: our breakfast had received his full blast. A silence followed. He looked straight at me and I looked from the sneezed-on tray straight at him.

Before I had time to consider my feelings on the matter, Gendun Rinpoche cut in. 'You are disgusting. It's a good job it's Shenpen with us; anyone else would have got up and walked out – and rightly so. Don't you have the first idea of how to behave? Not only are you totally useless, you are also a disgrace. You are just a parasite, living off others and giving nothing in return. You travel around as my attendant and the Dharma centres have to pay for your food and fares. You come along with nothing to offer. What kind of karma must I have to be landed with you? I used to keep company with great yogic practitioners, people who were a constant source of inspiration. But for the last twelve years it's been just you. What did I do to deserve that?' He scowled fiercely. 'You're useless. Anyone else in your position, with nothing else to do all day, and with Shenpen there to help, would at least have learnt some English. Then you could have been able to buy our train tickets or something. You are a drain on Dharma centre resources. God, what did I do to deserve this?'

Lama Phurtse's head was bowed throughout this tirade, and during the moments of silence that followed, I didn't know where to look. Whatever he was feeling, my being there must be making it worse – but I was rooted to the spot. When it became evident that Gendun Rinpoche had had his say, Lama Phurtse slowly raised his head. I was unprepared for what happened next. As he faced me, I saw his expression was rapt. His eyes shone with a deep joy and wonder. He brought his hands together with a bold and whole-hearted clap before his face, then turned to look at Gendun Rinpoche with evident love and gratitude. From somewhere deep within him he cried out, 'The Lama's Vajra Voice!' His expression suggested he was experiencing something profound, and I was overwhelmed by a sense of tremendous privilege to be witness to it. Gendun Rinpoche momentarily wavered as a slight smile crossed his face, but quickly resumed his fierce glare. He laid into Lama Phurtse once more, and Lama Phurtse lowered his head accordingly. This time I felt differently, heard differently, saw differently. 'All sounds are the guru's voice.' I had heard this said many times and wondered what it meant. Clearly Lama Phurtse knew.

Although everyone talked about Gendun Rinpoche as being Enlightened, nobody seemed to say that about Lama Phurtse. Nevertheless, I once had a dream of a long dining hall with a long table with a pure white cloth draped over it. On a dish in the middle of the table was a pure white dish on which was a pure white sausage-shaped item. People around me were whispering to each other that it was Lama Phurtse's turd. When I told Gendun Rinpoche of this strange dream, he said, 'That is a sign of a pure practitioner.' That remark left a deep impression on me, as did the dream.

On a number of occasions I was deeply grateful for Lama Phurtse's timely, no-nonsense interventions that rescued me from difficult situations. Once I was translating for Gendun Rinpoche and it was the end of one of his marathon three-hour sessions. The hall was crowded with over one hundred eager disciples and curious members of the public. Rinpoche had talked fast and at great length on complex and subtle points and everyone was baffled – the disciples, the public, myself, and not least Rinpoche himself when it came to question time. After the final chants, Rinpoche gave individual blessings to a stream of people approaching him, tweaking beards and smiling merrily. I'm sure none of them suspected how tired he was – but if he was tired, I was exhausted. Rinpoche pushed me like he pushed himself; the difference was that whereas he rested between the sections of his teaching, I had to concentrate while he was speaking, and then work hard to translate what he'd said. We made our way up the stairs, followed by Lama Phurtse carrying Rinpoche's books and glasses, and sat down together in Rinpoche's room to drink some tea before bed.

There came a knock at the door and a young Indian man ventured in apologetically. Lama Phurtse gestured to him to sit, and I was called upon to act as translator as the Indian started to put his questions to Rinpoche with a long and involved preamble about himself, his philosophy of life, his concerns, intellectual problems and so on. I struggled to wrest some kind of definite question out of the Indian so that I could put it to Rinpoche and get the interview done with. He kept rambling on, jumping from one idea to the next, all the time glancing up at the lamas earnestly as if seeking reassurance. Finally, I felt I had the essence of his question. I put it to Gendun Rinpoche. He looked baffled and was just about to launch into a reply when Lama Phurtse butted in. 'Look here,' he said, waving his finger in the Indian's face, their noses almost touching, 'what are you asking *her* all these questions for? You're an Indian, born in the Buddha's country, you know more about Buddhism than *she* does.' The Indian man, in surprise, replied that he was asking Rinpoche. Lama Phurtse laughed raucously. 'You are asking *her* in English and *she* is answering in English. You don't know what the old Lama is saying.' Then with a sudden graciousness he leaned forward and looked kindly into the Indian's face. 'Have a cup of tea.'

The Indian's anguished and earnest expression was suddenly replaced by a look of utter contentment. It was as if a load had been taken from his shoulders, and he was saying to himself, 'Is that really permissible? Just to sit here with no other excuse than a cup of tea?' He looked like a man come home. Lama Phurtse stroked him on the head, and made various conversational comments in a mixture of broken English and Hindi. Once it was clear that the Indian was well satisfied, Lama Phurtse turned to Rinpoche and said, 'Off you go, old Lama, you're tired. And you, Shenpen, it's time you were in bed. I will talk to this man.' Gendun Rinpoche looked from Lama Phurtse to me and shrugged. Then laughed. 'He's sometimes quite clever, old Phurtse, isn't he? Mad as a hatter, but he's sometimes quite clever.'

We had returned to Dhagpo Kagyu Ling in February, but soon set off again on another teaching tour, this time without Stace and Jim. Early in that spring of 1976, we were staying at the Dharma centre in Paris and making final arrangements to leave for the next stop, Brussels, by car. We were hesitating because Lama Phurtse was not well. A doctor who happened to be at the centre had been monitoring his temperature every hour that day. Although Lama Phurtse did not say much, I could tell he was in a lot of pain. Gendun Rinpoche thought it was just indigestion from eating too many greasy Tibetan New Year biscuits, but I was alarmed, remembering how Lama Phurtse had said in the plane, as we came in to land a few days before, looking out over the tops of bright pink-tinged clouds as the sun went down, that he would like to keep travelling on to Sukhavati, the Pure Land of Bliss. This is a place Tibetan Buddhists hope to go after death.

We were wondering whether to get him more medical help, but when someone joked, 'Suppose he died, and we arrived at the Belgian border with a corpse in the car?' There was an uncomfortable silence. Suddenly Gendun Rinpoche made up his mind. 'We will do what that doctor says.' The doctor pronounced, 'He needs to go to hospital immediately.' Suddenly I was in the back of an ambulance with Lama Phurtse, crossing Paris with the siren wailing. When we arrived, Lama Phurtse nearly got wheeled into the women's ward – I think the skirt of his monk's robe fooled them. Almost immediately, he was being prepared for the operating theatre and within a couple of hours he was being operated on for septicaemia as a result of appendicitis. We knew nothing of the details till late that night, after a nine-hour operation which involved a great deal of internal mopping up. Apparently if we had brought him there half an hour later he would have died.

The next morning, I went in advance of Gendun Rinpoche, just to get a sense of what the situation was. 'He is probably very frightened there all on his own,' said Rinpoche. 'Tell him not to worry and that I will be there shortly. I won't go to Brussels till he's better. He will need reassuring. He's never been in hospital before, he doesn't know what is happening and he doesn't speak a word of French or English. Poor Phurtse!' However, as I entered the ward and walked towards Lama Phurtse's bed I got an altogether different impression. He seemed completely relaxed and happy, idly making patterns with his forefinger on the wall in front of him as if doodling and humming to himself unconcernedly. 'How's the old Lama?' he asked when he saw me. 'Tell him not to worry about me. I am fine. He can go on up to Brussels without me. I will follow in a day or two.' We chatted for a while and I explained the drains and drips and so on that were hanging out of him everywhere. Later, when I reported to Gendun Rinpoche what I had found, he retorted, 'You are so stupid. He seems happy because he is doped up to the eyeballs with all the stuff they have been giving him. He is going to feel frightened later on when he comes to. I must get there quickly to reassure him.' We both went back there together, but as soon as Gendun Rinpoche saw Lama Phurtse, he laughed. They hardly said anything to each other, but Gendun Rinpoche was reassured and told me, 'It's ok. We can leave for Brussels this afternoon. He is fine.'

When Lama Phurtse joined us a week or so later he had to rest a lot and I spent time at his bedside talking to him. He exuded an air of complete ease and joyfulness that seemed to come from a deep and spacious place from within himself that could not be disturbed by anything in life, nor by death itself. 'Why do we pray to take birth in the Pure Land of Sukhavati when we die?' I asked him. 'Pure Land?' he asked. 'It is all the Pure Land right now,' he said quietly, stroking the cover of his bed as if contemplating it in wonder as he spoke. It was right there in his experience as if it were simply a way of looking.

Karma Ozer had once told me, 'As a child I used to think I could get to Sukhavati by travelling west, perhaps by aeroplane. Then one day I was amazed to learn from a lama that it was actually in my heart!' As she said this she looked really amazed as if somehow she had stepped into the Pure Land as she spoke, whereas by taking the whole idea to be simply a metaphor I had not found it amazing at all. Now, I felt like a blind man arriving in Paradise. I was right there in it, but I couldn't see it. Yet, by looking at Lama Phurtse's shining eyes and rapt gaze, I could pick up the atmosphere. 'It is all like precious jewels...' he said, as if entranced. He was in another world and somehow the reality of that communicated itself to me.

I asked him if he would start teaching Dharma himself. 'No,' he said. 'I can't teach Dharma.' 'Why not?' I asked. It seemed to me that he was teaching it by his very presence. 'Nobody would understand,' he replied. The way he said it came from a place of deep confidence, as if he knew the truth and realised it was too deep to communicate in words. I told him I had a lot of faith in him, but he said the person I should have faith in was Gendun Rinpoche. 'He is like one full vessel filled from another. You don't need me if you have Gendun Rinpoche.'

Although I had never heard Lama Phurtse praised as a realised yogin I was more and more convinced he must be. This was confirmed by Kalu Rinpoche's nephew, Gyaltsen, who said to me, 'You are very lucky to be travelling around with two great yogins like that.' When Lama Phurtse went in to see Kalu Rinpoche shortly after his illness, Kalu Rinpoche rose off his bed and greeted him forehead to forehead as lamas of equal status greet each other. Some time later I told Khenpo Tsultrim Gyamtso Rinpoche by way of a confession that I had more faith in Lama Phurtse, the attendant, than in Gendun Rinpoche himself. Rinpoche surprised me by saying, 'Ah yes, back in Tibet, Phurtse was known as a *chatralwa.*' *Chatralwa* is a way of referring to a highly realised yogin who has gone beyond ordinary conduct. When Lama Phurtse died in 2017 he stayed nine days in a state of post-death meditation – a well-known sign of an accomplished yogin.

Later, as my faith in him increased I asked him if he would give me an empowerment. He said he didn't know how to give one. Nonetheless, later that day he walked with me to the end of lane and sat me down among the trees. We shared together a very peaceful and relaxed moment – it reminded me of being a child. He picked a dandelion and broke off the stem. 'When we were children we used to do this,' he explained. He rolled the piece of dandelion stalk into a kind of bead shape and put it in his mouth. He sucked it for a while and then spat it out onto the palm of his hand. Then he handed it to me. 'That is what we used to do,' he said, looking at me meaningfully. I took the bead as somehow being a blessing, overcoming my slight sense of revulsion. I don't know what I did with it after that but I always remembered that moment as a transmission and a blessing.

There are many stories of great yogins appearing in eccentric guises and giving blessings in very strange ways, so why not?

Lama Phurtse, in fields at Dhagpo Kagyu Ling, Dordogne, France in the 1980s.

Lama Phurtse, **Gendun Rinpoche**, myself & Lama Zimbon, at Dhagpo Kagyu Ling, Dordogne, France, 1976.

The first summer at Dhagpo Kagyu Ling in front of the pigsty with (on the far left) Omzay la, **Lama Jigme Rinpoche**, Myself aged 30, Stace and Jim – the bare-chested chaps, plus volunteers Tashi Mannox (aged 12) and family, with his mother Sally Somersby (front row). Dhagpo Kagyu Ling, 1976 © Peter Mannox.

Khenpo Rinpoche standing with me on the right, Chryssoula Zerbini on the left. At Dhagpo Kagyu Ling within the first few weeks of Khenpo Rinpoche's arrival, 1977.

Khenpo Rinpoche (centre), I am sitting on the left (his right) in the front row, **Tenpa Gyaltsen** to Rinpoche's left, at La Poujade about 10 miles from Dhagpo Kagyu Ling in 1977, where Khenpo Rinpoche held a six-month study programme not long after he had arrived in France.

As a nun at Dhagpo Kagyu Ling. The ladder goes to my bedroom! Photograph ©
Peter Mannox.

Khenpo Rinpoche and **Gendun Rinpoche** at Dhagpo Kagyu Ling, 1977. In the
background: preparations outside the pigsty for the Karmapa's throne. Photograph © Peter Mannox.

A previously unpublished photograph of the **16th Karmapa**, Dhagpo Kagyu Ling, Dordogne, France, 1977. Photograph © Peter Mannox.

Eleven

Meeting Khenpo Rinpoche & Disrobing

Up to this point Dharma centres in the West were rather chaotic. The tendency was for serious practitioners to spend their time trying to cater for the needs of lamas and other visitors, so they didn't get time to practise in retreat much themselves. That was what was happening to me. So when I learned from Denys in 1976 that Kalu Rinpoche's plan for a three-year retreat centre in France was going ahead, I was very excited. Denys hoped I would join it, so I asked Gendun Rinpoche what he thought. 'You don't want to do a three-year retreat with a group of people,' he said. 'It only takes one bad apple to turn the whole thing rotten. Better to do retreat on your own.' In fact, Bokar Rinpoche had once told me more or less the same thing. I eagerly took up Gendun Rinpoche's suggestion to do a three-year retreat on my own under his direction, and Stace and Jim started looking out for a suitable site for a retreat house for me. It turned out that a Dutch couple, Johfra and Ellen, well known artists living several miles away, were willing to let us build a wooden retreat chalet on their land. Stace and Jim set to work and by June I had started a three-year retreat, with Johfra and Ellen providing me with my weekly shopping. I began by doing another full set of the preliminary practices and then focused on some other practices I had been doing for some time. For many months, it was idyllic.

Unfortunately, towards the end of the first year I became rather unwell. I felt as if I were in a permanent state of shock, such as one might suffer after taking a fall, except that it never wore off even after a good sleep. Gendun Rinpoche very kindly came to visit me, and I explained my condition to him. For some reason, instead of addressing this problem, he started giving me all sorts of teachings at a speed just a bit too fast for me to follow. The stress of this simply aggravated my condition. It didn't matter what I said, he just would not slow down, and I found myself struggling not to panic. I wanted to be heard – I wanted him to know this wasn't just wilful resistance.

Eventually Gendun Rinpoche got up to leave and I slipped out onto the veranda to escape at last. Lama Phurtse was sitting there, waiting to accompany the Lama back to Dhagpo. He saw the state I was in and sat me down opposite him on the floor. I looked at him in desperation, unable to mouth any words to express my distress. He looked at me thoughtfully and then poked my breast bone sharply with his long firm forefinger. 'You know how not to go mad,' he said decidedly and with good humour. And strangely, I did. His action and words brought me straight back to my senses. I knew exactly how not to go mad. I knew exactly how not to panic. Lama Phurtse may have delivered a rough poke, but it had the effect of touching my heart – my sanity. I never forgot that lesson and I have often told this story to people who have been verging on panic. It seems we always know how not to panic: we just need to be reminded some-times.

My strange condition continued to bother me, however, making it hard to sit in meditation all the time. I had realised that my relationship with Gendun Rinpoche was just not working out and again I longed to go back to Bokar Rinpoche in India.

It was at that moment that I received a letter from Karma Yangzom in Sonada telling me that her lama, Khenpo Tsul-trim Gyamtso Rinpoche, was on his way to Dhagpo Kagyu Ling. 'Please help my Lama' she begged. 'He doesn't speak English and will need a translator.' I was really excited about this news. We had been waiting for at least eighteen months for him to come and join us. Denys had tried several times to take him to Delhi to finalise his passport and travel arrangements only to find he had disappeared and would turn up several months later somewhere else, at which point Denys had to start trying to organise things all over again. Now, at last he was actually on his way. The Karmapa clearly had the idea that Gendun Rinpoche would be the lama in charge of the practice side of things and Khenpo Rinpoche the lama in charge of formal study. Dhagpo Kagyu Ling was going to be a fantastic place to learn Dharma, through both study and practice.

I was dying to meet Khenpo Rinpoche, but since I was only one year into my retreat, I would have to wait another two years before I could meet him or offer the help that Karma Yangzom had requested. Then quite unexpectedly a message came through to me from Gendun Rinpoche, telling me to come out of retreat to meet the Karmapa, who was due to visit Dhagpo Kagyu Ling in a matter of days.

It was weird to suddenly find myself back at Dhagpo after a year in solitary retreat. My re-emergence went without notice amidst the hundreds of people arriving to receive the Karmapa and his party. I was still suffering from my strange condition and this sudden change in circumstances added to my stress, so I tried to find a quiet spot to meditate. I was sitting in Gendun Rinpoche's room when the door was flung open by the Karmapa. 'What are *you* doing there?' he asked in surprise, but turned and left before I could explain myself. I felt excruciatingly embarrassed as I sat a little longer and then went to join everyone to welcome him formally.

The original shrine room Stace had had built in the hay loft in the barn had burnt down the previous year. Since then a new temple had been built in what used to be the stable and barn. The room was crammed with people gathered there to welcome the Karmapa, with many more queuing up outside. After he had spoken to us for a while, we all lined up to offer him a white greeting scarf and receive his hand on our head as a blessing. We were passing before him at a fairly brisk rate, but when my turn came, he looked at me wide-eyed. 'What are you doing out of retreat? You shouldn't have broken it. Go back and start your three-year retreat all over again from the beginning!' I hadn't realised he knew I was doing a three-year retreat but was more than happy to start again. 'Why are you not doing your retreat on our monastery land?' he continued. It was not the moment to go into it, so I didn't say anything. 'Why have you let your hair grow so long. Get it shaved!' There had been nobody there to shave it for me while I was in retreat. I felt very honoured to be receiving so much attention from him, even if it was a bit of a telling off.

'Did you see Khenpo Tsultrim Gyamtso Rinpoche?' someone asked as I emerged from the crowded temple. 'He turned up unexpectedly and is sitting alongside the other lamas.' I found myself flushed with excitement just on hearing his name. I didn't have a white scarf to offer him but someone kindly handed me theirs and I dived back in against the flow of the crowd and offered it to him. He greeted me warmly and said he had heard about me from Karma Yangzom and wanted me to translate for him. I was thrilled. Almost immediately someone else came up to me and said, 'We weren't expecting Khenpo Rinpoche to be arriving with the others and there is no room prepared for him. We are quickly commissioning one of the retreat huts for him to stay in, but could you serve him?' This was even better – a dream coming true.

He was about forty at the time, small in stature, with the walk and presence of a samurai warrior. There was something very direct and yet very kind in everything he said or did. Having shown him into his room, I sat down in the semi-darkness of the gathering dusk to listen to him talking and felt an immediate sense of rightness and connection. There was something in the way he was that made me think, 'So that is what not-self means.' It was an intuitive, not a reasoned, observation. Something was communicating itself to me through how he was more than what he said. I had never met anyone like this before and yet he felt strangely familiar, as if I had always known him.

I surprised myself by saying to him, 'I have faith in you.' He said, 'We will see.' Twenty years or so later he said to me in Oxford that I was a good student because I had always done what he said. So I guess that is what he meant when he said, 'We'll see.' It is now almost forty years later, and I still have great faith in him. It is like meeting someone and knowing you have *really* met them and they have *really* met you. It is more real than anything else in one's experience and makes all other experience irrelevant.

At the first opportunity, I told the Karmapa that I had a lot of faith in Khenpo Rinpoche and wanted to be his student. He looked thoughtful for a few moments. Then he said, 'Khenpo Rinpoche is...' He was silent again as if searching for the right word. Then he said 'Khenpo Rinpoche' again, somewhat wistfully. He looked at me opening his eyes wide in wonderment, then as if he had finally found the words he was looking for he said, 'Khenpo Rinpoche has very deep compassion.' Khenpo Rinpoche had many great qualities that the Karmapa might have named; I was very struck that what impressed him most was his compassion. The Karmapa told me that I should start my three-year retreat again and that Khenpo Rinpoche would direct me. I went to Khenpo Rinpoche to tell him what the Karmapa had said. Khenpo Rinpoche told me quite simply that if I was his student I was not to do a three-year retreat right now but should study instead. I was puzzled. All I could say was, 'But the Karmapa...' His reply was very clear. 'It is up to you then. You have to choose who is your lama. If it is me, you do what I say, and if it is the Karmapa you do what he says.' I was clear in my mind that I wanted Khenpo Rinpoche to be my lama, so I asked, 'What shall I tell the Karmapa then?'

Khenpo Rinpoche made no reply. There was a long, per-plexed pause. 'Should I excuse myself?' I asked, using an ex-pression I had heard Khenpo Rinpoche himself using when he declined to follow the Karmapa's instruction to stay at Dhagpo Kagyu Ling. 'If that is what you want,' Rinpoche re-plied.

This was the first time I had heard a Karma Kagyu lama say so openly that one's first allegiance is to one's own lama. Although the Karmapa is the nominal head of the Karma Ka-gyus, there is nothing in the Buddha's teaching to suggest one owes allegiance to a head of an institution. To give one's allegiance to a lama is a matter of personal choice. Luckily for me, when I returned to the Karmapa to excuse myself from the three-year retreat, he simply nodded his head in assent.

I was *so* clear that I wanted to be under Khenpo Rinpoche's direction that it didn't occur to me to ask Gendun Rinpoche what he thought. Yet Gendun Rinpoche had every reason to expect me to consult him. Up until then I had been in retreat under his spiritual direction and I had been his translator working closely with him for years. I could certainly have broken the news to him more gently than I did. I heard he was so upset that he wrapped his robe around himself, cov-ering his head, and refused to talk to anyone for twenty-four hours. By the next time I went to see him he had recovered enough to say to me, 'You have done nothing wrong and nei-ther have I.' That is when I realised how upset he was. I had elevated him into a class above other beings who have ordi-nary human feelings – it didn't occur to me he would care whether a student came or went. Yet we had a close Dharma connection. The way I had announced my depar-ture must have sounded like our relationship had no mean-ing for me, in spite of all the time we had spent together, let alone all the teaching and guidance he had been giving me over the past few years.

Gendun Rinpoche warned me that I was being seduced by my pride and ambition, hankering after learning so as to be like the rest of Khenpo Rinpoche's students. Maybe he was afraid that I would start to neglect my meditation in the way Karma Yangzom had feared for Karma Ozer. He had become Enlightened by simply following the special oral instructions of his guru, the Karmapa. He had complete, unwavering faith in the guru – he glowed with an inner light whenever the Karmapa was mentioned. Faith in the guru and oral instructions were enough for him and he simply couldn't understand why that was not enough for me. Why would I need to study? Years later I asked Khenpo Rinpoche about Gendun Rinpoche's attitude and he smiled in a special way. Then he said, 'If you have faith like Gendun Rinpoche then of course that is all you need. But if you have doubts, you have to study in order to understand the Dharma more deeply. Faith develops from that.'

I had left my three-year retreat very suddenly on receiving Gendun Rinpoche's message to come out and meet the Karmapa. Now that I wasn't going to continue the retreat, I needed to bring it to a formal end with the proper concluding ceremonies. I invited a number of the lamas who were present at Dhagpo Kagyu Ling at that time to come and take part in a feast offering in my retreat hut. When I asked Khenpo Rinpoche to come he said, 'I will come in my mind.' I thought this was his way of politely declining the invitation. The other lamas came, and at the close of the ceremony a rainbow appeared in the field by my retreat hut, which seemed a very auspicious sign. The next day I took Khenpo Rinpoche his portion of the feast offering. As I offered it to him he said, 'Is this the portion of the feast for those who were not present at the time?' I said it was. 'Well I don't need it, do I? I was there in my mind.' That left a deep impression on me. When he said something, he meant it and he remembered it. I was to discover subsequently that he always remembered what he'd said, sometimes after many years, even decades, had elapsed.

Khenpo Rinpoche was invited to give talks each afternoon to the hundred or so people gathered in the temple. One of his first talks was on love and compassion. He asked us how we would feel to see our own mother bound and beaten in front of us and said, 'That is how to feel love and compassion for *all* beings.' There was something about the way he said it, and the awful idea of *anyone* being tortured in front of me, that brought tears to my eyes and a deeper sense of what compassion meant than I had ever had before.

During one of his formal teaching sessions in the temple, he asked us all how we knew that what we were experiencing right now was not a dream. People came up with all kinds of answers such as 'dreams are not as clear as this', 'dreams do not last as long', 'dreams are not so consistent' or 'you wake up out of a dream'. To all of this Khenpo Rinpoche replied, 'So if a dream were clear, lasted a long time and was consistent, and if within the dream you dreamt you experienced waking up, then would that dream become waking experience?' We couldn't agree to that, so he asked what the difference would be if we had a waking experience that was unclear, short, inconsistent and seemed to involve waking up. Would this make it a dream? We couldn't agree to that either. I left the session feeling very puzzled. I had often heard this life compared to a dream, but I had never really questioned my assumption that waking experience was real to such a degree before.

Rinpoche was like a great treasure trove of teaching. Whenever I saw him he would say something arresting to wake me up. 'Everything is the vast expanse of awareness – emptiness inseparable. Do you understand?' he might say. The question seemed to come out of nowhere! At the time I thought perhaps I did understand, although I now know I didn't. Each day the penny drops a little more as to just how profound such a statement is. If I fully realise its meaning in this lifetime, I shall be well satisfied. Rinpoche never tired of reminding us of the nature of mind in whatever we were doing. Clearly it was also his own way of keeping himself awake. He was teaching by example. I have never seen Tibetan lamas gathering around a teacher in the way they gathered around Khenpo Rinpoche, asking him Dharma questions. He was always explaining Dharma to them and to us Westerners, at meals, while we were out walking, or just sitting around together.

Sometimes as I sat on the floor in front of him, he would talk to me in a gentle, intimate way, picking up on my unvoiced doubts and hesitations and answering them as if he were present in my mind, knowing my innermost thoughts. As if that were not amazing enough, he would then sing to me in a hauntingly beautiful way, looking at me so tenderly. It felt intensely personal, even though I knew he did this with his other students too. He was famous for his singing. Once he got me and another of his students to sit together focusing on our foreheads as he sang to us. I never asked him, but I got the feeling he was practising equanimity, equalising his love and compassion for each of us. He told his students to go and sit in a busy place where there were lots of people and practise equality and equanimity towards all the passers-by. He would go off to town and do that himself sometimes.

Virtually as soon as he arrived in Europe, Khenpo Rinpoche had gathered a large following of young students keen to learn Tibetan. More and more translators like myself wanted to come and study with him because there was a clarity and detail to the way he taught that was exciting and immensely helpful.

At one of his classes with translators he asked each of us how we would translate the word '*de pa*' (usually given as 'faith' in English). He turned on his tape recorder and recorded all the different answers, listening carefully. Finally, he declared that although he had been intending to learn English in order to teach Westerners, it was clear to him that translating Dharma into English was not a straightforward matter. There was so much difference of opinion, and if all of us who had studied English for so long couldn't agree, he didn't see the point of his trying to learn it. He never did learn to give teachings in English, even after travelling round the world for decades teaching Dharma. Instead, he made a point of teaching translators Tibetan.

Khenpo Rinpoche was keen to cut through all the confused thinking and blind faith that was rife among both Tibetans and Westerners. His solution was to train his students to set a good example to other Dharma students by focusing on study and discipline. He got us to learn traditional philosophical texts by heart in Tibetan and also started to teach us how to meditate on emptiness by giving instructions in what he called the 'Progressive Stages of Meditation on Emptiness'. I had to translate for him giving these teachings many times. Later I translated and arranged them into a book by that name.

Not long after he arrived, Khenpo Rinpoche had told all his students that he wanted to teach us in an intensive six-month long study programme. Since Dhagpo Kagyu Ling didn't have the facilities to host such an event, arrangements were gradually made for a group of about thirty of us to stay in an old chateau about ten miles away, starting the following spring. Until then, Khenpo Rinpoche was going to be away on a teaching tour around Europe, and he told me I should go back into retreat until he returned.

I gladly re-entered retreat, although in fact I was called out on a number of occasions to translate for Gendun Rinpoche, since there was no other suitable translator on hand. I also went travelling with him again, this time including a trip to England. I hadn't recovered my health so this was yet another exhausting month or so for me. During that time, Gendun Rinpoche told me that the Karmapa had informed him he should teach a three-week course on the 'Tibetan Book of the Dead' to all his European disciples the following summer. He was quite dismayed at the prospect saying, 'I've never had a transmission for that text and have never studied it. I don't understand why His Holiness is telling me to teach it.' The reason was no doubt that the book – already famous among Western Dharma students as one of the first texts on Tibetan Buddhism ever to be translated into English – had just been re-translated by Francesca Fremantle under Trungpa Rinpoche's guidance.

Because the book was so famous, the course aroused a lot of interest and hundreds of people planned to come to it from all over Europe. The timing of it overlapped with Khenpo Rinpoche's six-month course, which I was attending. As the date drew nearer, I became increasingly anxious. Knowing that Gendun Rinpoche was unfamiliar with the text and actually had no wish to teach it meant that it was going to be hard-going and I was determined not to be his translator this time. Every time I asked about it, the organisers would say, 'Someone will come. It's a matter of trusting the situation.' I had heard that line a bit too often and knew very well what it meant: it meant that a situation would be set up with hundreds of people in one place waiting to hear an eminent lama give teachings, and some poor translator would be roped in at the last minute, unable to refuse to help because it was 'an emergency'. I kept asking, ever more suspiciously, 'Who is the translator?' Finally, just before the course was due to begin, my good friend Tenpa arrived from India, sent by the Karmapa to help out. It would be his first translation job in Europe.

I was tremendously relieved. However, the night after Gendun Rinpoche's course began, I dreamt I was asked to do the translation for Gendun Rinpoche. In the dream I was so furious I threw a chair through the window. The next morning I laughed about it: I had been so worried that I might be asked to translate that I was even now having nightmares about it. Then came a knock on my door. 'The Lama wants to see you.' How exciting! I hurried to Khenpo Rinpoche's room. 'Good morning. How are you?' he said in English.

'Very well,' I replied. 'Lama Gendun needs you as his translator for the next three weeks,' he said in Tibetan. I can't remember what I did then. Khenpo Rinpoche reported to Gendun Rinpoche that he had told me to go and translate for him and all I had done was cry.

What had happened was that although Tenpa had agreed to undertake the job, he had found during the first day of the course that he just couldn't do it. He had exactly the same problem as I would have done. The Lama was stumbling along trying to read a text that he had never seen before and could not read properly, and would stop and wait for the translator to translate right in the middle of a sentence, which just doesn't work with Tibetan sentences, where the verb might not come till right at the end. Furthermore, Tibetan texts, unlike English translations of Tibetan texts, are not comprehensible just from the words. You need an oral commentary in order to get any meaning out of it at all. So the fact that neither he nor Gendun Rinpoche had had an oral transmission made the task extremely difficult. Tenpa had fled the situation, leaving a note of apology on the kitchen table: 'I am sorry, I came to serve Karmapa, but I am unable to do as I am asked.'

He had come straight to Khenpo Rinpoche to explain the situation, which is when I had been summoned, but when Tenpa saw the state I was in, he immediately relented. This time however, he prepared himself. He read Francesca Fremantle's translation each night and the next day explained the text on the basis of what he had read. No doubt everyone in the assembly had a copy of Francesca's translation with them and was referring to it even as Tenpa spoke. Apparently they were all very happy. How could they fail to be, sitting in the presence of a great lama such as Gendun Rinpoche and listening to that translation?

I, on the other hand, was rather disappointed by the study course with Khenpo Rinpoche. For some reason he had decided not to use me as his translator, so I had to sit for hours in a class, with a translator who knew less Tibetan than I did. At that time I was the most experienced translator around, and I had lived as a nun for seven years, which in those days seemed a long time. The other students thought of me as being streaks ahead of them in terms of knowledge and experience, which seems funny to me now because since then others have far surpassed me. It was a bizarre experience to have to sit in class understanding almost everything he was saying, but having to listen to people trying to translate who had to keep stopping to discuss terms with him that I could have told them, but I was never asked. The classes were tedious and slow, making life very difficult for everyone, especially me.

One day after class I asked him why, having asked me to be his translator, he was now ignoring me. He stood up and told me to follow him as he strode off into the middle of a field. He gestured to me to sit down opposite him as he told me very seriously that I should meditate on all my teachers above the crown of my head and have equal faith in all of them. It was a very powerful moment for me. Connecting me to all my teachers in this way told me I had done nothing wrong. Many years later I asked him why he had changed his mind about using me as his translator and he said, 'I will tell you one day,' but he never did. It is possible that he realised after asking me to be his translator that I was already spoken for as Gendun Rinpoche's translator and that Tibetan protocol meant he could not therefore use me himself. Nobody ever said that, so who knows? On the other hand, the answer might lie in his intuition that my path lay elsewhere. The whole painful affair was made bearable by the way Rinpoche used it to cut through my ego-clinging. He did this by making it clear that he could see how frustrated I was feeling. It wasn't that he was particularly sympathetic but at least he let me know that he knew. He would warn me against jealousy, which gave me food for thought. What I really wanted to do was to leave all this study behind and get back to meditation.

When the course with Gendun Rinpoche was over, Tenpa came to the chateau to join Khenpo Rinpoche's course as his translator. Having him to talk to made a huge difference to my time there that summer. We could talk about the teachings together and I regained my interest in study. He was a deep thinker and had a gentle way of taking me by surprise, exposing my hypocrisy and cutting through my pride. One time I was talking to him at length about my mother and how difficult she was. He listened very empathetically so that I felt really heard. I assumed he was taking my side, which was rather gratifying. He then very gently ventured to say, 'It is always easier to love people who you get on well with, isn't it?' His comment cut me to the quick, but I knew he was right. I had been trying to impress him with how wronged I had been, but his comment reminded me that the Dharma is about developing equal love and compassion for all beings, not for proving oneself to be in the right.

Once I was talking to him about a teaching we had just received on the three levels of the Buddha's teaching. After holding forth for a while on the superior nature of the Great Vehicle (Mahayana), with its emphasis on compassion and profound teachings on emptiness, compared to what is referred to as the Lesser Vehicle (Hinayana), I fell silent. Tenpa too was silent, and then in a thoughtful tone enquired, 'Do you think you could be a Mahayanist?' His question surprised me, as I had assumed all Tibetan Buddhists were Mahayanists so I said, 'Yes of course, aren't you?' He answered wistfully, 'It would be a presumption to call myself a Mahayanist.'

His words gently pierced the balloon of my own pretentiousness. 'But surely you have faith in the Mahayana?' I ventured. He warmed. 'Oh yes – of course, faith I have.' Again silence, then, 'I would say, if anyone asked, I aspire to the Mahayana. But in practice I think only in my better moments could I say I was even a Hinayanist. Most of the time I am a very ordinary person.' Then, in a more cheerful way he added, 'But even to aspire to the Mahayana is already a wonderful thing. Ah! How inspiring the lives of the great Bodhisattvas are and how profound the teaching on emptiness! Yes, I aspire to understand that, and one day to follow that path.' He then shook his head and said in an awed tone of voice, 'A Bodhisattva's compassion, though, is inconceivable.'

I found Tenpa's life story very touching in many ways. He came from the Kunu region of north India where the people are culturally Tibetan. His mother had left her husband and children to become a nun when Tenpa was about six and his sister was three. He remembered how abandoned they felt and having to go to stay with his mother in retreat sometimes, which he found very boring. When he grew up he became an English teacher in the Indian army and so was able to support his mother in retreat in Sonada. I had watched and even participated in the loving yet sharp dynamic between the two of them for years. His mother was poorly educated and to Tenpa's eyes a gullible believer in all and everything. Tenpa had trained for years with learned Gelugpa scholars and was very discerning. 'If she passes a Hindu shrine she prays at it as if it were the Buddha. She has no idea what she is doing half the time. When I was young I became so disillusioned at all the ignorance and superstition I saw in my mother and others like her that I felt I was losing my faith in the Dharma. It got so bad that I once sat at the feet of the Buddha in the temple and wept.'

As a young boy he went on pilgrimage with his mother in Tibet and was invited to stay at Tashi Lhunpo, a Gelugpa monastery, where he remained for his teenage years into his early twenties. He stayed on in Tibet longer than his colleagues because as an Indian he was not persecuted as the Tibetans were. When he got back to his home village in the early sixties his father didn't even recognise him. Although he then studied for many years with learned Gelugpa scholars it seemed to him he was learning intellectual arguments just for the sake of it. He confessed to me that if it were not for the pointing-out instructions on the nature of mind that he had received as a child from a Kagyu lama, he would have ended up with no faith in the Dharma at all.

Although not officially a lama Tenpa was a good Dharma friend to me and to many other people and I think of him as an important teacher of mine. He was nuanced and subtle in his approach to the teachings and would often take me by surprise. He was very humble and claimed to have little faith yet he clearly had very deep faith indeed. As Gendun Rinpoche's translator he wanted to listen to him in a detached way without entering into a special relationship with him as his lama, yet sometimes, he would find he was so moved by faith that it was hard to translate. When Gendun Rinpoche gave instruction in the *powa* ritual which means the transference of consciousness practice that is done for people when they die, he found his consciousness pushing at the crown of his head with the itching that is a sign the *powa* ritual is working. It was working even against his will because of the combination of the Lama's power and his own openness and faith.

Tenpa resisted Lama Gendun's style of teaching Dharma because it stressed faith and repetition of prayers rather than study and reflection. He much preferred Khenpo Rinpoche's approach as did I. Over the years I had been given many different practices which I was supposed to do every day. This took a couple of hours of my time daily and felt burdensome, so I was quite relieved when Khenpo Rinpoche told me I didn't need to do them anymore. It took the sense of pressure and busy-ness out of my daily practice. His view was that it was better to do a few practices well rather than rush through a medley of practices at speed just to complete one's commitment.

Nonetheless, many other Tibetan lamas when they give empowerments or teachings, enjoin those present to keep at least a token amount of the practice going everyday for the rest of their lives, even if it's just a verse or mantra or two. This may not sound much but since Tibetan lamas frequently give empowerments and teach different practices, one can, as in my case, end up having to chant for two or three hours a day in order to keep up with one's commitments.

In this way Khenpo Rinpoche completely changed the style of my practice. He said, 'You have had oral pointing-out instructions which have given you the essence and the right way of understanding Dharma. That is all you need for your own practice. Now you need to understand the broader context of Buddhist doctrine so that you can answer people's questions for them.' I didn't know what he was talking about. I had never been particularly interested in Buddhist doctrine as such. I wanted to realise the truth for myself through meditation practice as I imagined the Buddha had done. Then I would be able to answer people's questions from my direct experience. Nevertheless, I studied because I had confidence in him and wanted to be his student.

Curiously, after a while, whenever I went to see him for a personal interview he would tell me the story of a close disciple of the Buddha whom the Buddha had sent away. He had told the disciple that in order to reach Enlightenment he had to go away and practise by himself. I didn't understand why Rinpoche kept telling me this story. Was he going to send me away? I dreaded that.

One sunny afternoon when I went to see him, he was lying back in an armchair that he had asked to be put outside among the trees. His legs were stretched out in front of him and he looked so relaxed that I thought he might be sleeping. He slowly opened his eyes as I approached, then leant forward, and beckoned me to sit at his feet. I did so and he lay back again. He continued to lie there for a while with his eyes shut. Then he opened them and said to me, 'The trouble with you is that you are not prepared to listen.' I was shocked; all I could say was, 'I am!' He looked at me for a long time saying nothing and then looked away. I decided to break the silence. 'I have faith in you and I'll do whatever you tell me. Please tell me.' He then started making bizarre remarks about how I was an uptight nun. He used such senseless arguments that I became very doubtful about what he was getting at. After several days of this I was so disturbed by it that I went to see him and said, 'The only sense I can make out of all your comments is that you think I should stop being a nun.' He nodded and said, 'So you have understood.' I left the room dumbfounded.

Next time I went to see him he said, 'You will be able to help people in the West better if you are not a nun.' I didn't know what to make of that. I now remembered how strangely Lama Phurtse had been behaving earlier that year. He asked me on three separate occasions whether I was always going to be a nun or not. I was indignant. 'Why are you always asking me that?' I had exclaimed at last. 'Oh, I just wondered,' he replied casually. 'So many Westerners give up. That is all.' 'Well I am not like that,' I had said with finality. It then came back to me that all those years earlier Trungpa Rinpoche had said in his letter that I might have to discontinue being a nun in later life. I had always known that if my lama told me to give up my vows or to get married I would do it. I wasn't that attached to being a nun, but it had been my identity for seven years, and it was hard to get my head around what it would mean to give up. Wouldn't I be letting a lot of people down? Yet I found the whole situation very exciting.

'You need to go back to England, get a job and live an ordinary life,' Khenpo Rinpoche said. This was what Ato Rinpoche had told me to do, but this time I was clear about who my guru was. After a week or two of his talking to me like this each hot afternoon, one day in the shade of the avenue of tall trees, he suddenly announced, 'Now that you have cut through all your pride and attachment to being a nun, you must continue to be a nun for the rest of your life. I have only been putting you through all of this for the last two weeks in order for you to gain flexibility of mind. You should now forget all I have said.' I spent the next week or two trying to settle back into being a nun for the rest of my life. It was too late though. I no longer felt the same about it. Gone was the conviction that the only way to Enlightenment for me was to be a nun. Nevertheless, I tried to re-adjust and be prepared to do whatever Rinpoche required of me.

No sooner had I re-adjusted than Rinpoche said, 'Actually, I have been thinking about it. It would be better if you were to give up being a nun and return to England. You should think of what sort of job you could get.' Again it was hard to re-adjust. Was this for real? Rinpoche kept up this process of switching back and forth all summer. I reached the point where I could no longer revive the conviction needed to re-main a nun for the rest of my life. Perhaps that was because I had never really believed in it: I had just believed that my teachers did.

The next surprise was Khenpo Rinpoche saying, 'You have been learning Dharma in Tibetan for many years now. It is time you learnt Dharma in your own language. Go to America and learn from Trungpa Rinpoche.' 'I want to stay here and learn from you,' I told him. 'Anyway, it is not easy to go and live in America or to even to get to meet Trungpa Rinpoche.' I had heard that people sometimes had to wait months for an interview with him and even then it was not guaranteed you would get one. How was I going to be able to afford to stay in America waiting to see him? Khenpo Rinpoche listened to my objections. He just nodded and did not insist. Instead, he told me to take the first opportunity that came my way to go to see Trungpa Rinpoche.

My first opportunity came a year or so later when Trungpa Rinpoche was giving a weekend course in London. In line with Khenpo Rinpoche's wishes, I attended and put down my name for an interview. Waiting in line for my turn to see him I felt quite nervous and didn't know what I should say.

To my surprise Trungpa Rinpoche said he remembered me from ten years before. Doubtful though I was at the time that this could be true, on reflection I realise that he probably sent me to Karma Thinley Rinpoche because he was expecting him to come to join him in Samye Ling. It was Karma Thinley's decision to go to Canada that had resulted in my long sojourn in India and Nepal. It is likely Trungpa Rinpoche's intention had been for me to return to the UK with Karma Thinley all those years before. It is strange how life works out sometimes. When I next met up with Khenpo Rinpoche, he was very keen to learn the result of my interview with Trungpa Rinpoche. He was clearly intuiting that I had a strong karmic connection with him and was waiting for signs of its manifesting. I didn't have much to report at that point so Rinpoche let the matter drop for a while. Nevertheless, knowing how important Rinpoche considered my connection with Trungpa Rinpoche to be, I continued to look out for another opportunity to meet him.

At the end of Khenpo Rinpoche's six-month course at the chateau he told me to keep my nun's vows until he next saw me and then he would tell me what to do. As he departed on a teaching tour, I returned to my retreat hut on Ellen and Johfra's land. Before he left, he told me to do what he called a *Petsam* which literally means a book retreat. I was to sit as in meditation and read through the text we had been studying called 'The Jewel Ornament of Liberation'. I was to read it slowly and meditatively, reflecting on the meaning and learning as much of it as I could by heart. In this way I was to read it twenty-one times. If at any point I had trouble with understanding the text, then I was to pray to its author Gampopa, thinking that he was present before me. In this way, by his blessing, my mind would become clear and I would gradually be able to understand everything. I did as he told me and am very grateful for the experience. It gave me a blueprint for understanding the stages of the Buddhist path that I carry with me for reference in my daily life. There is a lot to be said for learning texts by heart or even, as in my case, getting an intimate feel for the whole text.

A great joy and comfort to me at that time was that Tenpa would often come to visit me in retreat to work on our translation of another text we had been taught that summer. It was a text on Buddha Nature called the Ratnagotravibhaga. Little did I know then just how significant this text was going to become for me in the years to come. Tenpa's sensitivity to nuances and the power of language in both English and Tibetan, meant I learnt a lot about how to translate from him. Although he was ethnically Tibetan he was Indian by nationality and spoke Hindi like a native as well as very good English. Since he was a scholar, he knew both colloquial and classical Tibetan for translation purposes and could explain the meaning of terms to me. Furthermore, being an original thinker he would question everything to try to get the essence and the full meaning of whatever it was we were translating or talking about. I owe a lot of my education to Tenpa, as did many others of Khenpo Rinpoche's students.

His familiarity with Hindi and Indian culture added a whole side to his character quite different from most Tibetans I met, for whom India was a foreign land. Hindi is much closer to English, being an Indo-Aryan language, and there are things you can say in Hindi and English you cannot really say in Tibetan. English or Hindi-speaking Tibetans have often told me that they cannot talk about emotional or psychological things with their parents the way they can with Hindi and English speakers. In Tibetan emotions are either negative and need to be remedied or positive and so need to be cultivated. Often psychologically we need to just experience our feelings in a non-judgemental way but to say that in Tibetan sounds like a deep Dharmic matter. One Tibetan friend told me that when she tried to talk to her parents about this they simply looked bemused and said she needed to talk to a lama. In other words, if you want to talk about emotions and feelings in a deep way you have to use technical Dharma language. Trungpa Rinpoche noticed that in English you can talk about Dharma in non-technical language using the same kind of language usually associated with ordinary feelings and emotions. It enables the teachings to become accessible in a way that is impossible in Tibetan. Tenpa said for this reason he could often understand a Dharma text better in English translation than he could in the original.

As had happened the previous year, after my spending a few months in retreat, Gendun Rinpoche asked me to travel with him as his translator, this time to England, Belgium and Holland. I was still thinking about what I might do if Khenpo Rinpoche again told me to give up being a nun. The only thing I had trained in over the last seven years was Buddhism and the Tibetan language. I wondered if there was a future in Buddhist studies at university level, so when I was in England I made some enquiries. It occurred to me that what I had learnt as a Buddhist nun might be suitable for a sociological study of some kind. I arranged for an interview with Professor Ninian Smart at Lancaster University, which specialises in religious studies.

'I would like to write a thesis about how Buddhist teachings that are standard in Buddhist countries have a completely different psychological effect on the Buddhists of those countries from the effect the same teachings have on Westerners,' I told him. I was thinking about the fact that on top of the differences in linguistic structure, the way we think in the West is very different from the world view in Buddhist countries. This means that the standard, rather formulaic way of presenting Buddhist doctrine does not have the effect on Western students that traditional teachers expect. 'As a translator I have seen that misunderstandings often happen without either the lama or the student noticing,' I explained. 'I want to study the gap between the message the student picks up and the message the lama intended.'

Professor Smart asked me what kind of methodology I had in mind. Since my first degree had been in sociology, I was to some extent equipped for a study of this kind, and I talked about using interview methods with Tibetans and Western Buddhists. He seemed to find my idea interesting, but thought it would be a pity to not make more use of my Tibetan language skills, and suggested I try the Sanskrit department in Oxford. He put me in touch with Dr Paul Williams there, who was a scholar of Buddhism in both Sanskrit and Tibetan in the Department of Oriental studies. I went down to Oxford to speak to him.

Tenpa happened to be in England at the same time, and he accompanied me to what I had assumed was an informal meeting. Instead we were shown into a room of eminent academics including Professor Richard Gombrich and several others. I was a bit puzzled about why they were all there. As we talked about the possibility of my coming to Oxford to study, I was quite frank in saying that I wanted to carry on pursuing my interest in Buddhism in the academic context. 'Are you thinking that a doctorate in Buddhist studies will lead to employment opportunities?' they asked. Beyond having been an undergraduate at Reading, I had never mixed with people from an academic background and I had little idea of what getting a doctorate would involve. I didn't even realise I would have to write a thesis. I said I hadn't given it a thought. 'That's good,' one of the academics replied. 'There's little chance of getting a job in this field.'

After about an hour Tenpa and I were back on the street looking for the friends who had brought us there by car. 'How did it go?' they asked eagerly. 'Not much happened,' I replied. 'They were friendly enough though.' At this point Tenpa interrupted, 'The whole event was clearly being conducted as a formal interview, except for the fact that Shenpen seemed to think it was some kind of tea party!' 'An interview?' I asked, mildly surprised. Then I thought back over the morning's conversation and realised that this was probably true. Indeed the last thing the professor had said was that I should try and get a government grant and apply to join a college. At that point I started to take the idea of studying at Oxford seriously.

I wasn't sure it made sense though. I was still accompanying Gendun Rinpoche as his translator at the time and when I mentioned the idea to him, he told me to forget it. 'You will just get caught up in worldly ambition,' he said and I was inclined to agree with him. Nevertheless, I needed to ask Khenpo Rinpoche, who was in Greece on a teaching tour. I rang him from a call box on a street corner and that is where my fate was sealed. I only had one coin big enough for a long-distance call, so I had to keep the conversation brief. His answer was immediate and categorical. 'Very good,' he said. 'Write a doctoral thesis on Buddha Nature. Go ahead and apply!' I went back to Gendun Rinpoche and explained what had happened. By then he seemed to have relented a bit and encouraged me by saying that I would be able to un-derstand the texts because I already had the right view from all my years of direct instruction and meditation practice. 'Without that experience, studying can just end up leading you astray,' he told me. He was saying in effect that I had sufficient understanding of the experiential inner essence of the teachings to be able to benefit from studying Buddhist philosophy without getting lost in the details of the polem-ics.

A few weeks later I was translating for Gendun Rinpoche in Brussels. Khenpo Rinpoche was due to arrive the next day and I had decided to stay on to see him. Gendun Rinpoche had been invited to teach in Lama Gawang's centre in Hol-land and was eager that I leave with him and Lama Gawang for Holland immediately rather than wait to see Khenpo Rinpoche. Something was brewing. The two of them tried so hard to persuade me to come with them that Lama Gawang even went as far as to promise me that I wouldn't have to translate. So what would have been the point of my going? It was all very strange, but I was determined to stay on to see Khenpo Rinpoche even if it meant making my own way to join them later in Holland. That evening Lama Phurtse took me to one side and said, 'Remember, we have put a lot of work into training you. You are always a Kagyu!' It was as if he had had a premonition and knew something major was going to happen to me the next day.

Lama Gendun and the other two left and Khenpo Rinpoche arrived as planned. Almost the first words he said to me were, 'Now is a good time to give up your robes. I am not ordering you to give them up. However, if you want to be my disciple that is what I am telling you to do.' The choice was clear.

I told Tenpa, who was accompanying Khenpo Rinpoche as his translator, what I intended to do. He looked concerned. 'You shouldn't just do what Rinpoche says – it's up to you what to do. You should judge for yourself. Of course, if he really is your teacher you have to do what he says. But I don't think he'd make you give up the robes if you didn't want to. I think Rinpoche is only saying you should give up your robes because you have been ill and he thinks being a nun is affecting your health. He probably thinks you would be happier and more relaxed if you weren't a nun.' I decided to check with Rinpoche whether that was true. I knew that the Karmapa and the other lamas would be very saddened if I gave up the robes since they looked to me to set a good example to other Westerners. I had a responsibility to the tradition. Khenpo Rinpoche had been saying that robes alienated other Westerners, but I was also aware that keeping them would be supportive for other Western monks and nuns who were trying to do the same as I was. I wanted to show everyone in the tradition that Westerners could be trusted as serious practitioners.

I told all this to Rinpoche and he agreed that the Karmapa and many other lamas would not like it. 'It is up to you,' he said. 'If you care what other people think, do what they think. I've told you what I think.' I wanted to be sure I was understanding him right. 'Why exactly do you want me to give up the robes?' His only answer was, 'so that you give up your pride'. 'It will take more than giving up my robes to get rid of my pride,' I said, but he didn't change his position. Instead he gestured graphically, grasping one of his hands in the other. 'We give up attachment to be free and then we become attached to non-attachment.'

I told Tenpa what Rinpoche had said. 'Well it's a question of your faith then. If he really means it then you have to decide whether he is really your guru or not.' I told Tenpa I was sure that he was and he said I was lucky. 'I have never found anyone I'm so sure of – not even the Karmapa.' I reminded him of the lama he had told me about who had given him mind instruction as a child. 'Not even him?' I asked. 'Not even him,' was the reply. 'I never found anyone I could trust enough to promise to obey. Sometimes I think perhaps I could have faith in Trungpa Rinpoche – it is my great wish and aspiration to meet him some day. I pray that by the power of my pure wish that I will meet him one day.'

Many years later his prayers were answered and he met Trungpa Rinpoche in a hotel restaurant in Gangtok in Sikkim. He told me that Trungpa Rinpoche had many amazing golden rings with coloured jewels on all his fingers. 'It seemed to me that I was seeing him in his transfigured form, as if he were shining directly from his Pure Land. To me he was really the Buddha.'

'What about Khenpo Rinpoche?' I asked, and he said, 'I suppose of all those I've met, he is the one I have the most faith in. But still, I feel there is still some regard for social convention there.' He explained that for him a guru must be completely free from the taint of that. He must be beyond hope and fear, beyond good and bad. 'Perhaps it is karma. Perhaps I will come to trust Khenpo Rinpoche in time.' I felt pretty sobered hearing all this from a Tibetan with as much devotion to the Dharma as Tenpa had. But for better or worse I felt my only way forward was to trust Khenpo Rinpoche.

I told Tenpa how comfortable I felt in robes, 'As a nun, you have the whole weight of two and a half thousand years of tradition behind you so that you feel that you are doing the right thing.' Tenpa agreed. Then I said, 'No one is going to understand, are they?' 'No, they'll just think that you got tired of being a nun. You can't even say that Khenpo Rinpoche told you. Tibetans won't believe you and he's not going to tell them. I know Tibetan society – we are not frank with each other like you Westerners are. If you say he told you to do it they will think that you are angry with Khenpo Rinpoche and say such things to discredit him. They won't believe you.' I asked Tenpa if he believed me. 'I think you are very sincere and I don't want you to do anything that you will regret. I think you're making a mistake, but I will always respect you – whatever you do.'

I was clear in my own mind that without doubt I wanted to be Khenpo Rinpoche's disciple. I knew Rinpoche was not telling me to do this for his own selfish ends or out of carelessness, but out of a deep concern for me and the teaching of Dharma in the West.

There was a Western monk with Khenpo Rinpoche on the day he arrived in Brussels. He was talking loudly about how he didn't want to be a monk any more, but that Khenpo Rinpoche had insisted that he continue until that day. Now he had given him permission to disrobe and it was the talk of all the students gathered at the Dharma centre. He was bad-mouthing the whole institution of monasticism in a way that I found gross and dishonourable. I spoke up for it and begged him to stop talking in that way because it was undermining for all the good monks and nuns there were in the tradition. I think everyone who heard me simply thought I was defending that way of life because I was a nun. Only I knew that I might well not be by the end of the day.

By the evening I was ready to tell Khenpo Rinpoche that I was willing to disrobe. I had been unwell all day, unsurprisingly. I was not at his evening teaching session because I was lying in bed. Suddenly I got up, determined to tell him I would disrobe. At the same moment he left the teaching session earlier than scheduled and came striding up the stairs to where I was standing, as if to a pre-arranged meeting outside his room. I was no longer wearing my robes.

At his bidding, I followed him into his room. As he sat down, I told him, 'I've come to give back my robes.' He sat up straight in his chair and looked at me intently. 'As a sign of my faith in you,' I said, 'I have come to give up my nun's vows.' In Vajrayana, an esoteric form of Mahayana Buddhism, the emphasis is on trusting the guru, and as a Vajrayana practitioner, I was giving up my robes solely because I trusted him. That level of trust in a teacher is mysterious. I cannot explain where it comes from. Traditionally it is explained as coming from karmic connections made in past lives. That is as good an explanation as any I suppose. At the time I just sensed there must be a deep meaning in my trust, otherwise I would never have given up my nun's vows. 'That's good,' he replied. 'You have always kept your nun's vows purely. You have never offended against your word. By the Buddhist monastic rules you are free to take them on again whenever you want to.'

I knelt, and he took from me the folded robes I offered him. He seemed very pleased with my decision and spoke to me very kindly. 'Come – we will do a ceremony. You took the robes originally with a ceremony; now you must give them up in the same way and with the same motivation. Repeat after me.' He then made up a ceremony on the spot, so that I recited something like: 'All the Buddhas and Bodhisattvas in all directions and all times – listen to me. I, Shenpen, took on the nun's ordination in order to follow the Lesser Vehicle discipline for my own liberation. My motivation was the Greater Vehicle intention to gain Enlightenment in order to liberate all beings from suffering. Now with the same intention, I offer up these robes so that I may continue my practice of the Greater Vehicle, the Bodhisattva path, without pride and attachment.'

I then renewed my Bodhisattva vow in his presence, vowing to follow the Bodhisattva path to Enlightenment for the sake of all beings. Rinpoche said that I was now free to live as was most appropriate for the benefit of others and told me to take my robes with me so that I would be ready to return to that way of life if I ever wanted to. Finally, he said, 'I am very pleased with you. This is Greater Vehicle. You are giving up your robes out of the Bodhisattva motivation, the sincere wish to gain Enlightenment for the sake of all beings. I am very happy about that.'

'I don't mind what you do particularly,' he continued. 'Think carefully and keep your mind open and relaxed. I have given you a lot of special instructions on the nature of mind. You have a good understanding – so go and keep my instructions close to your heart.' I asked him for his blessing. He said, 'You have it already,' but then seemed to have a change of heart and held my head lightly in his hands and chanted a blessing. 'Remember what I said about attachment!' he warned. 'And remember what I taught you: relax your mind in the expanse of space – let the wisdom mind shine through like the sun in space – and don't get fixed ideas!'

I felt pretty bewildered. I wasn't quite sure how my disrobing was going to benefit anyone. You invest your whole life in becoming a nun, and you really have to believe in it, the whole institution and lifestyle. I didn't know what lifestyle I believed in now. As I stepped out of my robes for the last time the thought had crossed my mind, 'How will I be special now?' It was at that moment that I realised with some embarrassment that defining myself as a nun had made me feel special and apart from others. Now who was I? The manner of my giving back the robes became legendary among Khenpo Rinpoche's Western students. People ask me sometimes, 'Is it true that Khenpo Rinpoche told you to?' I say, 'Well, yes, but it was my choice to obey him.'

Feeling at a loss, I wandered into the eating area of the Dharma centre where a couple of my colleagues were sitting drinking a late-night tea and casually chatting. I sat down and told them I had given up my robes. One of them looked at me oddly and said, 'What kind of joke is that supposed to be?' It felt disconcerting and so very different from the feeling of joy everyone had greeted me with when I first took ordination. Now it seemed as if I was going against everything I had believed in for so long. What were people to make of that? In myself I felt the same commitment to the path as I had always had, yet from now on there would be no outward sign of my chosen lifestyle. I had gone incognito.

I didn't meet Gendun Rinpoche and Lama Phurtse again for a year or two. Eventually, I was in the Dordogne and dropped by to see them. Gendun Rinpoche laughed awkwardly at my appearance. I couldn't help agreeing with him that my summer dress had none of the gravitas of my nun's robes. Wearing robes is like standing for something, upholding certain values for all to see. I felt less myself somehow, and that people couldn't really see who I was or what to expect from me. It was almost as if I were hiding from the world. I missed wearing robes because I wanted to stand visibly for what I believed in. Lama Phurtse said, 'Why did you deny you were going to give up your robes when I asked you?' I could tell that he was hurt about that. I told him that it had not been my idea and it was Khenpo Rinpoche who had told me to give them up. Lama Phurtse paused and reflected for a few moments. 'Well then, that is the main thing. The main thing is to do what the lama says.' I took what he said seriously and was determined to keep faith with my lama.

When, fifteen years later in Kathmandu, Karma Ozer came to visit me, I felt somewhat reserved, wondering what she would be feeling and thinking about my having given up my robes. As she entered the room, she took a few steps forward to greet me. She lowered her head respectfully and I lowered mine so our foreheads met. She offered me the customary white scarf and then held my hands in hers. She looked long into my face, smiling and shaking my hands warmly and reassuringly.

We sat down together on the bed and she started to relate to me all that had happened to her since last I had seen her in India. Her sister Karma Yangzom had died the previous year more or less alone in Bodhgaya, having been sick for some time, and having followed Kalu Rinpoche and Bokar Rinpoche there to be near them when she died. Karma Ozer had been in a three-year retreat so her sister had not told her how sick she was. When at last Karma Ozer had received a letter from Karma Yangzom telling her of the illness she was stunned. Knowing her sister, she realised it must be serious or she wouldn't have told her. She agonised over whether to break the retreat to go to see her, but within a couple of hours another letter arrived telling her Karma Yangzom was already dead.

It was sad news. I told Karma Ozer how sorry I was that I hadn't helped either of them very much since coming back to the West. 'Oh, but you did and have done always,' she cried in astonishment. 'The sponsor you found for me in Manchester helped me continuously up until a few years ago when he retired. He always helped both of us. Now you have started sending money to Khenpo Rinpoche for me. You've always helped me!' She frowned crossly as she smiled, looking sideways at me with her big beautiful eyes — a very characteristic expression of hers.

'You haven't changed at all,' she said happily. 'Stable as a vajra.' I recognised this as high praise indeed from a Tibetan. 'But now I am a lay person, how can you say that?' I asked. 'Your mind is the same. I don't care about superficial changes of lifestyle,' she laughed. 'But what did you think when you heard I'd given up my robes? I know you Tibetans, you hate that.' She told me that she had indeed been very shocked and upset when she first heard that I had given up being a nun. 'I thought that there was no hope for the Dharma in the West if even you could not keep your nun's vows. You were my great hope for the Dharma and for it spreading to the West and benefiting many people. So I went to bed crying. Then suddenly it came to me that it was all right and that you had not given up on the Dharma. I knew that you had given up the nun's vows in order to prac-tise Vajrayana. Maybe it was Khenpo Rinpoche telling me. I was praying to him and then it came to me. I felt very happy about that.'

We talked some more and she said, 'Rinpoche always said that the nun's vows and the Vajrayana vows were like this.' She made a gesture of holding her hands back to back. 'The vows are in opposition to each other. If you are practising Vajrayana then you cannot at the same time be attached to the lesser vows. The Vajrayana vows are the highest vows, the most sacred and the most difficult. After I remembered this, I felt very happy inside and I stayed that way. It is Rinpoche's blessing.' I was deeply impressed by her humil-ity, since she was herself a nun practising Vajrayana.

I didn't see the Karmapa after giving up my vows until the last time he passed through London, in 1981, on his way to the USA to get medical treatment for cancer. Hundreds of us had gathered at a patron's house on the Thames. We were shocked to see how wasted he looked, yet his pres-ence was as radiant as ever. We filed past his throne as he blessed us individually and when it came to my turn, I looked up at him as he touched me lightly on the head. He looked at me kindly and said, 'Rabjungma'. It is a respectful way of addressing a nun. As I moved away, I saw Lama Jigme stand-ing nearby handing out blessing cords for us to put around our necks. 'Why did he call me Rabjungma?' I asked. 'Does he not know I am not a nun anymore?' Lama Jigme's response was warm and kind. 'I think he is saying that it doesn't matter. To him you are still Rabjungma.' Tears welled up inside me. He died a few months later at the age of fifty-seven.

Twelve

Becoming a Scholar at Oxford

The very next day after returning my robes to Khenpo Rinpoche, I was travelling back by coach and ferry to London, heading into my new life, whatever that might be. By some strange chance, I was sitting next to a Christian nun. 'I am really enjoying talking to you dear,' she said. 'I am so glad it is not like before the Vatican Council when I would have had to believe you would go to hell for not being Christian.' I was grateful to be able to talk to a travelling companion who understood from the inside what a nun's life meant. We had something very deep in common in spite of our different religious traditions. In giving up my robes, I had given up far more than I had given up by becoming a nun in the first place. In my heart I was still a nun, but it was as if I were now living undercover. The problem was that at that stage I wasn't really interested in any other way of life than the one that I had just left behind.

I was in a kind of no-man's land. A monastic at heart pretending not be so in order to fit in with the world around me. I was to discover that even most Western Buddhists didn't particularly support monasticism. I was shocked when John Maxwell, one of my main supporters financially, and the man who had sponsored the Karmapa's visit to Birmingham in 1974, said to me, 'Quite honestly I have been thinking for some time that perhaps it would be better for your health to disrobe.' How many other people had been thinking things like that?

Coincidentally, soon after that I *did* recover from the health condition that had been affecting me since my year-long retreat in the Dordogne. I don't believe it was anything to do with no longer being a nun, but who can say? I attributed my recovery to an osteopath in Kington on the Welsh borders who sorted the problem out in a matter of weeks. It felt like having my life handed back to me. I spent the early summer living in Karma Ling in Birmingham, working as a supply Geography teacher at a local Grammar School, whilst at the same time finalising my application for a grant to study at Oxford.

I felt like a fish out of water during those months. Even getting used to wearing ordinary clothes again felt strange. The only thing that gave me a lift – almost moved me to tears, in fact – was the hymn singing at school assembly. The other teachers and probably most of the students hated it, but for me it was a joy to link back into the simple intuitive feeling of God's love that had sustained me through my childhood. I was still the same old me.

Trungpa Rinpoche had sent me to India to absorb the atmosphere, which I had done by immersing myself in Tibetan culture. Now Khenpo Rinpoche was telling me to let that go, at least in some sense. It was quite a remarkable thing for him to be doing. He was freeing me from a lot of Tibetan cultural baggage and sending me back to re-integrate with my roots, completely transforming my life. Something about it felt clean, somehow, leaving me naked. The image came to my mind of a peg that had been banged into the ground crooked and the only way to straighten it was to pull the peg right out and start again. I was not sure what the new angle needed to be, although I still had the same motivation as before. I wanted to do whatever was necessary in order to Enlighten myself and the world by following my lama's directions.

Once the school term was over, I went to join Khenpo Rinpoche and his other students in Brussels at a three-month residential course. My dear friend Tenpa was also going to be there. Still somewhat disorientated, I was hoping that during this time Rinpoche would help me understand better what it meant to not be a nun. In the event, although he paid me a lot of attention, which was rather exciting, he didn't clarify anything.

One morning a letter arrived for me saying that I had been given a grant by the Northern Ireland Education Authority. This was the final confirmation that I would be able to start at Oxford in a couple of months' time. Rinpoche was more delighted with the news than I was. He was astonished at my lack of enthusiasm. 'Anyone else in the world would be thrilled at the opportunity of going to Oxford University to study and you just screw up your nose at it,' he said. He then teased me mercilessly, saying to Tenpa, 'Look at her. She is never satisfied, always complaining. She will complain even when she reaches Enlightenment. She will say, "Oh dear, all my obscurations and mental disturbances have gone – I have nothing left to do!" Well, at least your parents are going to be pleased.' I said I doubted my mother would be, and he replied, 'I have no compassion for your mother.' As a Bodhisattva, he cannot have meant it truly, but the instant he said it I realised *I* had compassion for her. She had always rejected my attempts at kindness as not good enough, which had left me with the uncomfortable feeling that I lacked compassion for her. Rinpoche's comment cut through the self-doubt stemming from my childhood experiences, leaving me more connected to my feelings. It had a profoundly healing effect.

Rinpoche was very kind and encouraging to me at that time, letting me take a central role in many projects. He even encouraged me to pop in to see him at breakfast time each day and always seemed very pleased to see me. I was on a high. Then one morning, having cheerfully greeted me as usual, he said, 'I want you to go to England to translate for Thrangu Rinpoche.' It was like a bolt from the blue. 'Oh no!' I exclaimed. I absolutely did not want to leave Brussels and cut short the time I had with Khenpo Rinpoche. 'It is OK,' Rinpoche said kindly, 'you don't have to go yet.' Before I had time to gather my thoughts he went on, 'Tomorrow or the next day will do.' I fled the room in tears.

For about six months previously I had heard that Thrangu Rinpoche was planning a three-month summer school in England doing all the same things we were doing in Brussels. The organisers had said they didn't know who would be translating for it, but they weren't worried because someone would turn up nearer the time. I knew that old trick. Sure enough, at the last minute they were begging Khenpo Rinpoche to send one of his students to translate for their course, and he had chosen me. I was incandescent. How dare they manipulate me like this! My Greek friend Chryssoula found me fuming and she walked me round the block to help bring me to my senses. Gradually I calmed down, but I was completely devastated. How could Rinpoche be so casual about the whole thing? Why was he just going along with it? Why should I give up this last chance to see him before going to Oxford? I felt he had obliterated me as if I were of no consequence, killing my sense of self-importance. There was a moment as we rounded the corner on our last lap of the block when I looked up into the sky and thought with a sense of wonder, 'I am still alive. I have been killed but I am still alive!' It was like a profound revelation of no self or of there being life after death!

When Rinpoche next saw me out on the landing he said, 'Why are you crying? Anyone would think I was sending you to hell rather than to translate for a great lama.' From a certain perspective he was right, so there was not much I could say. I told him I was not complaining. I was just crying. After a couple of days, I had packed up and left.

On the evening that I left for England, Rinpoche sat me down in front of him and said, 'The most important thing about the guru and disciple relationship is that the disciple should not be attached to the guru nor the guru to the disciple. Gurus are for liberating their disciples. If they get attached to each other – it's the biggest joke in the universe.' I was deeply affected as I understood that this was not a rejection but a lesson in non-attachment, and I was touched that he applied this lesson to himself as well as to me. In fact, over the years I found that his sending me away taught me that the bond with the lama is closer than anything bounded by time and space could ever be.

This did not address my anger at the way translators were treated though. To add insult to injury, when I got to England, arrangements for my accommodation had hardly been thought about. I was expected to stay in a shared students' flat with a filthy kitchen and cater for myself. Thrangu Rinpoche told me that there had not been sufficient preparation even for himself and someone had had to step in at the last minute to rescue the situation by offering him the use of her house. The whole thing was a bit of a shambles. I did my best to translate for Thrangu Rinpoche and his students, but I hated to see him put into such a difficult position. I determined to help find him a place of his own in England so that he wouldn't be dependent on unreliable people next time he came.

At the end of the summer, the time came to start my new life in Oxford. I had been hankering after my old lifestyle of meditation retreat so much that I had hardly thought about the amazing opportunity that was opening up for me. The evening I arrived at Wolfson College I was given my key and room number at the porter's lodge. I will never forget the moment I opened the door to my room. I quickly closed it again, thinking there must have been a mistake: it looked so luxurious, and had an amazing view over the river, with punts floating by. But I double-checked and yes indeed, this was my room. I was bowled over. After all those years of simple living, I now had an extraordinarily comfortable space all to myself, and my own regular source of income. I was a normal person for the first time in years!

Yet I was completely naïve about the task ahead. I didn't have the faintest idea what writing a doctoral thesis involved. This meant that for the first year I had much more fun than I would otherwise have allowed myself! I loved going punting on the river and having dinner parties with new friends. I met all sorts of different academics from around the world, studying a whole range of subjects, and I attended various interesting events and lectures. Having been so single-minded and focused for so many years, I found the speed and variety of my changed life dizzying. I was amazed just how many different things one was expected to do – and *could* do – in a day.

I hadn't worked particularly hard for my first degree at Reading. None of my friends had – or at least that is how it seemed to me. I imagined working for a higher degree would be the same kind of thing, but I soon discovered that my time in Oxford was not going to be a re-run of the lax way I had sailed through my undergraduate days in the late sixties. 'You should think in terms of working ten hours a day, seven days a week,' my supervisor, Paul Williams, informed me at the end of my first term. What a shock! I never got anywhere near that number of hours, although I frequently worked myself into the ground. Sanskrit classes in particular were a nightmare: the pace was much too fast for me. We were handed a text book and told to read a chapter a week and do the translation exercises for that chapter without looking at the answers. I was well out of my depth. There was no way I could translate the exercises. Instead I spent each week looking at the answers at the end of the book trying to work out how the Sanskrit fitted with the English translation and vice versa.

Paul set me to work writing essays that would help me clarify the wider context of my field of study. This meant finding my way around the enormous volume of literature about what Buddhist philosophers and practitioners have said down the ages, a daunting task. Had I not spent ten years trying to understand these teachings experientially from within, I would have been completely at a loss. One of the essays he set me was on the Buddhist concept of mind. That just about covers everything in Buddhism! I wrote pages and pages of stuff, but struggled to organise it into an essay. At least I learnt a lot in my reading, which made the whole exercise worthwhile.

By telling me to study the Shentong explanation of Buddha Nature, Rinpoche had thrown me into a world of polemics that had occupied learned Buddhist scholars for over a thousand, perhaps even two thousand, years. This was bad enough but what made it worse was that I would have to defend a view that both my supervisor and most of the scholars in the field at that time saw as fundamentally mistaken. I wasn't going to have an easy time of it! Paul dismissed Shentong as mystical or even 'mistake – all' as he liked to put it. He kept trying to steer me in the direction of Buddhist commentators he was more familiar with, all of whom opposed the Shentong view. The custom is to have two examiners one from one's own university and one external examiner. Professor Ruegg, a formidable scholar of fifty years in the field and a world expert on Buddha Nature was more than likely going to be my external examiner and he too opposed the Shentong view. I was going to take him on like David and Goliath.

When Kalu Rinpoche had presented the image of gold covered with dirt, I had not understood what he was talking about. I was now encountering the controversy surrounding what he had been saying. The Buddha's teaching about impermanence, suffering and not-self, stress the illusion and dream-like quality of conditioned phenomena which are described as empty. It hardly makes sense to use the image of gold covered in dirt for emptiness like this. The image suggests something lasting and real hidden by false appearances. It makes more sense to use the image of gold for Buddha qualities such as the wisdom, love, joy and power to liberate others that are revealed as one reaches Buddhahood. What are these qualities and where do they come from? Were they always there in some timeless sense, waiting to be discovered or do they arise newly from causes and conditions? If the latter were true, they would be impermanent and so not a Refuge for beings. If the former were true, which is the Shentong view, the qualities themselves are synonymous with the Unconditioned. They are our changeless nature – the true nature of mind. When we drop our clinging to what is conditioned, impermanent and suffering, our true nature, with all the Buddha qualities, shines through like the sun from behind the clouds. The confusing thing is that this is also called emptiness – emptiness of other, Shentong. It is called emptiness because it is empty of anything that the conceptual mind can grasp.

Many Buddhists both past and present believe that everything is conditioned, including the qualities of the Buddha. In other words, everything is empty like a dream and an illusion and there is nothing other than this. This is the Rangtong (self-empty) view. The alternative view is the Shentong view, a term coined by the Jonangpa school but accepted by many Kagyus and Nyingmas. This view contrasts what is conditioned, impermanent and false, samsara, with the Buddha Nature with all its qualities that is unconditioned, unchanging, true and the nature of all beings, nirvana.

To understand what the controversy is about you would need to read the book of my thesis.

I chose as my main textual source a text called the Ratnagotravibhaga, which Khenpo Rinpoche had taught and I had translated with Tenpa a couple of years previously. Those with a Shentong perspective read this text as supporting their view and the more I studied the text the more convincing I found their position. Nonetheless, since Professor Ruegg was an expert on opposing interpretations, I was going to have to tread carefully. I would have to keep acknowledging his point of view before meticulously quoting sources for the opposing one.

Since Paul wasn't interested in the Shentong view, we could never have very satisfactory conversations about it. Instead he would blast me with his vast erudition, possibly in the hope that I would relent and decide to study something more in line with his own field of expertise. I didn't relent however and instead found myself losing interest in the academic approach altogether. An astrologer friend of mine looking at my chart said that from what she could see, this was hardly surprising. I wasn't really cut out for it. Nonetheless, I kept going believing it was good to finish what I had started.

During my first term at Oxford I was still waking each morning feeling angry with Rinpoche. I was angry at him for sending me back to England prematurely, for allowing me to be exploited as a translator and for never really making it clear why he had told me to stop being a nun. After some months Khenpo Rinpoche's teaching tour brought him to London and I went down to meet him there. I was shown to the door of the room where he was sitting talking to some other lamas. I looked in, and as soon as he saw my face he jumped up and took me to a quiet room alongside. He sat upright on his bed there and told me to sit on the floor in front of him. I didn't know what to say because I was still feeling very angry. After a moment or two he said, 'I never told you anything that the Primordial Buddha himself would not have told you.' I knew from that remark that he knew just how angry I was and I was relieved not to have to tell him. He then proceeded to stress to me the importance of always obeying the lama. I listened carefully, feeling sorry for my resentment and glad that we were at least talking about it.

A few days later Rinpoche and I were walking into Oxford together and he confided in me, 'You know, I know how you felt when you were so angry with me. I was angry with the Karmapa when he told me to come to the West to teach. I was building a nunnery and teaching my students. I didn't want to come to the West. It seemed a waste of time to me since I didn't even know the language. Yet I came and look what happened. It all turned out well. So it is right to do as the lama tells you.'

Alongside my studies, I was getting involved with other Buddhists and experiencing what it is like to practise Dharma in the midst of a householder life, including being present at a person's death for the first time. On pilgrimage in India I had once met a lady called Mala at a railway station and when I got to Oxford she invited me to talk to her Buddhist group in Worcester. Sadly, her cancer that had been in remission came back and I was with her during the last few days of her life, including the evening she died. Facing it together with the family and friends had a powerfully bonding effect on everyone involved. Death really focuses people on what is important in life – the heart. Everyone knows that. The heart is our Buddha Nature and it doesn't die. It is not of the nature of something that dies. I don't say this as an academic, but I do as a teacher of Dharma.

For the first few terms I was in Oxford, Michael Aris was giving a Tibetan class that I attended. When I told him about my idea to buy a house for Thrangu Rinpoche, he urged me to start raising money for it and get him to come to Oxford. I didn't give it much more thought there and then, but a year or so later, I was in London amongst the crowds assembled to greet the Karmapa as he passed through on his way to the USA for medical treatment. Waiting in line to receive a blessing, I heard a woman's voice behind me saying, 'Won't anyone take this money off me?' Even as I turned around to see who was speaking, I called 'I will'. I thought even a small amount of money would surely help kick-start fundraising.

As it happened, it was my friend Jenny Newton from the Worcester group, and she explained that she had received a good-sized legacy from her mother that she wanted to give to a good cause. Jenny was delighted at my suggestion to buy a house for Thrangu Rinpoche.

When I heard how much money she was talking about, I realised that buying a house for Thrangu Rinpoche had suddenly become an immediate possibility. I wondered if I shouldn't offer to buy a house for Khenpo Rinpoche as well or instead, but when I checked with him, he was quite adamant that he didn't want anything of the sort. Asked if he would prefer London or Oxford, Thrangu Rinpoche chose Oxford, so Jenny bought a small terraced house and paid to have it renovated. The whole Worcester group and the University Buddhist Society got involved in the project, and a Trust was set up to manage this asset as Rinpoche wanted. I discovered I thoroughly enjoyed getting involved with property – inspecting it, improving it, buying and selling it – which is curious given my general lack of concern about my living conditions. I tend to have luck with property when I do set my mind to it. The Karmapa must have sensed this because he took me totally by surprise once when I was in Rumtek by asking me about various houses and property and whether I liked them or not. At the time I had no idea what that was all about.

At the end of the first year I had to pass a Sanskrit exam in order to upgrade to D.Phil status. Had a most gracious classmate not coached me for a few weeks before the exam I am sure I wouldn't have stood a chance. As it was, I still had to re-sit it. This involved translating a piece of previously unseen Sanskrit text. I knew I was out of my depth but didn't want to have to tell Rinpoche that I had not even tried to do the exam. I was shown into the room where I was to sit on my own and do my translation. There was a big dictionary on the desk to help me, but I hadn't properly mastered the way to use it. I looked at the text I was supposed to translate and idly tried to read it, not expecting to be able to understand anything. To my surprise, I quickly recognised it to be a set of verses from the Ratnagotravibhaga, the precise text I had come to Oxford to study! I actually knew it by heart in Tibetan and could use the Tibetan as a crib for working out the Sanskrit. It turned out to be good fun and I passed the exam. If I hadn't, it would have been good-bye to Oxford and who knows where my life would have ended up.

Thirteen

Marriage & Reconnecting to Trungpa Rinpoche

'Look there he is!' I cried as I spotted a tall, well-built man in his mid-forties, head held high, looking rather pleased with himself threading through the crowds outside Oxford railway station. His thick dark-framed glasses, distinctive walk, high forehead and beard gave him a professorial or rabbinical air.

It was Michael Hookham and he was to be the speaker that night at the University Buddhist Society that my friend Jim and I had resurrected during our first year at Oxford. I had been very keen to invite him as I had heard he was an early student of Trungpa Rinpoche in the 1960s. I hoped that by making a connection with him I would be to some extent fulfilling the wishes of Khenpo Rinpoche. We had had to wait an hour for him in the car park in my friend's camper van because he had missed his train. This meant we had to go straight to the college where he was going to give his talk instead of going for a meal first. This didn't put me in a very good mood, but I nonetheless listened carefully to what he had to say.

I had never heard Dharma taught like that before. What he was saying sounded as if it might be very profound, but I wasn't sure he knew what he was talking about. Was it worth the effort to try to understand it or not? Afterwards, a small group of us went out for supper and spent an enjoyable evening talking about Dharma, which somewhat improved my impression of him. We drove him back to the house where he would be staying and as he realised that I was not getting out there too, he sounded so disappointed that I was immediately won over. I went in for a cup of tea with him and his host and that is when we got talking in earnest. Even then I was still not sure where he was coming from.

It was around midnight that I mentioned how fascinated I was by the Avatamsaka sutra and the idea of countless worlds interpenetrating. This is expressed as how within a single indivisible particle there are as many Buddhas as there are points in countless Buddha realms. Michael's face lit up and he became quite animated. He clearly took this teaching seriously and was not dismissing it as fanciful nonsense. It turned out that he was a mathematician and physicist and had begun a PhD on black holes, which he had abandoned due to illness some years before. This teaching about numberless Buddhas within a single point resonated for him with how one can demonstrate mathematically that infinity can be packed into the infinitely small by mapping every point outside of a sphere to a corresponding point within it. After this conversation about the Avatamsaka sutra I dropped my guard and started to properly appreciate the subtlety and depths of his understanding of the Dharma.

We talked all through the night and all the next day. There had been nothing romantic in our connection up to that point, but when my friend and I saw him off at the station in the evening, Michael kissed me on the top of my head. It was such an idiosyncratic thing to do that it charmed me. I definitely wanted to meet him again. When after a couple of weeks he hadn't rung me, I made up an excuse to ring him and to my delight he was clearly pleased I had done so.

Then came the earth-shatteringly sad news that the Karmapa had died in America at the age of fifty-seven. It was one of those moments that stick in your mind. I stood transfixed, staring at the message I had just found in my pigeon hole in the porter's lodge. What did it mean that he had died? We had all relied so much on his being there. He was like the sun in the sky. What would happen now? Yet as I read it again and again, I realised that for me the Karmapa couldn't die. His presence was all-pervading and always had been. 'You didn't know him all *that* well did you?' suggested a friend who was watching my reaction to the news. He couldn't quite gauge what kind of bereavement this was for me. I couldn't either. It was big and yet in a strange way it didn't affect me as much as I would have expected because for me he hadn't gone anywhere. Even to this day I cannot think of the Karmapa in any other way.

The message explained that his body was being flown back to Rumtek in Sikkim and early the next morning would be passing through Heathrow, where people were gathering to pay their respects. In what I thought was a bold move, I rang Michael and asked if he would be going and whether we could go together. As I had hoped, he invited me to stay overnight at his flat in Swiss Cottage. On the train to London, I kept asking myself what on earth I was doing. I didn't even know this man. He met me at Paddington and we took the underground to Swiss Cottage. He seemed quite excited, almost trembling, and I really hoped that I wasn't making a huge mistake.

The next morning, Heathrow airport was teaming with lamas and Dharma colleagues all looking lost and disorientated. Shamar Rinpoche was there and called us over to join him at breakfast. I remembered his saying to me once at Dhagpo Kagyu Ling that he wouldn't know what to do if the Karmapa was not there to direct him. It was poignant knowing how hard he must be finding this moment. We had all come to the end of an era.

Yet my feelings were in turmoil. Yes, there was the shock of the Karmapa's passing away, but at the same time there was the excitement of a new relationship starting up. I had at last found someone I could talk to about deep Dharma in my own language. It felt as if Khenpo Rinpoche must have intuited I would have a relationship like this when he told me I should return to Trungpa Rinpoche, learn Dharma in English and give up being a nun. A month after that I went to live with Michael in Swiss Cottage, and within days, he asked me to marry him. The year was 1981, he was forty-six and I was thirty-five.

When Michael first said, 'Let's get married,' I didn't say, 'Yes, let's,' or show any particular sense of surprise, gratitude, joy or even enthusiasm. I said, 'Not yet,' thinking that although I was sure I wanted to marry him, it would seem precipitous to others if we announced it so soon after having first met. However, it was what I had always dreamt of – a Dharma companion for life. I looked forward to our practising and working together. After living alone for so long, it felt good to have someone close to me whom I could rely on for simple love and affection.

We decided to ask our respective gurus what they thought of our getting married. If either of them had advised against it, we wouldn't have wanted to marry. As it was, both gurus were very much in favour of it. By happy coincidence, Trungpa Rinpoche was stuck in London for several days, en route to the States, because of snow. We went to meet him in the waiting lounge, where he was sitting surrounded by a party of his students. We knelt before him and asked what he thought of our getting married. 'About time too, for both of you,' was his warm response. I had a strange moment of déjà vu about that meeting. Then a month or so later we met Khenpo Rinpoche in Brussels. I asked him what he thought about it and whether he would marry us. He just said 'When?' and then immediately, 'Today or tomorrow?' He seemed very pleased. From the moment Khenpo Rinpoche met him, it was clear to me that he liked and respected Michael and recognised his strong connection with Trungpa Rinpoche and the Dzogchen tradition which points directly to the true nature of mind at the very deepest and subtlest level. Michael similarly took a liking to Rinpoche, and his respect was to turn into deep gratitude as the years went by.

The next day, Khenpo Rinpoche married us in an old farmhouse in the countryside. He was going there to give some teachings on Dzogchen and Michael was almost more interested in asking Rinpoche questions about that than in the actual marriage event. Rinpoche made up a special ceremony for us, telling us he had married us for all our lifetimes. Quite a challenge!

Khenpo Rinpoche's advice to us as a married couple was, 'Look at each other's faults as conditioned, and therefore as empty illusions. Look at each other's intrinsic good qualities as their unchanging, non-conditioned true nature shining through, like the sun from behind clouds. The faults like clouds come and go, but the sun never changes.'

It was one blessing after another that year because a few months after our marriage we were in Boulder, Colorado, asking Trungpa Rinpoche to bless our union which he did by placing his vajra, a symbol of stability and indestructibility, on our heads. Then later that year, Dilgo Khyentse Rinpoche came to England. Years before, Trungpa Rinpoche had impressed on Michael that it was vitally important to take teachings from him. I had first met him in Darjeeling in the early 1970s, because Bokar Rinpoche had similarly wanted me to make a special connection with him, as one of his own very important teachers. In fact, Dilgo Khyentse Rinpoche was the teacher of all my teachers and of the Dalai Lama himself.

He was a giant of a man with a massive and warm presence. Since we were so fortunate as to have a private audience with him we decided to ask him about Ngakpa ordination. We had heard it was an ordination for non-monastics and wanted to know more about it. No sooner had we mentioned it, than Khyentse Rinpoche called for his ritual implements and proceeded to ordain us. It felt a very special blessing, but we were none the wiser about what it meant.

After having been so amply blessed as a couple, we wondered whether a civil marriage was necessary, but Khenpo Rinpoche strongly advised us to have one. We were formally married at the registry office in Swiss Cottage in London, with family and friends in attendance. Christmas Humphreys, the high court judge who had founded the London Buddhist Society attended too. We had been talking to him at a meeting the week before and casually invited him along and to our surprise he accepted. My parents didn't come but Michael's father, my Auntie Mollie, my two brothers and two of my cousins did. In fact, my younger brother brought his whole family, who never forgot trying to follow Christmas Humphreys' erratic driving through the London traffic. It wasn't quite what they expected from a high court judge! The reception was a simple affair at our home in our big studio flat. We invited all and everyone saying contributions of food and drink would be welcome. In the event it lasted thirty hours with over a hundred guests coming and going in their own time. Loads of food and drink materialised and we had plenty of opportunity to chat to all our guests and they to each other. It was a joyous and memorable occasion in spite of our seriously constrained budget!

Living with Michael gave me ready access to the vastness and depth of his mind. Whatever direction I wanted to go to explore further, he was always there far ahead of me, trying to draw me closer to the truth. He could take me as deep as I was capable of going. This had a profound effect on my understanding of Dharma and worked to affirm my meditative experiences for me – a benefit that continues to this day. In turn I was able to help him with my knowledge of the Tibetan language and culture from my experience of living with Tibetans. Yet I was so much more a typical Westerner than he had ever been. He told me that talking to me helped him to understand better the kind of difficulties his students sometimes had with things like the imagery in Tibetan Buddhism, difficulties he had never had.

Michael's meditative experiences had begun in childhood which rather suggests he was a Buddhist practitioner in past lives. On meeting Trungpa Rinpoche in the early 1960s he was amazed that Rinpoche understood immediately where he was in his meditation and directed him accordingly. One of the first questions Michael asked him was about a Dzogchen text and this created the auspicious connection for Trungpa Rinpoche to explicitly teach him Dzogchen far earlier than he did elsewhere. They would meet up for whole weekends in Oxford, translating Dzogchen teachings and Michael took notes that he then checked word for word with Rinpoche meticulously making sure he had understood correctly. This meant I now had direct access to someone completely immersed in Trungpa Rinpoche's deepest teachings, just as Khenpo Rinpoche had wanted.

For his part, Michael now had, through me as a translator, direct access to the Shentong teachings of Khenpo Rinpoche, which enabled him to place Trungpa Rinpoche's teachings within the wider Buddhist tradition. I found it quite moving when fairly early on in our marriage over a meal in a Chinese restaurant, I looked up to see Michael gazing at me lovingly with tears welling up in his eyes. 'Why are you crying?' I asked and he replied that he felt overwhelmed with gratitude to me because I had made it possible for him to get such teachings from Khenpo Rinpoche.

Soon after that we learned that Dudjom Rinpoche was going to give a rare empowerment that Michael really wanted, at the Nyingma centre in the Dordogne. Word had spread rapidly so that by the time we arrived, there were already hundreds of other people gathered.

On the morning of the day that we all assembled for the empowerment word came through from Dudjom Rinpoche that because of an inauspicious dream he had had that night he was not going to give the empowerment Michael had hoped for and that was that. He gave other empowerments and teachings instead, with which I for one was more than satisfied. I was used to such sudden changes of plan based on auspicious or inauspicious signs (*tendrel*).

Dilgo Khyentse Rinpoche was also in the Dordogne at that time, staying at his own house nearby. At a private interview with him, Michael asked a question relating to an experience he had had, and Khyentse Rinpoche told him he needed further instructions. He hadn't time to give these himself, so suggested he ask one of his more experienced disciples, naming three great masters, Nyoshul Khenpo, Khenpo Tsultrim Gyamtso Rinpoche and Gendun Rinpoche specifically, perhaps because they were all in the vicinity. Michael chose to ask Khenpo Rinpoche, who graciously agreed saying, 'Because my own Guru Khyentse Rinpoche has asked me to do so.'

Nothing increases my faith in the whole tradition of Tibetan Buddhism more than this kind of respect that the great yogin practitioners have for each other, and the way they validate each other's experience.

Lama Thubden lived at Karma Ling in Birmingham and I had known him for a long time. He was an experienced meditator and he confided in me that for a few years he had had a problem with the subtle energies in the body and mind. 'I am only telling you this because you are a close Dharma friend and colleague. I wouldn't talk like this to just anyone' he assured me. I was touched by his trust. Then he said, 'I asked Khenpo Tsultrim Gyamtso Rinpoche about it and he told me it was not because of a fault in my meditation. I also asked Nyoshul Khenpo. He said he would meditate with me for a while to see if he could spot anything. We shut the door and meditated for an hour or so. Afterwards Nyoshul Khenpo told me it was not a fault with my meditation.' I was fascinated by the window this gave me into how yogins check each other out directly mind to mind.

The way yogins behave around each other leaves me feeling they see qualities in each other of which I am scarcely aware. My friend and colleague Larry Mermelstein described Khenpo Tsultrim Gyamtso Rinpoche's visit to Chogyam Trungpa Rinpoche in Boulder. Trungpa Rinpoche had been told that Khenpo Rinpoche, a very learned scholar, would like to meet him. Khenpo Rinpoche came in with trays of Saki as offerings, because he had been told it was Trungpa Rinpoche's favourite drink. Larry said that this was a first. Tibetans usually tried to either ignore the fact that Trungpa Rinpoche drank alcohol or tried to dissuade him from it. During the interview the two men barely said anything at all to each other. Afterwards Trungpa Rinpoche said to Larry, 'I thought you told me he was a *khenpo*.' Larry said that he was. Trungpa Rinpoche replied, 'Seems more like a yogin to me.' Just to be sure, Larry asked if that was good and Trungpa Rinpoche said, 'Of course.' Years later I read Khenpo Rinpoche's own account of that meeting with Trungpa Rinpoche. He said it was like meeting his own mind.

Lama Thubden once remarked to Michael with respectful appreciation, 'Your success as a practitioner comes from your faith and *samaya* connection with Trungpa Rinpoche.' I don't know how he knew either that Michael was successful as a practitioner or that he had good *samaya* connection with Trungpa Rinpoche, but he did. 'Westerners don't usually understand about faith and *samaya* connection,' he continued. 'That is why they don't succeed.' In a transmission lineage the *samaya* is the inescapable bond between student and teacher that makes the spiritual transmission possible. It is both the sign that the transmission has happened as well as the condition that makes it possible.

Khenpo Rinpoche would remind us when giving key instructions that he was doing so because of his *samaya* with Khyentse Rinpoche who had asked him to give them. He also

said, 'You are only able to receive and practise these profound instructions because of your strong *samaya* connection with Trungpa Rinpoche.' It was as if the *samaya* connection between yogins was the life line of the lineage via
which transmission was happening.   Blessing power
(*adhishtana*) flows through it like sap through a tree or one's
own life blood.

From the remarks I was hearing I came to understand that
yogins recognise each other directly mind to mind, heart to
heart through the power of *samaya* connections and this is
how transmission happens between them. The significance
of spiritual connections is something we in the West have
yet to recognise and learn about. This is how yogins gain the
reputation among other yogins of being great practitioners.
There are all sorts of hierarchical structures in Tibetan Buddhism that involve monastic institutions and the handing on
of authority when heads of institutions die. It is not always
the greatest yogins who take on the top roles in such hierar-
chies. Sometimes the greatest of yogins live quite obscure
lives, outside any institution and are only ever recognised by
other yogins or perhaps at death when they show extraordinary signs of accomplishment. It became increasingly obvious to me that yogins recognised Michael as a yogin. They
were clearly recognising in him more than I was yet
equipped to see.

About six months before I met him, Michael had left a job
he had at Marconi Space and Defense Systems in order to
spend three months in Canada at a seminary, a kind of training programme, with Trungpa Rinpoche. On his return, instead of looking for another job in the field, he wanted to do
something completely different. On meeting me he started
to consider doing a doctorate on Buddhism in Oxford himself. This led to our moving from Swiss Cottage into a flat in
north Oxford. On the same day we moved his blind father
from Surrey to a small terraced house in east Oxford to be
near to us. Two moves in one day was quite a feat of

logistics but it went through without a hitch – a combination of good organisation and a lot of luck!

I hadn't been finding it easy to adapt to the demands of the academic world and things were not made any easier by my marriage. Michael had never been practical on the domestic front and now his eyes were badly damaged by glaucoma, everything he did was painfully slow. I hated to see him struggling for hours at his turn at the washing up. I found I would rather do it myself, because it seemed such a waste of his time. This way all the practicalities of housework, shopping, accounts and planning for our life together came down to me. He helped once a week at caring for his blind father, while I earned money for us both through teaching English as a foreign language. He did some one-to-one tutoring in Mathematics for a while, but his eyes made it too labour intensive to be worthwhile. Anyway, his passion was the Dharma and he had so much to offer that I hoped to set him up as a Buddhist teacher with his own students to support him. This was a far more challenging task than I had anticipated. My life got so busy I was often in despair at how to get everything done. I longed to spend more time in meditation and appreciating the company of the yogin by my side.

Nevertheless, true to form, I was determined to finish my doctoral thesis. It was before the era of word processors so it was painstaking work on a manual typewriter. Even when computers were available they were still too expensive for my small pocket. However, there was a place I could hire one paying by the hour, so I ended up cycling into town late at night to a scruffy basement flat where six of us would be booked in on one each of the six computers, all working deep into the night to get our doctoral theses done. I would often be cycling home in the early hours of the morning singing to myself, feeling well pleased with my night's work. After two years of marriage, I at last submitted my doctoral thesis and a date was set for my viva. This is when the two examiners discuss your work with you and tell you whether it's a substantial enough contribution to the field to be accepted as a doctoral thesis or not.

The day of my viva came and I had very little idea of what to expect. I knew Professor Ruegg personally and he had always been very kind and friendly, so I was not feeling particularly anxious. I sat opposite him and another professor from SOAS whom I didn't know except by name. Professor Ruegg opened the proceedings by observing sagely, 'You have approached the topic of Buddhism from a religious point of view, which is an increasing tendency these days.' You may wonder how else one might approach Buddhism – isn't it always religious? For a long time, in Western academia, the main interest has been philological, tracing the history of ideas from ancient texts. To me this is a bit like comparing ancient instruction manuals without intending to follow the instructions. Buddhism gives instructions to reach a spiritual goal, so I was pleased to note that Professor Ruegg accepted a religious approach as academically valid. I was sorely disappointed therefore when instead of discussing with me my approach and the thrust of my arguments, he held forth for a full hour mainly to the other professor with barely a reference to my thesis. Any attempt by me to join in the conversation was met with an odd look as if none of this was anything to do with me. Then the other professor held forth for an hour in such a way as made it blatantly obvious that he hadn't even looked at my thesis. After two hours of this I was left feeling quite shaken up and without any sense of how I had fared. I was in tears when I joined Michael outside in a nearby café where he had been waiting for me. 'Knowing how much work a person puts into writing a thesis and how lonely a task that is, why would *anybody* treat someone like that?' I sobbed. 'It's a good job I have no intention of pursuing an academic career.'

It took a whole month of anxious waiting before I got a letter from Professor Gombrich telling me my examiners considered my work was a significant enough contribution to the field to warrant a doctorate. Professor Ruegg had done me the honour of making little corrections and comments on almost every page, which he wanted addressed before he would formally accept it. This meant yet another whole year working on it before it was finally accepted. Some months after my viva, I met Professor Ruegg at a conference and thanked him for having looked at my thesis so thoroughly. He was all kindness again and said warmly, 'I enjoyed it, and since I was assuming it would be published, I thought it was worth making the corrections for that.'

Nevertheless, when he gave a lecture on the topic at that same conference he didn't mention once the Jonangpa Shentong tradition that I had been writing about. It was as if for him it just didn't exist, even though he knew full well it did and what is more that it was a very important strand of the tradition. I was forced to stand up in front of an audience of over one hundred people to ask him why he had failed to mention it. It was interesting how he could dismiss my question simply by a tone of voice. 'Oh – you mean *that* tradition – well yes there is *that*,' he said, and moved swiftly on to the next question. Clearly what I had written about was too revolutionary in terms of his own field of expertise. He had led the field for so long in academic circles, who was going to think I had anything interesting to say if Professor Ruegg didn't think it worth commenting on? I wished I was more articulate and quicker on my feet. As it was, he effectively silenced me. I was pleased to hear that when he tried to do something similar at other conferences, he was challenged by heavyweight academics such as Paul Williams!

For graduation day, my proud parents came down to attend the presentation in the famous Sheldonian Theatre. We students all filed forward in our hundreds dressed in mortar boards and gowns to receive our degrees, kneeling before the Vice-Chancellor, who ceremonially placed a book, the symbol of wisdom and learning, on our heads one by one. It was strikingly reminiscent of receiving a blessing from a lama; they also sometimes use a book on the head in this way. Clearly the roots of these rituals run deep.

That was more or less the end of my academic career except for a few articles and lectures here and there. However, shortly after receiving my doctorate a request came from the State University of New York Press for permission to publish my thesis as a book. A fellow student of Khenpo Rinpoche was on their editorial board at the time and she was keen to learn more about the way Khenpo Rinpoche was teaching Buddha Nature. I began yet another long process of working the thesis into a publishable book.

As Michael and I were first getting to know each other, he had kept referring to the Longchen Foundation, but I could never quite make out what it was. At supper one memorable night in an Indian restaurant, I was asking him if it was a community or an organisation like a charity or something. Did it have members? Did it *do* anything? Who was in charge? How was it run? It turned out to have no structure at all. Yet he still kept talking about its vision and intentions. I was becoming increasingly puzzled as to what it was when I suddenly put two and two together and exclaimed, 'The "Longchen Foundation" is *you*, isn't it?' He rather coyly admitted that it was in a way, but said it seemed presumptuous to say so. It was his name for his own vision inspired by Trungpa Rinpoche's teachings. It wasn't the vision for an organisation as such, but of a spiritual movement of some kind.

Trungpa Rinpoche had spoken to Dilgo Khyentse Rinpoche about a vehicle for transmitting the Dzogchen teachings that he had given Michael in the 1960s and told Michael to connect to Dilgo Khyentse Rinpoche about this, which he did. Even before Trungpa Rinpoche had left the UK in the early seventies Michael had set up a small group which he later named the Longchen Foundation and Trungpa Rinpoche had written a blessing for it in Tibetan. I discovered that there was a group of about a dozen people who identified with the Longchen Foundation, but they each seemed to have a slightly different idea about what it was. Over the years I helped Michael to set up a trust with the name the Longchen Foundation to support our Dharma activity. We also started to build a Buddhist community (a sangha) by that name.

The students of the community would meet for weekend courses every six weeks or so, lasting from Friday evening to Sunday evening, meditating eight hours a day as well as Michael giving two or three Dharma talks a day. These courses were pretty intensive. As the years went by the students found it harder and harder to find the time and energy for the original format, so we had to shorten the weekends and relax the programme a bit. Most years Khenpo Rinpoche came and taught the group at least once. This was the pattern for fifteen years or more.

Over these years Michael and I lived together day and night, self-employed, working at home. We worked together as teachers of Dharma, with him taking the leading role as teacher and me taking the leading role in organising the students to receive the teachings. For several years we lived largely on my income from teaching English, until gradually our students started to take more and more responsibility for supporting us.

Khenpo Rinpoche used to comment about how much faith Michael's students and even his wife had in Michael. Living close to a teacher mercilessly exposes one to their foibles and weaknesses and one's faith tends to dwindle. He would quote a well-known saying in Tibet emphasising that if the wife and family of a yogin also had faith in him it was a sign of the yogin's great accomplishment. In the case of Milarepa, not only his enemies ended up with faith in him, but also his own betrothed whom he had abandoned, his sister, and his aunt!

Having faith in a lama doesn't mean believing they never make a mistake or that their every action is skilful. It means something much deeper than that. I had always assumed that a person's aptitude to deal with situations in life improved at the same pace as their realisation deepened, but the life-stories of great yogins show they often have problematic character traits and blind spots that mean their development of skilful action often lags behind the depth of their insight. Once I was describing my difficulties with Gendun Rinpoche to a lama friend, who tentatively suggested that this was because Gendun Rinpoche was as yet relatively weak in skilful means. In other words, although I found his insensitivity to my needs unskilful, this did not call into question the depth of his realisation nor indicate a lack of compassion.

Tibetans are used to handling this kind of paradox and have their own ways of dealing with it. Once when I was having difficulties translating for a lama, a Tibetan friend said, 'Old lamas get irritable. Come back later when he is in a better mood.' Surprised by her candidness I asked, 'Isn't that saying he is not always kind?' She looked thoughtful, 'Not really. He is a Bodhisattva and always motivated by wisdom and compassion.' In other words, she felt comfortable naming what I took to be a fault without it meaning she doubted his underlying character. Conversations like this stood me in good stead for my own life experience as the wife of an accomplished yogin.

As a married couple there were all the same tensions and difficulties as face most people. Just as I had habits that irritated him, he had habits that irritated me. Living with another person always tests one's patience and means making adjustments to accommodate each other's needs. Even simple things such as having a different rhythm of day and night can be problematic. I am an early riser and Michael a night-bird. When he was starting to really wake up, I had had enough and was ready for bed. What to do? He didn't notice or care about practicalities such as planning ahead and making ends meet, so I wore myself out trying to make up for this. I felt frustrated and overwhelmed and longed for a share of what to me seemed his relaxed way of life. The image of myself as a patient person was shattered! Outside of my comfort zone, I had to confront my limitations. Painful as this was, it opened my eyes to how deeply we can suffer, even when in so many ways our circumstances look perfect.

Michael and I cared for my father-in-law until he died in his early eighties, about five years into our marriage. After he died, we sold his house and moved into a larger semi-detached house in Beechey Avenue, a quiet leafy cul-de-sac just half an hour's walk through the meadows into town. It had an unusually large extension that meant there was a room big enough to hold meetings for up to thirty people if they didn't mind being a bit squashed. We ran courses and hosted Khenpo Rinpoche there for many years.

We also hosted a young lama called Ponlop Rinpoche, a fellow student of Khenpo Rinpoche. I had first met him when he was about five years old, at Rumtek. The Karmapa introduced me to him when he ran into the room while I was having an audience. He had just been given his first set of monk's robes and was dancing around in them very sweetly. I later met him as a young man in Nepal when I was at one of Khenpo Rinpoche's courses there. He was teaching a small group of translators and I was impressed by his great presence of mind in reminding us to switch our tape recorders on and off whenever he started and stopped speaking. I would often forget, but he would remember for me! Similarly, when he visited us in Oxford, I might exclaim, 'Oh dear, where is my purse?' not expecting any reply, and Ponlop Rinpoche would say, 'You left it on the table by the chair in the sitting room.' He had noticed and remembered when I had not!

He had just completed a twelve-year study programme taught by Thrangu Rinpoche and Khenpo Rinpoche in

Rumtek and shared with us his view that the essence of all that study could be given in just a few years, and it is the essence that matters in terms of practice. We all hoped that he would come to study in Oxford, but sadly it didn't work out.

We were very pleased however that Trungpa Rinpoche's eldest son, known as the Sakyong, came to study in Oxford for a year or two before his father died. He stayed with us for a week or so when he first arrived and was looking for accommodation. I thought he was going to be very Americanised because he had been raised in America since the age of eight and could no longer speak Tibetan. I was however immediately struck by the gentle dignity of his comportment. While watching American football on television, at one point he turned to me and said, 'People think I am very American, but I am not. I am Tibetan.' 'Yes,' I thought, 'I can sense that.'

My parents hadn't believed in my marriage at first because it followed on so quickly from my having met Michael. That is why they were not at our wedding. As they realised we were settled as a relatively ordinary married couple, they came to visit and we visited them sometimes in Essex. My father was highly impressed by Michael's depth of learning, which he deduced mainly from carefully perusing his bookshelves. My mother was rather bemused by him. Neither of them stopped talking long enough to ever let him speak. Consequently, they never got to know him and I don't think he ever felt much connection with them. There had been the same sense of disconnection in regard to his father, who had been vaguely proud of his son, but as with my parents had no real interest in what he thought and did.

What we lacked in a sense of connection to our own families was more than made up for by our connections among our teachers, colleagues and students. We visited Trungpa Rinpoche at his home in Boulder on several occasions. It always felt like stepping into a whole different world. Trungpa Rinpoche was building a cultural context all of his own. It was neither Tibetan nor Western but a strange mixture of both with a lot of Japanese Zen thrown in.

Rinpoche was very kind to us, giving us access to whatever teaching materials we wanted. Rinpoche's students were all very kind and friendly and curious about Michael and who exactly he was in terms of Trungpa Rinpoche's world. Michael, always the loner, was unconcerned.

Trungpa Rinpoche rarely travelled to Europe and we only saw him in England a few times and very briefly. My strongest connection occurred when I received an empowerment from him in Marburg in the mid 1980s. I had to be given special permission by Trungpa Rinpoche himself in order to attend because I didn't meet the usual requirements. Michael and I both went and stayed in a hotel along with his other students, many of whom we knew already. We all had to sit in meditation for eight to ten hours a day for several days, constantly being told Rinpoche would be along in another hour or two. It reminded me of waiting for my ordination in Rumtek, except there was a whole roomful of more than one hundred people in the same situation. Finally, Trungpa Rinpoche arrived and the empowerment ceremony began. Rinpoche was sitting on a throne with a Tibetan monk in attendance. Everything was suddenly very Tibetan and familiar. I had been very struck by the words of one of his students the day before. 'You open your heart and he enters you.' I was so moved by his presence at the ceremony that I had a lump in my throat and tears came to my eyes, even though for much of the time he seemed a bit out of it and kept forgetting where he had got to in the text. Later, when I told Khenpo Rinpoche what had happened, he eagerly asked me, 'Did you *receive* the empowerment?' I didn't know how to answer so just told him that it had brought tears to my eyes. At that Khenpo Rinpoche nodded as if in satisfaction. 'That is a sign you received it,' he said.

At a personal interview with Trungpa Rinpoche in Boulder, he welcomed me very gently. I felt he knew me intimately. We talked about how even after all that time and my best efforts, I still found Tibetan iconography alien. I knew what the images were supposed to point to, but somehow all the associations were wrong. He showed no surprise and simply told me that I should practise without focusing on particular iconographical forms and leave such practices for later. I assumed he meant the forms would come alive from out of the spaciousness of the formless practice. I was grateful for his encouragement. His advice conformed with what all my other teachers had told me. We then started talking about teaching Dharma. 'You should teach Mahayana,' he said firmly. Since Mahayana is the path that brings all beings to Awakening, I had no objections to that!

The last time Michael and I saw Trungpa Rinpoche for a joint interview in Boulder, he was sitting in an elegant arm chair, upright and relaxed, in a smart grey suit and tie, fingering a tumbler of water or maybe whisky. During our conversation, Rinpoche said the Dharma would gradually move from America to Britain, that it would take a long time to establish itself there, but that nevertheless, when it did, it would be so firmly established that it would remain stable there for a long time. I said, 'So Rinpoche, if we were to find you a property in Britain, would you come?' At this he made a sudden movement towards me as if about to rise out of his chair. 'Yes,' he said, as if an invitation like this was all he was waiting for. I was determined to make this my next major project as soon as I had finished preparing my doctoral thesis for publication.

After our last meeting something mysterious started to happen to Trungpa Rinpoche. We would receive news that Rinpoche was 'in retreat', with the added suggestion that perhaps he wasn't well or was in some strange state. Very few people were able to see him and he was not answering any of the questions his students were asking him about how to take the community forward. Typically, he would answer, 'It doesn't matter,' or 'Whatever.' One has to suppose he was practising equalness and equanimity, but it was making life very difficult for his followers.

Michael went to America to see him, but of course couldn't get the teaching he had hoped for. I was awaiting his return from the airport just as I was about to leave for Surrey for the weekend to translate for Ngakpa Yeshe Dorje (famously known as the Dalai Lama's Rain-maker). Was I going to have to leave before he got back? Just in the nick of time Michael's taxi pulled up and he jumped straight out into our car and came with us. He was astonished to find that the teaching Ngakpa Yeshe Dorje was about to give was exactly the teaching he had hoped to receive from Trungpa Rinpoche. It felt as if Trungpa Rinpoche himself had choreographed the timing precisely for Michael's benefit!

At the end of the weekend, Michael still had questions he wanted to ask, so we stayed on to ask Ngakpa Yeshe Dorje the next day. At first Yeshe Dorje would not engage with Michael's questions, just giving general answers that did not help him go deeper. The wardrobe door swung open and the attendant quickly closed it again. Michael persevered with his questions, and Yeshe Dorje once more evaded them by giving general answers. The wardrobe door swung open again. The third time this happened, Yeshe Dorje stopped in his tracks and said, 'The door has swung open three times when I refused to answer your questions. That is a sign that I should open the door of the treasury of the teachings to you.' This was one of quite a few occasions I saw lamas giving teachings in response to signs that told them it was the right moment to do so. Yeshe Dorje gave Michael instructions that took his breath away. I had heard them before, but they had not struck me as very important. For Michael they were like a key. Tears came to his eyes. He was so grateful to the Lama for the teaching and to me for being there to translate for him.

Trungpa Rinpoche's condition meant Michael was left very much to his own devices in terms of how to carry Rinpoche's vision for Longchen Foundation forward. When we discussed the situation with the Sakyong, he said that Michael was in a relatively easy position in regard to it all because he worked independently from the Shambhala organisation, which had always been very dependent on Trungpa Rinpoche for direction. Longchen had more freedom to do what it liked. The situation led Michael to turn increasingly to Khenpo Rinpoche for advice, direction and instruction.

During this time of Trungpa Rinpoche not being available, Michael and I went to visit Trungpa Rinpoche's retreat centre in Colorado, the Rocky Mountain Dharma Centre. Khenpo Rinpoche was giving teachings and many of his translators as well as Trungpa Rinpoche's translators were gathering to discuss translation issues. While we were there the Sakyong invited Khenpo Rinpoche, Michael and me for tea in his apartment. As we entered, I was struck by the beautiful little hummingbird hovering stationary by the flowering plant just outside the window. The beauty of the bird suspended in space and time captured the poignancy of what was happening in the room between the four of us. Khenpo Rinpoche asked after Trungpa Rinpoche's health and the Sakyong described the strange nature of his condition. Khenpo Rinpoche explained how great yogins sometimes go through odd states where it seems their minds have left their bodies. It is not clear whether they are ill or in some deep meditative state. The Sakyong was reassured and said that he had always assumed something of the sort.

A day or so later we received the news that Trungpa Rinpoche had suddenly insisted on flying from Boulder to Halifax and everyone was in a state of shock. We were all asked to pray for his long life and the fear was that he might be about to die. The evening Michael and I were about to leave, Khenpo Rinpoche said to us, 'Don't leave until I have left.' That put us in a tricky position as we had had barely enough money to buy our original airfares. Where would we get the money to get replacement tickets at such short notice? I was aghast because I didn't want to disobey Rinpoche. He didn't withdraw the instruction, but he didn't insist, so we quietly slipped away. We worried that Rinpoche's prescience was warning us of some kind of danger and perhaps it was. As soon as we got back to Oxford, news came through that Trungpa Rinpoche looked as if he was about to die. Michael caught the next flight to Halifax. Although Rinpoche did recover that time he was back in hospital a few months later, expected to die very shortly. Michael once more went out to Halifax to be near him.

Meanwhile I was leading a Longchen retreat at Amaravati monastery, near Hemel Hempstead. We were earnestly praying for Rinpoche to remain with us and connecting to the power of his blessing as best we could while Michael sent us updates from Halifax whenever possible. The evening Rinpoche passed away, as I sat on my own in the dining room watching a brilliant red sun setting in the West, I felt a powerful sense of passing into another world that was both strangely familiar and yet deeply moving.

The year was 1987 and Rinpoche was only forty-seven. It was a huge blow for the Kagyu lineage to lose first the Karmapa and now such a great teacher who was still so young. Year by year there were ever fewer great lamas who had had a thorough training in Tibet. This was going to impact the training of the whole next generation of teachers.

Michael often talks about the profound effect it had on him to be present in the room where Trungpa Rinpoche's body was on display after he died. His heart remained warm for five days and during this period his students were allowed to meditate alongside him. A couple of months later Michael was back in America for the funeral. All this travelling to America had been very costly but I regret now that I didn't throw caution to the wind and just go with him anyway. I comfort myself that Michael had gone there on my behalf.

Khyentse Rinpoche presided over the funeral ceremonies in the company of various other eminent lamas. Michael was able to ask Khyentse Rinpoche about an idea Trungpa Rinpoche had talked to Michael about many years before, which was to build a lake and an island with a Guru Rinpoche image on it. Khyentse Rinpoche said it was a good idea and he should look for a lake and island west of London. Later that year in Paris, we asked him if he could be more precise, at which he marked a map of Britain telling us to look for a suitable place in north-west Wales. The hunt was on, but what exactly were we looking for?

Marrying Michael Hookham (now **Rigdzin Shikpo**) 1982, Swiss Cottage, London.

Rigdzin Shikpo, **Lama Denys**, **Khenpo Rinpoche**, **Karma Ozer** & myself, Dhagpo Kagyu Ling, 1990s. Rigdzin Shikpo & myself are wearing *Ngakpa* robes.

Dilgo Khyentse Rinpoche who directed us to make a base in Wales and build a stupa. Photograph printed with kind permission © Matthieu Ricard.

Khenpo Rinpoche and **Kalu Rinpoche** in Bodhgaya when I was attending Khenpo Rinpoche's teachings and visiting Kalu Rinpoche just before he died in 1989.

Khenpo Rinpoche tossing flowers from the palanquin that carried him up the drive on his last visit to the Hermitage, north-west Wales, 2005.

Khenpo Rinpoche and Ari Goldfield dancing with a dragon on the front lawn of the Hermitage, myself and Jonathan Shaw in the background, 2005.

Myself, **Rigdzin Shikpo** and **Lama Phuntsok** at the consecration of the stupa at the Hermitage, October 2011.

The Hermitage of the Awakened Heart and the Enlightenment stupa.

Fourteen

What is Buddha Nature?

The search for the lake and the island did not begin in earnest for some years, partly because we couldn't afford to buy a property and partly because I was too busy finishing writing up my thesis as a book.

During that period, I saw Kalu Rinpoche for the last time in Bodhgaya in India. It was my first time back in India since I had left twelve years before and I was there for Khenpo Rinpoche's course held at the Burmese Vihara guest house. It brought back poignant memories of living there as a simple Buddhist nun in my twenties with nothing in the world and without a care. Now I was a married woman in her forties with a home, responsibilities and bank account, my life and relationship with everything around me were so much more complex! I noticed this particularly when faced with the poverty of the local population. Strangely now I had more, I actually felt I could give less, at least in proportion to what I had. Bodhgaya had changed a lot since I had been there. Beautiful new temples had sprung up everywhere, sponsored by different Buddhist communities around the world and there were far more tourists among the pilgrims.

At the heart of Bodhgaya is an ancient 150-foot tall stupa, known as the Great Stupa, built on the spot where the Buddha is said to have attained Enlightenment. One morning I was sitting by the lotus pond in the park near the stupa, when I noticed a Tibetan woman in the middle distance, paying attention to a stray dog. It was so mangy it had lost all its fur and it was standing shivering pathetically. The Tibetan woman reached under her dress and pulled down her underskirt, laying it gently over the dog. I was so touched and at the same time reminded of Sherab Dolma, one of the five nuns in retreat with me in Sonada. It was so typical of her to do something like that. The woman came towards me and sure enough it was her! She cried out with delight when she saw me. She joined me on the bench and we excitedly exchanged news. She had got pregnant by one of the monks in the monastery and so was no longer a nun. Noting that I was no longer a nun either, she giggled and said, 'We are naughty nuns, aren't we? But the important thing is to repent our sins and practise loving kindness isn't it?' That is exactly what she had been doing and I was full of admiration for her.

Although I never spent a lot of time with Kalu Rinpoche, over the years we had many meetings and interchanges that have meant a lot to me. As so often happens with lamas with whom one has a significant connection, he always seemed to know me well and precisely, expressing this with startling simplicity. For me his special quality is the way he pervades one's being, a haunting presence that when remembered seems always to have been there – radiant, with a gentle but wry smile. I expect to see it on his face as I arrive at the threshold of Enlightenment, as if Rinpoche were wondering how it took me quite so long to get there, given there never was any non-Enlightenment.

Kalu Rinpoche often appears to people in dreams even if they have never met him. Soon after I met him I had a dream of him holding Denys's head in his lap and tears streaming down Rinpoche's face. It was very moving. Once I dreamt that he was whispering a profound instruction in Tibetan down a tube into my ear. He said, 'The Guru's and your heart/mind are inseparable. Don't let the mind be distracted. Give up questioning.' The older I get the more this simple piece of advice means to me.

The last time I had met him before this visit to Bodhgaya was at Karma Ling in Birmingham. As we filed by his throne to bid him goodbye at the end of his visit, we had each offered him a scarf and received a hand blessing on our head. As I bowed before him to receive my blessing he softly muttered, 'the Omniscient Dolpopa Sherab Gyaltsen'. This was the name of a famous 14th century lama of the Jonangpa school whose work I defended in my doctoral thesis, so I took him to be referring to that. As Michael followed me in line, he placed his hands on his head and said very softly, with a barely perceptible, mischievous smile, 'the wife of the Omniscient Dolpopa Sherab Gyaltsen.'

On arriving in Bodhgaya, I heard he was very sick, and although a public talk was advertised, we were warned he might be too tired to speak for long, if at all. In the event he spoke to a gathered crowd of perhaps a hundred Westerners for a full three hours without a break – tirelessly going over familiar ground, stressing the same points with the same enthusiasm and the same light sense of irony sparkling through as he spoke from his heart in a ceaseless outpouring of benign energy. Finally, he brought it all to a close, and leaning on the shoulder of his translator who had shown such remarkable stamina, he raised his tall and frail frame, and strode purposefully out of the room. I thought perhaps that this would be the last I would ever see of him. I was content with that.

To my surprise the next day I received a message saying that he wished to see me. Apparently, he had been trying by all manner and means to contact me over the preceding couple of years. He wanted me to join the team translating a multi-volumed 19th century work called the *Encyclopedia of Knowledge*. It was a project very dear to his heart and although I felt drawn to help with it, my other commitments wouldn't allow it. I was excited to have this opportunity to talk to him.

As I entered, I found Rinpoche sitting up on his bed – half reclining, his long thin and frail form wrapped in a soft white angora jumper. I prostrated and made my offering of fruit.

He thanked me, blessed me, and gestured to me to sit down. I sat at his feet, and he began to chat. 'What do you think of my translation project?' he enquired, and I said it was admirable and would be of great benefit to many people. 'How long do you think it will take?' he asked, and I said if everyone worked flat out then perhaps ten years. 'Oh, we will be dead by then,' he replied.

He asked after me and my husband and what we were doing by way of practice. I told him we were mainly practising devotion to Guru Rinpoche. He smiled and in an almost wistful tone, as if to himself said, 'Guru is Guru, Rinpoche is Rinpoche – Lama Rinpoche – very good.' These words, so simple and yet so profound, come to me again and again as the years go by. Why? They remind me that Guru Rinpoche is the essence and union of all my gurus. He was not some alien figure belonging to a different culture, time and place. I didn't have to think of him in any special iconographical form. He was real like my gurus, my lamas who embodied the lineage and linked me to its blessing power. As in the case of many Westerners, in spite of more than twenty years exposure to the forms of Tibetan Buddhism, and in spite of being convinced by the principles they represented, they did not in themselves evoke any particular response in me. It was as if Kalu Rinpoche could see this and was saying the iconographical forms were beside the point. What mattered was the guru, the lama, meaning all those who awaken us to our true nature, the essence of the lineage that brings Enlightenment into this world.

Kalu Rinpoche leaned back on his pillows, and gently ran his trembling, long, thin fingers along the edge of the sill beside him. 'Wherever I am, I am in retreat,' he informed me. 'But you've been travelling so much recently, Rinpoche, that's hardly retreat.' 'Sometimes I'm in retreat in the West, sometimes in the East, sometimes in the aeroplane, sometimes in the car or train. It's all the same, it's all retreat. It could be Karma Ling or Bodhgaya. It could be with lots of people. It could be when I am alone. It's all the same, always relaxed, nothing encroaches on my practice. It is like one long retreat...' As he spoke, I aspired to experience my life like that. 'Beyond meditation and non-meditation, then you can help everyone effortlessly.' Those were the first words the Karmapa ever said to me, and my heart had leapt to hear them. My whole aspiration in a nutshell, the deepest longing of my whole being. It is the simplicity that I intuited and longed for as a child. Looking at Kalu Rinpoche, his eyes shining with an inner strength and joy, I glimpsed something of how such a state would be and wondered at the blissful ease of it.

A few months after that Rinpoche died aged eighty-four: yet another reminder that a whole generation of great masters trained in Tibet was coming to an end. He had hoped to live to see the translation project completed. I sometimes wonder if he would have lived longer if I hadn't made it sound impossible!

About a year before this Khenpo Rinpoche had told Michael and me to do a three-year retreat together in our home in Beechey Avenue. We couldn't work out how, in practice, we could do a three-year retreat at the same time, so we arranged for me to help Michael on the understanding I would do a three-year retreat later.

Friends and neighbours were intrigued to learn that Michael was doing a three-year retreat in the back bedroom of a suburban semi. It caught their imagination as much if not more than if he had gone off and done it in a remote cave somewhere. He came downstairs at night to stretch his legs a bit and when he was not in meditation sessions he and I talked more or less as usual, which I think made it more challenging for both of us than if he had stayed completely in silence. However, it did enable me to keep alive the link between him and his students and to discuss with him what I was teaching them.

Khenpo Rinpoche had expected me to be practising along-side Michael during his retreat, which I did to some extent, but most of my time was taken up with bringing in the money, running the household, developing a distance course for new students, looking after our existing students and finishing off writing my thesis as a book. In other words, I was very busy and in retrospect I wonder if I should have been bolder and tried harder to find a way that we could both do the retreat together. It was a unique opportunity to be directed in a three-year retreat by Rinpoche, and I would have learnt more and translated Rinpoche's teachings much better had I been practising more alongside Michael.

Writing the distance course for new students was however an invaluable learning opportunity in its own right. The idea started with an eight-week so-called 'beginner's course' Michael had given in the weeks running up to his retreat. He was experimenting with a new way of presenting the experiential essence of the Dharma in terms of the three qualities of openness, clarity and sensitivity. These three words in English have rich resonances that relate to our immediate experience and what is important and meaningful in life. I like to point out that were we to say to our non-Buddhist friends we were going to a retreat to learn Buddhist practice, they might feel alienated. If we were to say we are doing it in order to become more open, clear and sensitive, I think they might encourage us enthusiastically saying 'Yes – do that for all our sakes!'

At first, I only intended to write up the transcripts of the course as study material for the group. Although it was supposed to be a course for beginners, as I started to teach from it, it quickly became evident that it was already advanced and needed a year-long course to break it down into digestible chunks. Even then, the one-year course often takes students several years, since it is experiential rather than intellectual in content and it takes time to plumb the depths of one's experience. Trying to break the course down like this was an illuminating experience for me from the point of learning how to teach Dharma here in the West. Similarly, listening to students struggling to understand and express their experience and noticing the way the nuances of English words affected them was a revelation to me as a translator, teacher and even as a practitioner. Although our aim was to go deeper, much of our discussion was about the power and effect of the words we were using.

It had taken me by surprise when Khenpo Rinpoche had told me I needed to learn Dharma in my own language and now I was beginning to understand how right he had been. Subsequently he said, 'The truth may lie beyond words, but words emerge from it and point back to it.' How words express meaning is quite magical!

Michael was not unaware of how problematic teaching Dharma can be. Before he began his three-year retreat, he had said to Khenpo Rinpoche, 'My students already say I am talking way over their heads. How is it going to be after three years in retreat?' Rinpoche laughed understandingly saying, 'Yes, there is that, but don't worry about it.' I took that to mean the benefits of his going deeper far outweighed his present concern and I for one was satisfied with that.

Rinpoche directed Michael's retreat by coming once or twice a year to stay a few days at Beechey Avenue as our honoured guest. There was not much room to spare, but somehow, we managed not only to host him, but also to clear the downstairs living room into a big enough space for him to give teachings to a room full of people crammed together, mostly sitting on the floor. This was at the same time as, unbelievably, Michael remained quietly in retreat upstairs.

Rinpoche's visits were joyful occasions. Many extraordinary things happened, often in the form of weird coincidences.

One day he told Michael that he should test his realisation by going into scary situations. 'Have you a roller coaster in this country?' he asked. 'Yes, in Blackpool,' we replied. 'Turn on the television,' he commanded. We did and our jaws dropped. On screen was a documentary about a man doing a record-breaking ride on the Blackpool roller-coaster for weeks on end!

Each time Rinpoche came he would ask Michael to tell him what experiences he had had since he was last there. Michael wouldn't know where to begin. What was significant and what was not? I was struggling as the translator. How can one translate another person's experience? I did my best and somehow Rinpoche picked up on what Michael was saying and vice versa. I say 'somehow' because whatever it was they were talking about was way beyond me! Most of the time I think Rinpoche and Michael were communicating directly mind to mind in some way and the translation was simply acting as an affirmation of this. Rinpoche sometimes told me to just relax and simply to listen to Michael and that would be enough. It was if he just needed me there to enable him to interject at the right moment. This became evident when I found myself between Michael and Rinpoche speaking to me at the same time, making it impossible for me to translate. Yet when I listened, I could tell they were both saying the same thing simultaneously in Tibetan and English respectively. It was as if their minds had completely merged and mine with theirs.

It is worth mentioning Guru Yoga again here and how it relates to the connection (*samaya*) between student and teacher. Literally Guru Yoga means union with the guru and for this the connection (*samaya*) with the teacher is vital. By means of *samaya* the yogic transformation of the body and mind is mysteriously brought about. Obviously, there is a limit to what I can say about this, but having seen first-hand the nature of that process at least in part puts me in a very privileged position. It feels like having had a glimpse into a whole different dimension of the Universe. I was amazed at what was being said and passing between us. So was Michael.

The way Rinpoche asked Michael questions about his experience showed he was checking for definite signs of what stage of the yogic process he was at. Mostly, while Michael talked, Rinpoche would from time to time simply say, 'Yes, and then?' Every so often, however, he would stop him abruptly and double-check, before suddenly giving extraordinary instructions and getting us to do bizarre things. For example, he might make us sing and dance very loudly and wildly for several hours until we were completely worn out -at which point, he would tell us to meditate. The pointing-out instructions that Rinpoche would give at such times often had quite a dramatic effect on Michael. These were oral instructions that could not be given to or in the presence of someone unsuitable. Not only could they be spiritually dangerous if misunderstood or misapplied, they were also a response to the specific situation that was unfolding between the teacher and student. Khenpo Rinpoche was at pains to impress on us that he could not have given the instructions he gave had I not had the necessary connection (*samaya*) for him to give me the teachings too. A translator without the necessary *samaya* would not have sufficed.

Being so intimately involved in what was going on between Rinpoche and Michael taught me a lot about the stages of the yogic process of transformation on the path to Enlightenment. Rinpoche explained that the stages can be dramatic or subtle depending on the individual and repeatedly emphasised that it was Michael's *samaya* with Trungpa Rinpoche that made it possible for him to teach him at this level.

Finally, Rinpoche said, 'I have given you absolutely everything. I have not held anything back – there is nothing else up my sleeve. It is now up to you to work on it and realise it for yourselves.' That was an amazing statement. There have been things that he taught us since that time, but I suppose he meant he had given us all the essentials. At the end of the retreat, Rinpoche told me that Michael's students and I should no longer call him Michael but instead should call him 'Rigdzin Shikpo' in recognition of his deep realisation. 'Rigdzin' (*Vidyadhara* in Sanskrit) means someone who has seen the profound nature of reality; 'Shikpo' literally means 'collapsed one', a kind of wastrel or layabout. There is a sense of irony here because wastrel in this context means that the yogin has achieved a state where all concepts have collapsed and as a result his mind is so relaxed that it seems completely lazy from an ordinary perspective. This is the name by which I have addressed him ever since. Rinpoche insisted that we never shorten his name to Rigdzin. If we shortened it at all, it must be to Shikpo. From then on Rinpoche always addressed us fondly as Rigdzin Shikpo and Shikmo – Shikmo being the female form of Shikpo.

Witnessing Rigdzin Shikpo's yogic process opened for me a dimension of what Vajrayana (Tantric) Buddhism was about that I hadn't even dreamed of. It also meant I knew I could trust Rigdzin Shikpo's experience and realisation as authentic because Khenpo Rinpoche had recognised it as such. In fact, Rinpoche had said that even before going into retreat Rigdzin Shikpo had the signs of yogic accomplishment. His doing the retreat would help his activity for the benefit of others because it would give others confidence in him – it was a recognisable outward sign that he had completed his training. In addition to this, what gives me confidence in him is that the more deeply I question him the more subtle and convincing are his answers. This is true even when his only answer is to say thoughtfully that he is wondering about something. It gives me the confidence to wonder about it too.

By the end of his retreat Rigdzin Shikpo had become a tremendously important influence and teacher for me, although he never took the place of Khenpo Rinpoche as my main teacher. It felt natural to treat him respectfully as my teacher at the same time as having a quite ordinary and straightforward marriage relationship with him. Ours was (and is) a deep Dharma relationship and much more than a marriage. Ultimately, as with all our heart-connections with others, it is not in time and space. Whatever happens we are forever inseparable. On this he and I are agreed.

The ending of Rigdzin Shikpo's retreat coincided with my thesis being published at last as 'The Buddha Within'. That was the culmination of ten years of work. What a load off my back! Shortly after it was published, I met Ringu Tulku Rinpoche, a lama who subsequently was to help both Rigdzin Shikpo and myself with encouragement and guidance on many occasions. Among his many other qualities, he was also an academic in the western sense and was one of the main examiners for *khenpo* degrees in Rumtek. He told me that he had read 'The Buddha Within', and I was eager to know what constructive criticism he might be able to make. 'Well,' he said, 'generally speaking when Westerners write on Buddhism there is always *something* they get wrong.' I waited to hear what it was in my own case. He then took me completely by surprise by saying that in the case of 'The Buddha Within' he didn't find anything wrong. I was relieved, although I would have expected there to be *something* wrong with it. Ringu Tulku Rinpoche also read the distance course I had written and told me it was just the kind of course students needed as a preliminary to doing other practices in Tibetan Buddhism. I think of it as introducing the Shentong view of Buddha Nature in a direct, intuitive way that uses a minimum of technical language. It is our nature of openness, clarity and sensitivity, which is our indestructible heart essence. We already can sense it in our heart of hearts.

It is taking me decades to realise the full significance of the Shentong view and its practical implications. In Buddhism a lot of emphasis is put on realising the non-reality of the conditioned, impermanent world which is without self-nature or true existence (i.e. self-empty, *rangtong*) and that taking it to be real is the cause of suffering. This in itself is not enough though. One has also to take on board the unconditioned that remains when all that is false falls away. It is not something that one can grasp with the conceptual mind, but that doesn't mean it is not there. Through proper instruction we can discover it within our experience and use it as the basis for our meditation practice. The unconditioned is our changeless Buddha Nature, but is ever ungraspable and in that sense, perhaps, mystical.

In retrospect I realise that when I rejected my childhood intuition of an all-pervading goodness that I called God, I had to a certain extent rejected an important aspect of Buddhism. As a child I had found so much inspiration and comfort in St John's Gospel, particularly 14:20:

'On that day you will realise that I am in my Father, and you are in me, and I am in you.'

Yet that had been no different from what I now recognised as the all-pervading presence of the Buddha Nature.

By focusing so strongly on the nature of mind, I had somehow been splitting my mind from my heart and my intuitively devotional side. I had dropped the doctrinal side of Christianity with such ease because I probably never really believed in it. What I loved wasn't the belief system, but what the word 'God' intuitively meant to me. I know I am not alone in this. I meet many Buddhists for whom God-language is profoundly meaningful and for whom Buddhism has helped appreciate more deeply what truth may lie within the Christian tradition. Tibetans seem less surprised by this possibility than Westerners are. Indeed, the Dalai Lama has famously said on many occasions that for many people it is better to stick to their own religion than to convert to Buddhism. Presumably he says this because he senses there is at least some truth in other religions and also because he realises how difficult it is to successfully go through the whole process of changing one's religion. On the other hand, many Western Buddhists have very negative associations with Christianity and God-language and for them the attraction of Buddhism is that it seems completely different in its approach. For them it is more scientific than mystical. Indeed, that is what first attracted me.

Maybe it is because of this that for a long time, I translated the term 'bodhichitta' as Enlightened Mind rather than Awakened Heart. Both are acceptable translations. By focusing so strongly on nature of mind without using the word heart very much, Enlightenment or Awakening seemed to be more about insight into the nature of mind than about the love, compassion and joy we feel in our heart.

Again, faith can be understood as a response from the heart. If we talk only in terms of the nature of mind, faith doesn't seem to come into it. Although *chitta* is both heart and mind, it makes a big difference in practice whether we translate bodhichitta as Awakened Heart or as Enlightened Mind. Because the true nature of mind is also our true heart, glimpses of insight into the true nature of mind, open or awaken the heart, so qualities such as faith, love, joy and compassion can shine forth.

We all experience longing in our hearts because of our primordially existing Buddha Nature. This is the bodhichitta longing for all beings to be happy and free from suffering. When fully emerged, it will have the power to effortlessly respond to the needs of all beings and bring them to Enlightenment. What a fantastic message for the world!

When Khenpo Rinpoche met up with me again each year instead of asking me how I was, he would ask if my bodhichitta was increasing. I used to think he meant was my thinking changing. Was I becoming less selfish and thinking more about others? He might have meant this, but I now suspect he was more interested in whether I was realising my true nature which is not so much *thinking* as simply letting go into the spacious, all-pervading goodness of the Buddha Nature. We learn how we can help everyone without having to *do* anything. As the Karmapa said to me, 'When you go beyond meditation and non-meditation then you can help everyone easily.'

In other words, our true nature is love. This is similar to the teachings of some theistic religions. Once I was watching a video of a conference in which the director of the World Community for Christian Meditation explained that in Christianity, ultimate reality is equated with love. The Dalai Lama, who was also a speaker, looked very interested and acknowledged that there were Buddhist schools that also taught that. These were the schools whose interpretation of Buddha Nature conformed to the Shentong view that I had written about in my thesis.

Gendun Rinpoche used to say, 'You let go of what isn't, and you rest in what is,' and would roar with laughter, yet I wondered what he was talking about when he said 'rest in what is'. He would refer to 'the real', sometimes as the 'clear light' or the nature of mind, but most often as 'the Guru'. This puzzled me because I had always thought from my first encounter with Buddhism that to say something was real was to grasp at concepts and therefore to be wrong by definition.

Eventually I found myself re-examining the idea I had had for a long time that the Buddha taught there is no self. This is what all the school text books on the subject say. Yet the Buddha didn't say this exactly. What he said was that the truth lies beyond all concepts, including the concept that the self is conditioned and impermanent. He used self for our true nature which is actually unconditioned and beyond concepts. In all the pointing-out instructions I had had from my teachers I was taught to notice that whatever I *thought* was my self was just a concept, to let go of it and then to rest in my own true nature.

Who thinks of their true nature as fleeting and illusory? Doesn't the very term suggest an ineffable reality beyond concepts?

Nature of mind, bodhichitta, Buddha Nature, indestructible heart essence, all-pervading love, the Guru, and ultimate reality are all names pointing to that ineffable reality beyond concepts. As a child this is what the word 'God' evoked for me. I already had an intuition of what I was looking for. By turning my back so completely on God, I had closed my mind to it. No wonder it took me so long to relate to all the devotional aspects of Buddhism. As a child, in turning towards God, my thinking mind would stop momentarily and I would find myself in a state of open wonder that included everything, a mysterious place, full of meaning, that was overwhelmingly good – words like 'holy' and 'glorious' come to mind here. What I was lacking was a teacher and a path to take that fleeting intuition deeper.

So there I was after all those years of following my Buddhist teachers re-discovering what I had intuited as a child! It is hard to explain how it is that the spiritual path yields insights that are so fresh and new, yet, you kind of knew them all along. You know your understanding and experience are deepening yet the way you describe them sounds just the same as before.

For a long time I had thought I understood emptiness when all I was seeing was what is termed self-emptiness, the fleeting nature of experience. Once when the Dalai Lama was giving a series of talks about emptiness, he explained how the way things appear to us is actually illusion, implying that simply to realise this would end all our suffering. Eventually someone asked the obvious question. 'Are you saying that all beings are illusions? If so, what would it mean to have compassion for illusions?' The Dalai Lama just laughed. I am not sure why because it was an important question. On another occasion he dismissed a similar question as too technical to answer simply. I assumed he was alluding to the

Rangtong/Shentong controversy and I appreciated his difficulty.

Some years later, after talking for hours about how everything is empty like a dream and an illusion, someone asked Khenpo Rinpoche the same question. 'What is the use of having compassion for beings if they are not real?' Khenpo Rinpoche was silent for a moment or two, then stated boldly and authoritatively, 'Beings are real and it is important to realise that.' He was clearly speaking from the Shentong point of view at that point, but he didn't say so.

We know other people are not just our imagination and to doubt their existence is madness. That is why when as a child I asked my mother how she knew she existed she was so scared. Yet, already I was noticing that there were no logical arguments to prove it. In other words, all our moral arguments take the existence of people and even their importance as axiomatic.

What this demonstrates is that our sanity depends on our intuitive wisdom and our rationality as humans hangs on this. Logical reasoning could drive us mad. What we rely on is an intuitive sense of what is right and good and we know this in our hearts. The wisdom in our hearts is our Buddha Nature. We sense that and talk to each other about the heart intuitively without resorting to conceptual analysis. We know it's beyond concepts.

When Bokar Rinpoche described to us all the amazing qualities of the Buddha such as his physical appearance with golden skin and mound on his head and so on, it meant nothing to us. As soon as we were told the Buddha was in our heart, Buddha suddenly meant something. Connecting to the Buddha means connecting to our hearts. This still doesn't tell us what the Buddha is though. When I asked Kalu Rinpoche all those years ago he told me the Buddha was the Guru. The trouble was I didn't know what the Guru was either.

I got an inkling one day when I came across Bokar Rinpoche sitting staring into space in amazement. On becoming aware of my presence, he slowly turned his eyes towards me and said, 'Kalu Rinpoche'. I waited and then after a moment or two he said, 'He is Buddha!' as if he had just had a profound shock. I wonder to this day what he had seen exactly. Recognising one's teacher is Buddha is a major revelation next only to realising one's own mind is Buddha.

Fifteen

Becoming a Lama

'You should stay in retreat here for one year,' announced Khenpo Rinpoche suddenly as Rigdzin Shikpo and I were about to leave Lama Denys's centre, Karma Ling in the French Alps, where Khenpo Rinpoche had been giving a week of teachings. I changed my plans on the spot. Lama Denys provided me with one of the retreat cabins in the enclosed compound where the three-year retreatants stayed and arranged for me to be supplied with food from the retreatants' kitchen. Thus, without more ado, I embarked on a year-long retreat.

It was in the period after Rigdzin Shikpo's three-year retreat had finished. I had stayed several times at Karma Ling over the years, sometimes in retreat, sometimes teaching short courses. Lama Denys was always very generous, hospitable, and eager that we all work closely together for the Dharma. Many a time Denys and I talked for hours on end about Dharma and our ideas around how to set up Buddhist communities in the West.

I didn't fully realise it at the time, but in retrospect, I can see that I was at a critical point in my life. I could feel that something was changing between Rigdzin Shikpo and myself, but I couldn't quite put my finger on what was happening. Trying to build a sangha in the West was proving complicated and even stressful. We lacked a shared vision of what we were trying to do exactly. The year I spent in retreat in Karma Ling was a welcome respite – a return to the simple life I always longed for.

As the months went by, I watched in contentment as the position of the sun each evening set further and further north over the rocky peaks of the valley, the slopes of which rose steeply either side of us. As the days got shorter it got colder and colder. There was no heating in my cabin, so at night I wrapped myself up in every article of clothing I had with me. My computer made ominous crackling noises from the cold, but to its credit, survived the winter. Fortunately, I could spend my days in a small, warm shrine room that nobody else was using, a few yards away from my retreat cabin. As well as many hours of meditation, I also spent time studying the Mahayana Sutras and the life of Milarepa in Tibetan. At my suggestion Lama Denys had invited Karma Ozer to come from India to live at Karma Ling as part of the community. It was a great joy to me when she was able to visit me in retreat as it was a chance to ask her Dharma questions and practise speaking Tibetan, not to mention have a good laugh. Each evening a blackbird would sing its heart out from the top of the fir tree opposite my cabin, touching my heart.

Sadly, during that retreat, my eldest brother died, aged fifty, from a brain tumour. He left a wife and five boys, the youngest of whom was barely three years old. Mercifully my mother had died several years before that happened; she would have found that situation very upsetting. I rang my father when I received the news about my brother's illness and told him I was wondering if I should break my retreat to come and see him. My father said, 'I wouldn't bother if I were you. Neither of you ever made much effort to keep in touch before he was ill, so what is the point now? Even if you came you would just be chatting away as if nothing was happening. That's how he's handling the situation.' I got the sense that I was better off staying where I was, making strong connections for him through my prayers rather than letting myself be distracted from my retreat. Rigdzin Shikpo attended the funeral on my behalf, for which I was very grateful. Sometime later Bokar Rinpoche passed through

Paris on one of his rare visits to the West. I agonised on whether to break retreat to go and see him but in the end simply asked Karma Ozer to take a letter from me explaining my situation. He replied saying how glad he was that I was in retreat. Little did either of us know this was our final communication with each other.

When my retreat ended the next summer, I spent several happy weeks having a fun time in Karma Ling, joining in various activities such as belly and whirling dervish dancing and swimming in a nearby lake. Rigdzin Shikpo joined us for a few days and I have fond memories of his trying to learn to swim in the lake, with Karma Ozer in fits of giggles, trying to conceal his modesty with a towel!

Khenpo Rinpoche came a week or so later to teach at Karma Ling. He was in the mood for fun too and one afternoon we all watched him and Lama Denys have a go at hang-gliding from a nearby hill resort. Strapped in behind his pilot, Khenpo Rinpoche sang happily all the way down about the vast open space of emptiness. That was a first for the pilot who was highly amused by his unusual passenger. For Rinpoche, the next stop after Karma Ling was our home in Oxford so off we all went together by car to the airport.

To my surprise, as we left Karma Ling, I found tears were streaming down my face and I couldn't stop crying for a long time. Rinpoche noticed it and remarked that anyone would think I was leaving my lover behind. I was puzzled. Although I felt sad to be leaving as I had enjoyed myself so much, the tears seemed to come more from a sense of foreboding about what was waiting for me in Oxford. In Karma Ling my life had been easy. I had been among good friends and completely free of responsibilities. Back in Oxford things were going to be very different and I hardly knew what to expect after a year away.

While Rinpoche was with us at Beechey Avenue it was as wonderful as ever to be there, but soon after he had gone, I started to get the strange feeling that I was like a ghost hanging around a home that had been taken over by others. It was as if I didn't belong there anymore.

Rinpoche had told Rigdzin Shikpo that having done a retreat in Oxford, the centre of Britain, he should now do retreats on all the coasts, to bless the whole Isle of Britain. It was a wonderful idea, but Rigdzin Shikpo wasn't keen, and was quite happy when Rinpoche told me to do them instead. I undertook these retreats over the next six months. I would sit or stand for hours in meditation looking out to sea – at the distant horizon and beyond, into infinite space. Yet the uneasy feeling that something was wrong between Rigdzin Shikpo and myself grew ever stronger. I hoped that if we moved to Wales as Khyentse Rinpoche had directed, things would improve, so after my retreats on the coasts, I focused on finding a place in Wales.

Almost a decade earlier, when Khyentse Rinpoche had told us to look for a lake and island in north-west Wales, we had immediately found a property with a lake and an island there, called Tyn y Gors. Dilgo Khyentse Rinpoche had done a divination and said it was a suitable place for our residence, but not *the* place. Rigdzin Shikpo wondered if his saying '*the* place' meant we were looking for a sacred place, something that in Tibetan Buddhism is referred to as a hidden land. We kept looking, sending Khyentse Rinpoche lists of place names that felt sacred to us and of these he named two areas as special and told us to find suitable land for sale there. I had kept up the search while Rigdzin Shikpo was in retreat and I also went out to Nepal to ask Khyentse Rinpoche for more details about his vision so we had a better idea of what we were looking for. Khyentse Rinpoche told me we should take our time finding the place because it would last for hundreds of years. He also said that when we found it, we should build a purpose-built temple or stupa there. As for a hidden land, he replied, that was in the heart.

While Rigdzin Shikpo was in his three-year retreat, I and a few other Longchen students were out on Madryn Mountain, one of the areas Khyentse Rinpoche had named as special, when the news came through by mobile that Khyentse Rinpoche had passed away in Bhutan. With Trungpa Rinpoche, the Karmapa and Kalu Rinpoche gone already, it was like being plunged into ever gathering darkness. How were we to find *the* place now? Khenpo Rinpoche told us not to worry, but to look for what we felt were good places to meditate and to practise there, drawing the blessing of the Dharma into them to increase their sacred power.

Ever since Khyentse Rinpoche had told us Tyn y Gors was a good place for our residence, I found my mind kept returning to it, even though it had now been sold. We looked at other properties but never found one we liked anywhere near as much. As we were driving past it one day, we somewhat cheekily dropped a note through the owners' door telling them that if they ever wanted to sell, we would be interested in buying. We didn't expect a reply, but a couple of years later, the owners suddenly wrote to us asking if we were still interested. This time, thanks to the generosity of our students, we managed to get enough money together for a mortgage.

So, after ten years of having thought about it, we were actually moving to Tyn y Gors at last. I was ecstatic. After being cooped up in a suburban semi for years, Rigdzin Shikpo and I were suddenly the proud owners of an extended six-bedroomed farmhouse with a conservatory housing a very fine grapevine. It included ten acres of land and a small lake with an island, at the foot of a hill famous for the fortified iron-age village on its summit. It is in an area steeped in history and legends, including that of a Druid priest telling his chieftain disciple to retrieve from a cave in the side of that hill a sacred wisdom text in a casket guarded by demons. It is an exact parallel to the stories from Tibet about treasure texts hidden by Guru Rinpoche being revealed by yogins called Tertons.

Both Rigdzin Shikpo and I felt it was a very special place, almost as if it were in a different dimension of reality, especially when shouting the mantra of Guru Rinpoche across the lake and listening to its echo clearly repeating itself from the hill opposite, *'Om Ah Hum Vajra Guru Padma Siddhi Hum!'* It was as if Guru Rinpoche himself were calling to us. The plan was for Rigdzin Shikpo to spend half his time in retreat in Wales and half his time teaching in Oxford. In the event he chose to spend the majority of his time in Oxford, while I remained in Wales taking care of Tyn y Gors.

I was devastated to find Rigdzin Shikpo and myself living separately like this, but it spurred me on to to develop as a Dharma teacher in my own right. I had begun teaching Dharma in a small way as soon as I arrived in Oxford giving a few talks at the University Buddhist Society and other places such as Worcester, London, France, Germany and Gampo Abbey in Canada. I had been present to give spiritual guidance at the deaths of several students and been asked to preside at their funerals. The more I taught, the more I realised that teaching was a spiritual path in itself because it forced me to gather my thoughts and reflect on what I genuinely knew for myself from direct experience.

I sometimes visited and still do visit an old lama called Lama Lodro at Karma Ling in Birmingham. He spends most of his time in semi-retreat. 'These days anyone who knows a bit of Dharma sets themselves up as a teacher,' he told me almost disdainfully. 'I have practised all my life and I don't presume to sit in front of lots of people to teach.' I considered the matter seriously before replying, 'When I give a Dharma talk, I find I say things I didn't realise I knew until I said them. From then on, I try to really practise what I have just said, so it's not just words.' The Lama looked thoughtful. 'That sounds good,' he replied as if reconsidering his position. 'That way you help yourself and help others at the same time.' This reassured me but at the same time led me to reflect on just what I thought I was doing trying to teach Dharma at this point.

Originally I had not intended to become a Dharma teacher until I was Enlightened so I am pausing here to consider what happened exactly to change my mind. Thinking back, I realise that it was my teachers who had brought about this change. From my earliest years in India first Karma Thinley Rinpoche, then Kalu Rinpoche and later Bokar Rinpoche had talked to me as if it were a given that I would be teaching and helping to spread Dharma in the West. When Bokar Rinpoche was giving me instructions, he surprised me by saying, 'You should practise like this for three years before starting to teach.' It seemed far too soon to me. Yet within a couple of years of his saying that the Karmapa sent me back to England to teach 'all I knew'. A few years later again Khenpo Rinpoche told me to study so I could answer people's questions obviously on the assumption I would be teaching. All this led me to conclude that it is enough to be able to glimpse and have confidence in the true nature of mind in order to help others on their way, at least to some extent.

When the Karmapa sent me back to England, I was not convinced that the way I had been taught was either suitable or possible in the West. I needed time to think deeply about how to share what I'd learned. However, having to translate Gendun Rinpoche's instructions pointing out the nature of mind was almost like having to give them myself. I was looking for words to express what I had understood experientially from the Lama. This meant I had to reflect deeply both on what I had understood and the words I was using to express that understanding. In other words, I was reflecting on how best to teach Dharma in English.

When Khenpo Rinpoche had told Rigdzin Shikpo and me to teach he told us, 'I don't really know the best way to teach

Westerners, because I don't know the language and culture the way you do. You are going to have to work it out for yourselves. Don't get bogged down in problems inherited from the complexities of Tibetan history and culture.' This made sense because I understood what it was like being a Westerner from the inside and could be a bridge between two radically different languages, cultures and world views. There were so many wrong assumptions that my Tibetan teachers kept making about their western students, and vice versa.

The last time Khenpo Rinpoche visited Tyn y Gors, just as he was leaving, he called Rigdzin Shikpo and me into his room, where he had laid out two sets of his robes along the back of the couch. Then rather shyly he said, 'Please don't think I am just off-loading old clothes on you. We Tibetans have a custom where the lama gives his robes to his disciples and it is considered an honour.' He then gave one set to Rigdzin Shikpo and one to me. It did indeed feel a great honour and an affirmation of the trust he had in us as Dharma teachers.

After I had been teaching my own sangha for a while, one of my students came to me and said, 'Are you a lama?' She had just returned from a weekend course on Mahamudra where it had been stressed that for this kind of instruction you had to have a lama, hence her question to me. 'It is true that you have to have a lama,' I said, 'But I don't know if I can say I am one.' Did I count as a lama? In those days the term 'lama' was almost synonymous with being a Tibetan monk and more particularly a monk who had done a three-year retreat in a retreat centre.

At the next opportunity I asked Khenpo Rinpoche what I should answer my student. He said, 'Say "yes" of course.' It was as simple as that. So you could say that is how I became a lama. I didn't use the title but did allow the fact to be known that Khenpo Rinpoche had said I was able to fulfil the function of a lama in the context of teaching Mahamudra. My students needed to know it. Eventually some of my students talked amongst themselves and decided they wanted to call me 'Lama Shenpen'. They thought it accurately reflected their relationship with me and would help other people understand the opportunity I presented as a teacher. I didn't encourage them, but I didn't stop them either; their thinking made sense.

Having the title of lama is not without its problems. The very title itself invites projections of various kinds. However, to say one is *not* a lama seems to imply that one is not qualified to teach. There are problems whether one uses the title or not. One reason for this is that the term is used in such a general way that it is unclear what it implies even among Tibetans, let alone among Westerners. Although it is a translation for the Sanskrit term Guru, it is often used loosely for any monk or teacher of Dharma. It *should* imply a person with good *samaya* connections playing the role of guru for students who have faith and good *samaya* with him or her. It doesn't have to mean an Enlightened person, even though this would be ideal. Someone like myself with good *samaya* connections can play the role for students who have confidence in them to teach from their own experience. In other words, I am good enough to link students with faith in me to the lineage of Awakening.

It has not been easy trying to educate my students as to the meaning of the term 'lama'. On one occasion I was in a conversation with Khenpo Rinpoche and told him that my students had difficulty with the concept of lama. 'That is a problem Westerners have made up for themselves,' he said. 'It is nothing to do with us Tibetans. We don't have a problem with the term lama.' I was shocked by his response and the sharpness with which it was delivered. It triggered such a reaction in me that I couldn't contain myself. This was a serious issue that I as a Western teacher needed help with. Tibetan teachers needed help with it too if they were to teach Westerners. What did he mean by saying it was nothing to do with the Tibetans? In retrospect, I realise the

strength of his reaction was a sign that he had been triggered too. He must have had a lot of trouble with Westerners misunderstanding what 'guru' or 'lama' meant. He was
probably as frustrated about it as I was. I didn't think that
at the time though. Oh no! I was just triggered.

I stood up and stormed out of the room. I stormed downstairs into the hall and when people asked me what was the
matter and where I was going I simply brushed them aside
and strode out of the main door. I charged off down the
nearest lane and kept going with my mind more or less a
blank – blank with rage and frustration.

At last, after five or ten minutes, I cooled off. I came to my
senses. I realised I had been rude to walk off like that and
so I had better make reparation. I was still upset. Nevertheless, I needed to apologise for my rudeness. I walked slowly
back to Rinpoche's room. I knocked and he called out to say
'Come in.' He was standing by the partition door and he
looked at me attentively. 'Yes?' 'I have come to apologise
for my rudeness.' There was a moment of silence as he continued to look at me attentively and then said, 'Right. Now
you know what ego-clinging is.' How did that land with me?
Well, it caused me pause for thought. The guru is there to
cut through our ego-clinging and that is what he did. Later
in the day he gave a Dharma talk to all of us and in it clarified
many points in regard to the guru or lama. He *had* heard me
and he tried his best to help, but there still remains a whole
nest of interrelated issues around language, culture and assumed conceptual frameworks that needs sorting out. It is
true that we need the guru to cut through our conceptual
grasping, our fixed ideas, habitual patterns and ego-clinging,
but not all our teachers know us well enough to do this. Furthermore we need the guru to play a good many other roles
for us as well. Over the years I have written reams and
reams about the guru-teacher relationship and yet it is only
now that I feel I have enough understanding to write a book
on it.

After moving to Wales, every few weeks I travelled down to Oxford to teach the beginner's course I had been developing. After my talk on one of these occasions, a twenty-year-old undergraduate called Jonathan Shaw remarked that my teachings were good and asked why, therefore, did I not have more students. I told him I didn't know how to attract more, at which he asked, 'How many students would you like?' I told him I wanted enough students to form a viable sangha community. 'The more students there are, the more they can support each other and the more we can do to bring genuine Dharma into the world,' I said. 'Fifty to a hundred would be a good number to start off with.' Jonathan boldly announced he would get them for me. Ten years later, his older self remarked, 'So much for the arrogance of youth!' Be that as it may, his entry into my life transformed it.

He came up to Wales for several weeks in his summer vacation and plied me with every kind of question about Dharma and what my vision was for the sangha. Since I was living on my own, I had plenty of time to try to answer all his questions, so we talked for hours on end. He set to work on planning how to publicise and deliver the distance learning course I had written in collaboration with Rigdzin Shikpo. Rigdzin Shikpo was no longer interested in that course. Since coming out of retreat he was fired up with ideas for a whole new course that he wanted to teach. This developed into a series of new courses as time went on. In this way he gradually made it clear to me that he wanted the Longchen Foundation to be about his own Dharma teaching activity. He was supportive of the idea that I have a separate charitable trust for mine. This left me free to continue to develop and teach the distance learning course on my own. Jonathan helped me to set up a charity, a website and the marketing for it. It was exciting starting something completely new. When we were all ready to go Jonathan called me to his desk and said, 'This is the point of no return. When I press this button we will roll. Is it yes or no?' 'Yes!' I cried and with a cheer we went for it and never looked back.

We called the course 'Discovering the Heart of Buddhism' which has since become just one part of a lifetime of experiential and structured training called 'Living the Awakened Heart'. Students started to enrol online at a steady rate, each with their personal mentor, of whom we had very few to start with. We were learning as we went about what was needed and how to do things. In order to build up a sense of community where students could meet me and each other we held events in London and retreats in Wales. A few students came to join us as residents at Tyn y Gors and a handful of local people started to show interest. After a year or so I had a small, widely scattered community of people who identified themselves as my students. The community needed a name and a sense of direction. I called it the 'Awakened Heart Sangha' and started working on a follow-up course for my longer-term students.

Although I was sorry that Rigdzin Shikpo and I were working separately, in retrospect I can see that it was good for my students that I had that independence. Rigdzin Shikpo and I kept in touch and I continued to learn from him, spending many a happy hour in conversation with him either in Oxford or Tyn y Gors. Working separately was more about a difference in *modus operandi* than of any disagreement in principle. We were and still are very different in the way we approach the student-teacher relationship, due to differences between us of personality, conditioning and experience. When we worked together, I tended to defer to him and think of the students as chiefly his students and myself as an assistant. Working independently allowed my students to work with me as their main teacher without any confusion. From the beginning Rigdzin Shikpo was always very supportive of our sangha, accepting many invitations to teach us. He says he feels a close affinity with my students and enjoys teaching them; so much so that he sometimes carries on talking to us for hours after the end of the scheduled programme. Since I regard Rigdzin Shikpo as one of my most important teachers, his generosity and support for our sangha gives my students a strong sense of authenticity and connection to the lineage.

Jonathan and I wanted to develop Tyn y Gors as a retreat centre and an administrative hub for our sangha community. It soon became clear that this did not fit with Rigdzin Shikpo's vision for the place and things became somewhat uncomfortable. For the next few years, Jonathan and I kept our eye out for another property where I could live and develop the Awakened Heart Sangha. Meanwhile I wanted a quiet place where I could live alone in semi-retreat. No sooner had I articulated this wish to Jonathan than he found one. He came bursting into my office saying, 'Guess what! Wyn is the nicest person in the world!' Wyn was a lonely Welsh farmer who was normally very retiring, but who had surprised me the first time I met him by saying that I was welcome to come and visit him any time, even if I was not going to buy his farmhouse, the original purpose of my visit. He had obviously taken a liking to me. On his land was a small, almost derelict, cottage that I had fallen in love with. I had seen a hare run past in front of us the first time we approached it, which added to its magic and charm.

As soon as Jonathan asked if I could rent it, Wyn had readily agreed. He was not commercially minded at all and hesitantly asked me what I thought the rent should be. Once that was settled, I moved in the same day, with my students loaded with my stuff, splashing through muddy fields in the rain with poorly packed blankets trailing in the puddles. Dear Wyn had carried up loads of wood and got a roaring fire going, to dry the place out a bit. As I waved everyone off that night, it was with a sigh of relief that I settled to my evening meditation. I felt I was back in my element, the simple life.

There was no road access, so I had to approach it on foot through fields of sheep and it was easy to miss my way in the mist and fog. Yet on a clear day, I could see Tyn y Gors a few miles away and the view across the hills and sea was stunning. The cottage was leaky, and the window frames were so rotten they were only held in place by annual layers of paint. There was no running water; only a simple well outside with a bucket and some milk churns to store the water. Although there was a sort of outside loo there was no plumbing or bathroom.

'Are you not frightened living up here all on your own?' Wyn asked after a week or two. I could only say that it never occurred to me to be afraid. Although I am not psychic at all, it felt as if I was being welcomed there by the local deities. Wyn couldn't do enough for me and we became good friends. Thus started a three-year period of my life in semi-retreat. Rigdzin Shikpo, Khenpo Rinpoche and Ponlop Rinpoche came and blessed the place while I was there and Khenpo Rinpoche named it Wenling, meaning 'remote place'. While I remained in Wenling, Jonathan and my other students carried on living and working at Tyn y Gors.

Khenpo Rinpoche came to visit Oxford and Tyn y Gors a number of times over the following years. His visits were inspiring, galvanising and fun with plenty of yogic singing, dancing and hilarity. From the early eighties onwards, he emphasised the importance of singing songs of yogic realisation – predominantly songs of the great yogin saint Milarepa and his own spontaneous compositions. Early in the morning when I took him his tea in bed, he might suddenly sit bolt upright and start composing a yogic song extemporaneously, about the drinking of the tea or the clouds he could see out of the window. 'How amazing that it isn't there, but it appears!' he might say with a look of wide-eyed astonishment. Whatever was happening was an inspiration for a Dharma song. 'Sing a song!' he would say cheerfully to his students. It was one of the few phrases he knew in

English. He often handed the words of a song to a translator to translate and put to a melody by the next day – sometimes even on the spot. These were songs of deep realisation that were difficult to translate at the best of times, but even more so when under pressure of such a tight deadline! However, it turned out that these songs were destined to be sung by hundreds of people all over the world for years to come.

Rinpoche's idea was that by singing yogic songs with language and melodies that we as Westerners found easy to relate to, we could sing them over and over again until we knew them by heart. Once we knew them by heart, because of the power of the blessing of the lineage, he sensed the deep meaning of the songs would come through, in spite of any mistakes in the translation. For many people this is what happened. Although the melodies and translators' choice of words were not always to my taste, particularly when compared with the haunting melodies of the songs I had heard my friend Tenpa and his mother singing in Tibetan, over the years I came to appreciate that in fact Rinpoche had hit on a brilliant teaching strategy. For many people with busy lives in the modern world, being able to bring to mind these songs has been a lifeline – the most effective means of keeping their practice going through good times and bad.

Rinpoche had a gift for creating a wild party atmosphere at the drop of a hat. Sometimes, unbelievably, he would start us off at breakfast time. 'Dance around the table as if you were drunk!' he would say, and we all would find ourselves swaying and stumbling round the breakfast table, singing at the top of our voices. Rinpoche would be rolling about giggling and telling us to sing even louder and jump even higher. 'Let go and relax more and more into appearance-emptiness, sound-emptiness, bliss-emptiness, awareness-emptiness,' he would say. Then he would suddenly snap his fingers and tell us to settle into meditation right there and then. After several minutes he would snap them again telling us that this was how we should cut through our concepts. From morning to night he would find ways to cut through our concepts like this.

Since Rigdzin Shikpo did not want the Awakened Heart Sangha to have its headquarters at Tyn y Gors, Jonathan and I wondered whether it made sense to start another centre close by or would it be better to move far away, perhaps even to England, Ireland or Scotland? I didn't know how to make up my mind so in 2002 I asked Rinpoche for his advice. Rinpoche's response was to tell Rigdzin Shikpo quite forcefully, 'You live in Oxford, you don't need Tyn y Gors. Shenpen supported you in retreat for three years. Now you should support her to do a three-year retreat in Tyn y Gors.' He told me to continue teaching from time to time over the course of my retreat, but to do nothing else. Rigdzin Shikpo agreed to this plan, but it soon became clear that he wanted Tyn y Gors to be available for his students to use for retreat as well. This didn't fit with my students being there to look after me. Something had to give. Would Rinpoche be satisfied if I could find a suitable place nearby?

He said he would be and by some miracle, which I always attribute to his blessing, I found a property just twenty minutes' drive away, twice as big but for the same price that we'd paid for Tyn y Gors. Even though we took a year to come up with the money, once the price had been agreed the owners waited for us, steadfastly refusing to put the place back on the market despite pressure from the estate agents, saying, 'We have given our word and we will stick by it.' I am sure the karmic result of their doing so will connect them to the path of Awakening forever! Bless them.

When the exchange of contracts finally came through, we were in the middle of a month's group retreat at Tyn y Gors. Jonathan had carefully prepared everything in advance in case this happened and with unbelievable efficiency he stage-managed us to move house and continue our retreat at the new house within just a matter of days. Even more remarkably, since Khenpo Rinpoche happened to be in the country at that time, we fitted in a weekend Lama-visit, before settling back into retreat for another two weeks. The timing had been perfect for Rinpoche to be there to thoroughly bless the place on our arrival. He named it Changchub Dzong, Citadel of Awakening.

We called it 'The Hermitage of the Awakened Heart' and 'the Hermitage' for short. Although in general everything had gone smoothly, in fact on the day we arrived, almost the first thing that happened was someone's chair leg went through a hole in the floor, causing much hilarity. All through the rest of the retreat we noticed a strong musty smell of mushrooms in that room, but at no point did we suspect a connection between this and the hole in the floor. After the retreat however, we found the cause of both – we were infested with dry rot – a magnificent mushrooming growth sending out its hyphae and spores, with the potential to destroy the whole house. I was impressed with how such a delicate thing could undermine the whole edifice of a solid stone building, just as the subtle wisdom of insight can undermine the whole edifice of samsara. The dry rot proved easier to remedy than samsara though. It was costly and inconvenient at the time, but that was all.

From then on when Rinpoche came to visit Tyn y Gors he also visited the Hermitage. Towards the end of one of these occasions he told Rigdzin Shikpo and myself to accompany him to Holy Isle, just off the Isle of Arran in Scotland. 'I feel that it is a place where yogins have practised in the past and I want all my students to practise there too,' he told us. He took us to the cave on the island where a 6th century Christian saint had meditated. Like other Tibetan lamas he had no problem with the idea that saints of other religions might be yogins or siddhas and honoured them accordingly. There were about a hundred people from many different countries on his week-long course on Holy Isle, where again he had us singing yogic songs and dancing with abandon. As we left Holy Isle, Rinpoche insisted Rigdzin Shikpo turn and look back at it, telling him to remember it and to practise there sometimes.

On Khenpo Rinpoche's last visit to the Hermitage, we went by car to pick him up from Manchester. As he climbed into the car, he looked up at the sun in the cloudless blue sky and sang in Tibetan:

> *What appears is clarity,*
> *Emptiness is clarity,*
> *Wisdom is clarity as well.*
> *The meeting of these clarities three*
> *Is like the sun in the sky cloud-free.*

'Translate it and compose a tune for it,' he said. Then, 'Sing it over and over again.' I did as he said and as we drove the two hours to the Hermitage, I could tell he was listening as I sang by the way he slightly nodded his head in time with it. When the car pulled up at the end of the Hermitage drive there was a palanquin waiting for him and eight strong men of the Awakened Heart Sangha asking him to step onto it. He did so without batting an eyelid, as if it were the most natural thing in the world. They lifted him onto their shoulders and carried him up the drive. Everyone had gathered to welcome him so a whole crowd accompanied him up the drive singing and dancing as he stood up on the palanquin above us happily tossing flower petals into the air as he went, as a sign of auspiciousness. Once he was settled in the house, he told me and my students to dance on the lawn in front of the house singing the song I had been singing to him in the car. We created a dance that ended with us all lying in a star shape looking up at the sky, while Rinpoche watched us from an upstairs window. Afterwards he remarked that our looking up into the sky like that was an auspicious sign that our sangha would be closely connected to Dzogchen, the realisation of the true nature of mind.

I followed Rinpoche's instruction to stay in retreat for the first three years at the Hermitage, only coming out now and then to teach. Six of my students including Jonathan undertook a year's retreat at about the same time. We were experimenting with how best to set the ethos of the place. Was it mainly my residence, a retreat centre or the headquarters of the Awakened Heart Sangha? It continues to function as all three with the inevitable tensions that involves but also a lot of joy.

In 2004 further darkness fell with the passing away of Bokar Rinpoche at the age of sixty-four. His death came as a huge shock to everyone. Apparently on the morning he died he had seemed well except for a curious cough. He was going to the hospital to have it checked and died in the car on the way there. This was a terrible loss for the lineage as Bokar Rinpoche was an important meditation teacher for the younger generation of lamas, including the 17th Karmapa, Ogyen Trinley Dorje. He was one of the few younger lamas who had managed to complete their training after fleeing to India and had formed the next generation of teachers on whom the future authenticity of the lineage rested.

After receiving the news, I sat for several hours in our shrine room meditating and making prayers to keep a strong connection with Bokar Rinpoche in all our future lifetimes. Strangely, shortly before he passed away, I had had a strong dream of him visiting me in Wales. He said he loved the place and that he would come and we would work together even more closely than before. I thought in the dream that this would not be possible because of all his other commitments. Now suddenly those were all finished.

I had seen him only once since leaving India all those years ago although he was always present in my heart and mind. He had been teaching on a Dzogchen text at Kham House in Essex and I had been translating for him. It was a joy to spend time with him again, but it was a joy accompanied by a tinge of sadness because I realised that he didn't under-stand what had happened to me. The openness that had been there between us was no longer the same, and we were not together for long enough to get used to this change or for me to explain anything. Now he had gone.

I quickly booked a flight to India and attended his funeral ceremony at his monastery in Mirik, near Darjeeling. People told me of the miraculous things that had occurred since his death, such as beads of light raining down on the lamas in the shrine room. I wished I had seen it. A few days after I arrived, there was a lot of excitement among the hundreds of people from all over the world who had come for the fu-neral and the hundreds of local Tibetans and Nepalis for whom Bokar Rinpoche was an important lama. The 17th Karmapa Ogyen Trinley Dorje was due to arrive any day and elaborate preparations were afoot. He was coming as Bokar Rinpoche's disciple to pay his last respects to one of his most important teachers. As if in response to his grief, as he stepped out of the car, there was such a downpour of rain, that all ceremonials had to be left aside and all he could do was go straight to the shrine containing Bokar Rinpoche's body. When it came for me to leave a week later, I did the same. I sat in front of it, praying that I had done everything necessary to honour the connection between us. As if in an-swer to my prayer, as I walked out of the temple, I met Khenpo Donyo, whom I had known in Sonada and was Bokar Rinpoche's main companion and successor. He recognised me and invited me to his room where he gave me some of Bokar Rinpoche's sacred relics. It was more than I had dared to hope for!

After Khenpo Rinpoche's last visit to the UK in 2006 his health began to deteriorate and when I went to see him in Kathmandu in 2007, I was deeply affected to see how sud-denly he had aged ten years since last I saw him. He was shuffling along instead of walking properly and nobody seemed to know why. He gave me a big bag of apples and told me to sit in his shrine room and eat them meditatively, savouring every morsel. Did he somehow know I hate apples? One time I was sitting chatting with him, when he asked musingly, as if out of the blue, 'What *is* two?' He was clearly contemplating an experiential mystery. I told him this was the sort of thing mathematicians think about, in a much more precise language than anything available in Buddhism. He looked very pleased to hear this, so I told him Rigdzin Shikpo was looking for ways of using this kind of language to teach Dharma. 'He must do that,' he urged, 'that is very important.'

That Rinpoche was reflecting on deep questions such as 'What is two?' right into his old age, shows just how important questions are. I love questions because they stimulate me to reflect more deeply. As a teacher I encourage my students to ask questions, which like Rinpoche's question above, can sound deceptively simple. Yet the more we ask them and the more we realise that we cannot answer them, the deeper our understanding can go. In my dream of Kalu Rinpoche he told me to finally give up questions when my heart or mind had completely merged with that of the guru. It is only then that they are no longer necessary. Perhaps the point is that only when one's heart or mind has merged with that of the guru are all questions answered.

Asking simple and direct questions about our experience takes a certain kind of courage. The courage of turning towards the unknown and allowing oneself to not know. That is to be completely open. It is surprising how the truth somehow pours out of that space of honesty. Dharma transmits itself from a place of confidence and honesty.

The opportunity to ask deep questions only arises in the presence of someone open enough to be willing to discuss them. I am acutely aware of the fact that I have only been able to make progress in Dharma because of having had such opportunities all my adult life. As a result, I find I want to provide the same opportunities for my students and aim to work with them long term, on a personal basis, so that I can observe how the teachings I give are actually being received and used. My focus is on giving them a range of methods that suits their life situation and will enable them to both live and die with confidence. Although in Tibetan Buddhism there are many elaborate practices one can learn, the important thing is to focus on deepening one's understanding of one's own experience.

While I was in Kathmandu Rinpoche had been unsure about what he was going to do next. I offered to stay on to help him if he needed me but he couldn't give me a clear answer. After I left, he accepted an invitation from Ponlop Rinpoche to go for medical treatment in Seattle. When I went to visit him there he seemed quite spaced out, but we were able to have a meaningful conversation about the teaching of Rangtong and Shentong. He was concerned that I might try to teach Shentong to students who did not understand Rangtong. I told him it was impossible to teach Shentong without teaching Rangtong at the same time. He agreed. I then reiterated to him what he had always said to me, 'Without Shentong there is nothing to have faith in.' Again he agreed. I promised him that I would come to see him every year wherever in the world he was. He seemed pleased and asked me to dance for him. He then promptly got up and left the room, so I didn't. Maybe I should have done anyway!

Every year since 2009 I have travelled to Kathmandu to his nunnery just ten minutes walk from the great Boudhanath Stupa, not far from where I had stayed in retreat all those years ago. His nuns look after him very lovingly, but year by year he has been able to do less and less so that now he cannot even speak. Nonetheless when his students come from all over the world to visit him, they feel as I do that the power of his presence augments year by year. Simply to step into his room brings tears of devotion to the eyes even of those who have never met him before. When he first got sick, he told us he was resting in the clear light nature of mind and that we would meet him there if we could do that too. Whenever I think of him, I experience an increasingly strong conviction that this is true.

Once I started teaching my own personal students, I quickly realised how vital it was to build up a community that could work with me in supporting each other's practice and training and that eventually they would have to start teaching each other. If the community was successful it would end up with more than one guru or lama. Who would recognise those people as lamas? I asked Rinpoche if I could authorise others to teach Mahamudra and he said, 'Yes if they have faith in you'. I asked if I could authorise them to teach Mahamudra to others and he again said, 'Yes if their students have faith in them'. Clearly transmission is as much about *samaya* connection and faith as it is about the level of realisation of the guru.

There are so many aspects to establishing a community it is hard to know where to start. On top of all the usual problems, ours is a cyber-age community that has gathered students via the internet who live quite distant from each other. How are we to build strong personal connections in our sangha community in such a situation? It is not like in a traditional Buddhist country where a community would all be living in one locality, if not the same establishment such as a monastery. When I was talking privately to Sangharakshita once, he confessed that the building of a sangha community is such a relentless task that he wouldn't wish on anyone – even his worst enemy. A Tibetan monastic lama once commented to a Western colleague of mine, '*We* only have to take on one or two well-defined roles within a monastic institution for a given period of time. You people trying to set up sanghas in the West have to do *everything* for yourselves, all the roles, all the different tasks, and you then have to keep doing them indefinitely because there is nobody to take over from you.' He is right. We have to teach texts, give meditation instruction and lead rituals, organise communities and events, fundraise, troubleshoot, maintain discipline, keep archives, take care of property and buildings and more – and we are not trained for any of it. After my mother died, my father, who was himself a pioneer in the field of engineering, came to stay with me for a month at Tyn y Gors. He watched carefully what I was doing and commented thoughtfully that he had never had to work so completely from scratch as I was.

It took a long time for my students to recognise what was needed for a sangha to cohere and be able to support new students coming in as well their own ongoing practice. They needed to learn even simple things like recognising that teachers need support financially and organisationally in order to be able to be there for their students.

After ten years we had succeeded in establishing a sangha with a strong core of a dozen students sharing the same values and culture, committed to preserving its teaching activity and delivering it to others. One of the first decisions of this group, called the Shrimalagana, was to build the stupa I had been planning for many years, in accordance with Khyentse Rinpoche's wishes. At the centre of our stupa at the Hermitage is a much smaller stupa blessed by Khenpo Rinpoche set in the central pillar and around the pillar is wrapped the text of the Ratnagotravibhaga on Buddha Nature. The stupa also contains relics of many of the Karmapas, as well as Trungpa Rinpoche, Khyentse Rinpoche, Bokar Rinpoche and others. In 2011 Lama Phuntsok consecrated the stupa at the Hermitage in the presence of Rigdzin Shikpo and our students from all over the world plus many local people who had contributed to the building of it.

For me this symbolised and embodied the power and stability of the lineage at the heart of the sangha community. Since the stupa was built the sangha has gradually gone from strength to strength, developing its own training programmes and strategies for caring for students over the long term. When all those years ago Khenpo Rinpoche had said, 'Connect to Trungpa Rinpoche and learn Dharma in your own language,' I hadn't been sure why. Now when I look back at the trajectory of my life, it is as if he saw it all laid out before him. As with passing fire from one firebrand to the next, Dharma has to be kept burning through the transmission process. Only future generations will be able to tell how successfully I and my students have handed the torch on.

Glossary of People

Akong Rinpoche (1939 – 2013) was a Karma Kagyu teacher who, together with Chogyam Trungpa Rinpoche, came to the UK to study and went on to establish Samye Ling monastery in Scotland. I met him in Samye Ling the year after it opened in 1967.

Apho Rinpoche (Pron. Apo) (1922 – 1974), full title Apho Yeshe Rangdrol Rinpoche, was a Drugpa Kagyu teacher who established retreat centres in the northern Indian himalayas, finally settling in Manali where I spent time in retreat.

Ato Rinpoche (b. 1933) is a Karma Kagyu teacher who came to live in Cambridge where, alongside his Buddhist teaching, he married and worked as a hospital nurse until his retirement. He gave me advice when I first returned to the West.

Avalokiteshvara (Skt.) (Tib. *Chenrezig*) is not a historical figure but known as the much-loved Bodhisattva of great compassion who is regarded as the patron saint of Tibet. His mantra 'Om Mani Padme Hum' is to be heard and seen inscribed everywhere Tibetan culture spreads. Both the Dalai Lama and Karmapa are said to emanate from him and he is said to emanate from Amitabha the Buddha of boundless light. He appears in many different iconographical forms; the four-armed white form is particularly popular.

Bokar Rinpoche (1940 – 2004) was a close disciple of Kalu Rinpoche who became a holder of the Karma Kagyu and Shangpa Kagyu lineages. He was the three-year retreat master at the Sonada and Rumtek monasteries for many years and became an important teacher for 17th Karmapa Ogyen Trinley Dorje. He built a monastery in Mirik in east Nepal where he died suddenly aged only sixty-four. He was my main teacher directing my practice while I was in India after Karma Thinley Rinpoche left for Canada.

Chokyi Nyima Rinpoche (Pron. Chochi Neema) (b. 1951) is the eldest son of Tulku Urgyen Rinpoche, one of the greatest Dzogchen masters of our time. He trained from the age of thirteen at Rumtek monastery where he stayed eleven years, after which he became abbot of Ka-Nying Shedrub Ling monastery, Kathmandu, which continues to be the centre of his worldwide teaching activity. I met him when he was a teenager in Rumtek and we still continue our connection today.

Dabzang Rinpoche (1929 – 1992) was a Kagyu teacher who established a monastery near to the Boudhanath Stupa and who I credit with saving my life when I was stung by a hornet.

Dalai Lama (b. 1935) is the overall spiritual leader of Tibet and winner of the 1989 Nobel Peace Prize. He belongs to the Gelug school of Tibetan Buddhism, is based in Dharamsala, India, and continues to travel widely to teach. Although I have been in his presence many times, I have not yet had a personal interview with him.

Dilgo Khyentse Rinpoche (1910 – 1991) was a very eminent Nyingma teacher, writer and preserver of practices and texts of all Tibetan Buddhist schools. The teacher of all my teachers and the person who guided Rigdzin Shikpo and me to set up a centre in north-west Wales. He became head of the Nyingma lineage when Dudjom Rinpoche passed away.

Dudjom Rinpoche (Pron. Doojom) (1904 – 1987), full title Dudjom Jigdral Yeshe Dorje, was a scholar, practitioner and teacher and was appointed head of the Nyingma lineage of Tibetan Buddhism when the Tibetans first arrived in India from Tibet. He revealed and preserved many teachings and texts, travelled widely and established centres around the world. I met him a number of times in India and France.

Gendun Rinpoche (1918 – 1997) was renowned for having spent decades in retreat in Tibet and India and having his realisation publicly recognised by the 16th Karmapa who sent him to be the head lama of his main seat in Europe at Dhagpo Kagyu Ling in France at the age of fifty-seven. He went on to set up a huge retreat centre in Le Bost (France) for monks and nuns. He became an important teacher of 17th Karmapa Thaye Dorje. I was his translator for several years when he first came to the West.

Guru Rinpoche (c. 8th century) is a semi-historical figure who is accredited with first establishing Buddhism in Tibet by miraculous feats of defeating opposing forces and practising meditation in many places, converting the king and teaching his wife Yeshe Tsogyal who became a great Guru in her own right. Guru Rinpoche and Yeshe Tsogyal hid holy texts and objects in many places to be discovered in later times when they would be needed. This is called the Terma tradition, which is especially associated with them and the Nyingma lineage of Tibetan Buddhism. He is known by many names among which Padmasambhava, the Lotus Born, is the best known. There is no record of his ever having died, and his manifestations have continued to appear down the ages, into the 20th century. Sometimes referred to by Tibetans as the second Buddha bringing Shakyamuni's teaching to us today via his transmission lineage.

Gyaltsab Rinpoche (b. 1954) is one of the four main lineage holders (regents) of the Karma Kagyu school. I met him when I visited Rumtek and once when he taught in South Wales.

Jamgon Kongtrul Rinpoche (1954 – 1992) was another of the four main lineage holders (regents) of the Karma Kagyu school. I met him at Rumtek and was once asked to translate for him at Dhagpo Kagyu Ling.

Kalu Rinpoche (1905 – 1989) was a meditation master, scholar and teacher and one of the first Tibetan masters to teach in the West. Holder of the Karma Kagyu and Shangpa Kagyu lineages and main teacher of Bokar Rinpoche. I received teachings and transmissions from him many times beginning with when I first arrived in India.

Karma Ozer (b. 1942?) is also known as Lama Lodro Palmo. She and her sister Karma Yangzom were children when they escaped from Tibet in a party of nuns led by Khenpo Tsultrim Gyamtso Rinpoche. She studied at Varanasi and has spent many years in retreat. She is now in Tenga Rinpoche's retreat centre in Sikkim. We spent a lot of time together in India and France, and she visited me in Wales.

Karma Thinley Rinpoche (Pron. Tch-rinley) (b. 1931) is a meditation master of the Sakya and Kagyu lineages and close friend and colleague of Trungpa Rinpoche. He gave me meditation instruction when I first arrived at the nunnery in Tilokpur, India, until he left for Toronto in Canada where he set up a centre. The Karmapa sent me to teach at his centre in Manchester when I first arrived back in the West.

Karma Yangzom (1937 – 1991?) was the older sister of Karma Ozer (see above). She did three-year retreat at Sonada and stayed on there until she died quite young on pilgrimage in Bodhgaya. We used to live together whenever I stayed in Sonada.

16th Karmapa Rangjung Rigpe Dorje (1924 – 1981) was the spiritual head of the Karma Kagyu lineage whose main seat was Rumtek monastery in Sikkim. Known as the holder of the Black Crown. I met him in India and Rumtek and various places in Europe. He took a keen interest in me, ordained me as a nun, sent me back to Europe to teach and appointed me as Gendun Rinpoche's translator.

Kechog Palmo (1911 – 1977), born Freda Bedi, was an English woman who married an Indian, B. P. L. Bedi, and worked for the Indian nationalist cause before becoming a Buddhist nun. She was abbess of the nunnery at Tilokpur where I received teachings from Karma Thinley Rinpoche and did many months of retreat. Several biographies have appeared recently – 'The Revolutionary Life of Freda Bedi' by Vicki Mackenzie, 'The Spiritual Odyssey of Freda Bedi' by Naomi Levine and 'The Lives of Freda Bedi' by Andrew Whitehead.

Khenpo Rinpoche (b. 1934), full title Khenpo Tsultrim Gyamtso Rinpoche, is a prominent Kagyu scholar and meditator. In a style similar to the great yogin Milarepa he often taught through singing songs of realisation. He has nunneries in Tibet, Nepal and Bhutan. He travelled around the world teaching for about twenty-five years before his health deteriorated. He now lives quietly in his nunnery in Kathmandu. He was appointed as one of the main teachers of 17th Karmapa Ogyen Trinley Dorje.

Lama Denys (b. 1949) is a French student of Kalu Rinpoche and a holder of the Shangpa Kagyu teachings with a centre in France called Karma Ling. I met him first in Sonada and later stayed with him in Kalu Rinpoche's centre in Paris. I have stayed at Karma Ling in retreat and taught there on many occasions.

Lama Jampa Thaye (b. 1952), previously Dave Stott, is an English student of Karma Thinley Rinpoche and Sakya Trizin. He teaches within both the Kagyu and Sakya schools. I was sent by the 16th Karmapa to teach him what I knew when I first returned to the West.

Lama Jigme Rinpoche (b. 1949) is the nephew of the 16th Karmapa and brother of Shamar Rinpoche. Lama Jigme was appointed as representative of the 16th Karmapa in Europe and the spiritual director of the Karmapa's main seat in Europe at Dhagpo Kagyu Ling in France. I spent a lot of time in his company during the early years of setting up the centre there.

Lama Phuntsok (Pron. Puntsock) (b. 1951) is a Himalayan-born monk in the Kagyu tradition who trained to become a lama and established a monastic school in Kathmandu as well as many other projects in Nepal. He is renowned for having built stupas all over the world including the stupa in Samye Ling in Scotland and our stupa at the Hermitage in Wales.

Lama Phurtse (Pron. Putsee) (1929 – 2016) was a Kagyu yogin who accompanied Gendun Rinpoche to France in 1975 as his attendant. Leading a simple life with great devotion to practice, he was an inspiration to many people including myself. After his death he remained in meditative absorption for eight days which is a sign of great spiritual accomplishment. I was deeply affected by him while spending a lot of time in his company when acting as translator for Gendun Rinpoche.

Lama Rigdzin Shikpo (b. 1935), born Michael Hookham, is an early student of Chögyam Trungpa Rinpoche in the UK. Trungpa Rinpoche and Khenpo Tsultrim Gyamtso Rinpoche both affirmed his experience and realisation of Dzogchen and encouraged him to teach. Trungpa Rinpoche and Khyentse Rinpoche appointed him as the director of the Longchen Foundation. We married in 1972 and worked together in teaching our students for a number of years until I set up the Awakened Heart Sangha. He continues to be one of my main teachers and often teaches my students too.

Lama Tenpa Gyamtso (b. 1938?) is originally a monk from Pawo Rinpoche's monastery who did three-year retreats under the direction of Kalu Rinpoche and Bokar Rinpoche. He was sent to France as the retreat master in the first three-year retreat in the West at Kagyu Ling in the mid-1970s and has spent most of his life since then in retreat or semi-retreat. I spent many hours discussing the Dharma with him when I was in Sonada and later in Europe.

Lama Thubden (Pron. Toobden) (born early 20th century and passed away in 1989) was a close student of the last Situ Rinpoche. He came to Karma Ling in Birmingham with his companion Lama Lodro shortly after it was founded and taught there until he died. Lama Lodro continues to live there in semi-retreat where I occasionally visit him. Birmingham is greatly blessed from having these two great practitioners living there for so many years. The 16th Karmapa consecrated Karma Ling on his first visit there, regarding it as the heart of Britain.

Milarepa (1052 – 1135) is probably one of the best-known Kagyu lineage teachers because of his extraordinary life story. His teacher, Marpa, set him various trials to atone for his previous negative deeds. Once he had received teachings and empowerments from Marpa he practised in strict mountain retreat in Tibet and went on to share his realisation by means of innumerable songs.

Ngakpa Yeshe Dorje Rinpoche (Pron. Nakpa Yeshee Dorjay) (1926 – 1993) was a close student of Dudjom Rinpoche and a Nyingma practitioner and teacher. Because of his special powers the Dalai Lama would call on him to keep the rain away when he was about to hold special events. In this way he became known as the Dalai Lama's weather maker. Rigdzin Shikpo and I received important transmissions from him and special personal instructions.

Nyoshul Khenpo Rinpoche (1932 – 1999) was a renowned meditation master and learned Rime (non-sectarian or ecumenical) scholar in the Nyingma lineage. I met him often in the Dordogne when he came to visit Dhagpo Kagyu Ling.

Pema Chödrön (b. 1933) is an American student of Trungpa Rinpoche who was ordained as a nun in 1975 just as I arrived back in the West. We met when the 16th Karmapa visited Birmingham and again at Gampo Abbey, Nova Scotia, Canada in 1989. She is well-known worldwide for the many books transcribed from her talks.

Ponlop Rinpoche (b. 1965) is a tulku in the Nyingma tradition and trained under the 16th Karmapa in the Kagyu tradition. I first met him when he was a child at Rumtek monastery, Sikkim. He is a close student of Khenpo Rinpoche and founder of Nalandabodhi Institute. He is based in Seattle and travels widely. He is married with a young daughter.

Ringu Tulku Rinpoche (b. 1952) is a close disciple of the 16th Karmapa and Dilgo Khyentse Rinpoche. He taught as professor for seventeen years at the Namgyal Institute of Tibetology in Gangtok, after studying at the Sanskrit University in Varanasi. He is the official representative of 17th Karmapa Ogyen Trinley Dorje in Europe and founded the Bodhicharya Institute in Berlin. He travels tirelessly teaching worldwide. I have met him many times in Europe and Nepal and spent many hours in conversation with him, asking him questions and seeking his advice. He read my thesis and Discovering the Heart of Buddhism course materials and commented on them positively!

Sakyong Mipham Rinpoche (b. 1962) is the eldest son of Chögyam Trungpa Rinpoche, born in India of a Tibetan mother. He was enthroned as the Sakyong after his father's passing away and thus succeeded him as the head of Shambala International. He was recognised as the tulku of the great Mipham Rinpoche and practised under the guidance of Khyentse Rinpoche for many years, teaching widely within Shambala. I have always felt a strong karmic connection with him since he stayed with Rigdzin Shikpo and me for a while when he came to Oxford to study shortly before

Trungpa Rinpoche passed away. He resigned from his role as head of Shambhala in 2018.

Sangharakshita (1925 – 2018) was a pioneering British Buddhist teacher who went out to India towards the end of the second world war and spent many years as a monk studying and promoting Buddhism particularly among the 'untouchable' community. He was a prolific writer and founder of the Triratna Buddhist community. He was one of my very first teachers and directed me to meet Chögyam Trungpa Rinpoche. I have gained a lot of inspiration from my many friends and students associated with the Triratna community. I last saw Sangharakshita several weeks before he died.

Shamar Rinpoche (1952 – 2014) was the 14th incarnation in this line of lineage holders in the Karma Kagyu school. The Shamarpas held the Red Crown and were considered equal in status to the Karmapas, holders of the Black Crown. The 14th Shamarpa was the 16th Karmapa's nephew (brother of Lama Jigme Rinpoche) and was always regarded as his successor until the passing away of the 16th Karmapa when a dispute broke out among the four 'regents' (Shamarpa, Situ, Jamgon Kongtrul and Gyaltsab). The 16th Karmapa appointed Shamar Rinpoche as the head of his main seat in Europe, Dhagpo Kagyu Ling in the Dordogne, and of Karmapa International Buddhist Institute (KIBI) in Delhi, as well as various other institutions. Shamar Rinpoche recognised and enthroned Thaye Dorje as the 17th Karmapa. I met him in Rumtek, France and London, and always felt a strong connection with him.

Situ Rinpoche (b. 1954) is another of the four main lineage holders or 'regents' of the Karma Kagyu tradition. He was brought up in Rumtek together with the other three 'regents' (Shamarpa, Jamgon Kongtrul and Gyaltsab). He founded a monastic centre in Sherab Ling near Bir in northern India and various other institutions worldwide. He recognised and enthroned Ogyen Trinley Dorje as the 17th Karmapa. I met him a number of times in Rumtek, India and Europe.

Tenpa Gyaltsen (referred to as Tenpa, b. 1938 or thereabouts) is the son of one of the Tilokpur nuns and a good friend of mine both during my time in India and also subsequently in Europe. He was born in Kunu on the Indian side of the border with Tibet and spent many years studying with Gelugpa Geshes. He later became a fellow student of Khenpo Rinpoche and translator for Gendun Rinpoche. He helped me to translate the Ratnagotravibhaga and was an important source of information and inspiration in my life.

Jetsunma Tenzin Palmo (b. 1943) is an English nun of the Drukpa Kagyu lineage. She was given the title of Jetsunma in recognition of her spiritual achievements and her work at promoting the training of female practitioners from Himalayan regions. She was a role model for me from when I first arrived in India. Vicki Mackenzie wrote a biography about her called 'Cave in the Snow' and she has since become well-known worldwide as a Dharma teacher. We have kept in touch over the years and she has visited me twice in Wales.

Thrangu Rinpoche (Pron. Trangoo) (b. 1933) is a tulku of the Kagyu lineage renowned for the depth and breadth of his learning. I met him in Rumtek and then again in Europe where I helped him set up Thrangu House in Oxford. He became one of the personal tutors for 17th Karmapa, Ogyen Trinley Dorje.

Thukse Rinpoche (Pron. Tooksay) (1916 – 1983) was a Drukpa Kagyu lineage holder and a renowned yogin. He came to the West in 1982 to teach, where he established the foundations for the Drukpa centres in France and other European countries. He is the lama who gave me the name

Shenpen Zangmo. Andrew Harvey in 'Journey to Ladakh' vividly describes his encounters with him.

Trungpa Rinpoche (1939 – 1987), full title Chögyam Trungpa Rinpoche, was an eminent reincarnate Tibetan lama of the Kagyu Nyingma tradition. A tremendously influential figure both among Tibetans and Westerners. He co-founded Samye Ling in Scotland and founded Shambala International. He also co-founded with Khyentse Rinpoche the Longchen Foundation which Rigdzin Shikpo now leads.

NB: Some of the lamas mentioned in this book have since been accused of serious misconduct. As this has been widely reported and is a matter of public record but isn't part of my story or experience, I haven't referred to it here.

Glossary of Terms

Abhisheka (Skt.) (Tib. *Wong*) 1. Empowerment, initiation: The process by which disciples realise the unity of their mind with that of their Vajrayana guru. 2. Transmission, anointing: A ritual intended as a vehicle for this process.

Adhishtana (Skt.) (Tib. *Chinlab*) Sustaining power, grace, blessing; the living presence of the lineage, which empowers our practice.

Awakening The goal of the Buddhist path which is to wake up to the wisdom and compassion that is the true nature of reality. Also referred to as Enlightenment, Nirvana, Liberation from samsara and Buddhahood.

Bodhichitta (Skt.) The heart or mind as that in a being which can awaken. It is translated variously; for example, as the awakened heart, the heart of awakening, the heart's awareness or the Enlightened mind. Often used synonymously with 'Buddha Nature' and/or with Bodhichittotpada (Tib. *Sem kye*), the heart or mind set on Buddhahood expressed in a vow to realise Buddhahood for the sake of bringing all beings to that state.

Bodhisattva (Skt.) A being who has realised emptiness and who is committed to attaining complete Enlightenment for the sake of liberating all beings. More loosely, an aspiring Bodhisattva, i.e. anyone who takes the Bodhisattva vow and who is committed to following the Bodhisattva path, the Mahayana.

Chitta (Skt.) (Tib. *Sem*) Usually translated as 'mind' but thought of as in the heart. In English heart and mind are used in various senses all of which could be translated as chitta or sem, although for Tibetans sem is definitely in the heart, where we point to when we say 'I'.

Dakini (Skt.) A mysterious term used in a number of different contexts. It is generally taken to be a term for female adepts on the path of awakening, possibly fully awakened.

Yet the term is also used for wrathful female inhabitants of charnel grounds, yoginis, consorts of yogins, prophetic guides or messengers emanating from some kind of Dakini Pure Land. A Paradise of Dakinis is often referred to in the stories of the great siddha practitioners and it is where they go on leaving this earth. The term is also used for unawakened female beings who can take on various forms including that of flesh-eating demons and witches. It is not clear what, if anything, links all these different usages to a particular kind of being that would warrant them all being referred to as dakinis. Western writers tend to equate dakinis with what they call the feminine principle, a term Trungpa Rinpoche used and maybe even coined. Tibetans, in general, tend to be very vague about what the term dakini signifies and don't in general use any term that suggests a feminine principle of some kind.

Dharma (Skt.) A term used to mean truth or reality with the understanding it is what the Buddha discovered when he awakened and then taught, revealed and demonstrated to others. It has come to be used synonymously with the path to awakening, so we talk of practising Dharma, meaning following the path to awakening. However, since it also means the truth revealed at awakening, the true nature of the living truth of the universe that is drawing us to itself, we also talk of Dharma as a force in its own right, rather than simply a path that we follow. The term is also used more generally for any texts or teachings concerning the Dharma as truth or as path within the Buddhist tradition.

Dharma protector A term used for beings who have been bound by oath to protect the Buddha's teachings and those who practise them. They are typically beings who were once demons and who were tamed by a siddha practitioner such as Guru Rinpoche or Milarepa. Some Dharma protectors are

Enlightened beings who are in the role of Dharma protectors and some are worldly beings who can get annoyed and make mistakes, so offerings are made to them to keep them sweet.

Dzogchen (Tib.) Sometimes translated as the 'great completion' or the 'great perfection'. It is another name for the goal of the Buddha's path and a series of teachings within the Nyingma tradition that outline methods for advanced practitioners to speed up their progress. The term is also used for the whole tradition of the Nyingma school of Buddhism which is open to those of all levels of practice.

Empowerment See 'Abhisheka'.

Guru A teacher. See also 'Lama'. The principle of Enlightenment as embodied in teachers of the lineage.

Guru yoga The practice of opening out to the essence and union of all the Buddhas in the form of a guru or lineage of gurus so that the adhishtana of their presence unites their heart and mind with your own.

Karma (Skt.) The word karma is now in the English dictionary. The word itself means 'action' but in Buddhism it has the specific meaning of volitional actions that are regarded as wholesome or unwholesome dependent on their results. Actions resulting in happiness are wholesome and those resulting in suffering are unwholesome. The results manifest not only in this life but also, more importantly, in future lives. The details of what actions lead to happiness and which to suffering is a major subject of Buddhist teachings and discourse and relate to the whole Buddhist cosmological view, without which the import of these teachings cannot be understood except in the broadest terms.

Lama (Tib.) The Tibetan term for Guru or teacher. It is also used for the essence and union of all the Buddhas in the form of persons within a transmission lineage. As such the Lama can take the form of teachings or the words of the

Buddha, symbolic expressions of the Dharma as well as ultimately referring to one's own Buddha Nature, the ultimate Guru/Lama. As such it is more a principle than a person and could be thought of in terms of being the world or mandala of awakened or awakening beings and their teachings.

Mahamudra (Skt.) (Tib. *Chag ja chen po*) Literally 'the great seal' or 'symbol', where all experience symbolises, seals or points to the true nature of reality; the mind, heart of awareness that is the Buddha Nature in all beings. It is a term used in the Dzogchen tradition for a level of realisation that falls short of Dzogchen, however, since the time of Rangjung Dorje the Third Karmapa, it has been used by the Kagyu tradition synonymously with Dzogchen.

Mahayana (Skt.) Literally 'the great vehicle', the Bodhisattva path leading to complete and perfect Buddhahood. It is called 'great' because it contrasts itself with what it refers to as lesser vehicles (Hinayana) that aim at one's own liberation and do not explicitly aim to bring all beings to awakening.

Mantra The Chamber's Dictionary gives the Buddhist and Hindu definition for this as 'a word, phrase etc. chanted or repeated inwardly in meditation'. It often has the name of a particular awakened being embedded in it and is similar in effect to reciting such a being's name in order to invoke them in one's heart and receive their adhishtana.

Ngakpa (Tib.) (Skt. Mantrin) A specialist in mantra. A term used for a person responsible for performing rites to protect the local community. There are various traditions of ngakpa ordination, each with its own customs. Westerners sometimes adopt the title on completing a three-year retreat or if they wish to practice as an ordained householder rather than as a monastic.

Nirvana (Skt.) The cessation of suffering in the Buddhist sense of liberation from samsara. It is also used for ultimate reality itself and as such can be entered into.

Om Mani Padme Hum (Skt.) The mantra of Avalokiteshvara.

Pranidhana (Skt.) (Tib. *Monlam*) Often translated as 'wishing prayer' or 'aspiration'. It is more like a blessing (or curse), in the sense that it has within it the power or ability to fulfil itself. Pranidhanas are fundamental to the path to awakening. It is by our aspirations and wishes that we are able to meet teachers and follow the teachings from one life to the next.

Preliminary practices (Tib. *Ngondro*) The foundation practices of Vajrayana Buddhism that consist of 100,000 prostrations, Vajrasattva mantra recitations, mandala offerings and guru yoga prayers. Before embarking on these special preliminaries, students have to reflect on the four ordinary preliminaries which are the precious human birth, impermanence, karma and suffering. Both sets of preliminaries are designed to reinforce faith and renunciation, accumulate punya and purify obscurations as a preparation for deeper teachings.

Punya (Skt.) (Tib. *Sonam*) Somewhat misleadingly translated as 'merit'. It is the power of goodness inherent in kushal-amula (roots of karmically wholesome states) and is often used more or less synonymously with that term.

Rangtong (Tib.) – see Shentong

Renunciation The attitude of mind that aims only at the path of awakening with no worldly ambitions or hankerings after worldly goals. It arises from the conviction that everything other than awakening traps one in the endless cycle of suffering (samsara).

Rinpoche (Tib.) A title meaning 'precious one', given to respected Buddhist teachers.

Roshi A respectful title for a Zen Buddhist teacher.

Samsara (Skt.) The endless cycle of birth and death in the six realms of different kinds of suffering beings (including gods, demigods, humans, animals, hungry ghosts and denizens of the hell realms). As long as we do not recognise our true nature (Buddha Nature) we will be subject to birth in different states of suffering as a result of haphazardly ripening karmic actions. We never know what will ripen next even from day to day, hour to hour, moment to moment.

Sangha (Skt.) The community of practitioners of the Dharma, used in general for the whole Buddhist world of practitioners. It is also used more specifically for monastics or those who are on the Bodhisattva path. It is also used these days for communities of practitioners following the same tradition or who regard themselves as members of a specific Buddhist community.

Sem (Tib.) See 'Chitta'.

Shentong (Tib.) Literally 'emptiness-of-other'. Shentong is used to refer to absolute reality, the non-compounded, true nature of mind that is empty of what is compounded, conditioned, contingent and mere illusion. The non-compounded, in other words Buddha Nature, is empty of the confusion and veils that conceal it, but not empty of itself. In contrast, all that is conditioned and contingent is self-empty or empty of self-nature, which is called 'rangtong' (self-empty). So rangtong emptiness means lacking any reality, whereas Shentong emptiness means that absolute reality exists as the unconditioned, beyond concepts of existence and non-existence. The distinction between emptiness-of-other and self-emptiness is the subject of a scholarly controversy in Tibetan Buddhism as to whether Buddha Nature is self-empty or empty-of-other.

Siddha (Skt.) An adept practitioner having super-normal powers (siddhis), in particular the power, upon Enlightenment, to cause others to awaken.

Stupa A sacred monument consisting of a square base, dome and spiral depicting the body, speech and mind of the Buddha and containing relics, texts and prayers.

Taking refuge Taking refuge in the Buddha, Dharma and Sangha means to commit oneself to following the Buddha, his teachings and those who teach them. It is central act for any Buddhist and is taken very seriously.

Tendrel (Tib.) (Skt. *Nidana*) An auspicious connection, sign or link. Good tendrel are indications of good connections between past, present and future events, persons and deeds, and so can be read as predictive signs of auspiciousness. They can also be deliberately forged so as to lead to auspicious situations in the future. Similarly, inauspicious signs (tendrel) are a warning and efforts can be made to avert evil by creating corresponding good tendrel. Sometimes the term is translated as luck because we call auspicious signs lucky. However in Buddhism the assumption is that the good tendrel have come from our own wholesome actions in the past and so are not simply lucky chance.

Transmission This term is used for a range of rituals and processes in the Buddhist tradition. It can be understood as the transmitting of adhishtana through rituals, ritual objects, teachings and the direct influence of one mind on another. This removes obstructions to realisation and strengthens faith and confidence thus allowing insight and the qualities of awakening to awaken in another person.

Togden (Tib.) A term for a realised siddha.

Vajrayana (Skt.) Also referred to as Tantra or Mantrayana. It is presented as a swift and possibly dangerous esoteric path to awakening requiring great faith and spiritual aptitude on the part of both student and teacher to whom the student owes absolute obedience. In practice however in the Tibetan Buddhist tradition, everybody is expected to engage in the Vajrayana whatever level of faith or aptitude they have. Because of this the special features of Vajrayana are no longer clearly defined. Students and teachers often have very little to do with each other even though the students are supposed to have received abhisheka simply by their presence at an abhisheka ritual. It is doubtful whether much of what is called Vajrayana is strictly speaking worthy of that name, nonetheless, it is thought to create good tendrel and strengthens student's faith and connection to the lineage.

Vedanta (Skt.) A strand of the Hindu tradition that arose after the time of the Buddha and is thought to have been strongly influenced by it. The teachings are very similar to each other if not identical.

Yidam (Tib.) A term often translated as 'deity'. It refers to the Vajrayana practice of meditating on a particular Enlightened being first as a figure separate from oneself and then in stages drawing closer and closer until one merges with it so that one realises one's own Buddha Nature is no different from that of the figure. It is the same principle as guru yoga and in fact the figure of the deity is transmitted in an abhisheka ritual making it clear that the guru giving the abhisheka and the deity are inseparable from each other and also inseparable from the chitta of the student. All this assumes a deep understanding of emptiness in both the rangtong and shentong senses, or at least a strong intuitive understanding arising from karmic connections. Strong karmic connections (tendrel) can cause powerful faith to arise spontaneously making it unnecessary to engage in much learning.

Yogin (Skt.) A practitioner who devotes their time to meditation and retreat or whose realisation is so advanced they can maintain their realisation and practice in whatever they are doing.

The Teachings of Lama Shenpen Hookham

The main body of Lama Shenpen's teaching is contained within the **Living the Awakened Heart Training,** of which Lama Shenpen is the author and principal teacher. The Living the Awakened Heart training has been devised especially for Westerners to explore the most profound teachings of Tibetan Buddhism in an accessible, experiential way. It is equally suitable for those who have read about and practised Buddhism for years and for those who are completely new to it.

The training is based on some of the most profound Buddhist teachings: the Mahamudra and Dzogchen teachings of Tibetan Buddhism. It is a search for truth: a process of exploring our experience and coming to understand and relax into our true nature. In the midst of all the pain, doubt, hesitation, stress and confusion of our lives, there is something that keeps us going. We talk of losing heart and yet, somehow, there is something deep inside us that spurs us on, restores us and gives us hope. The path of Buddhist training is to uncover this heart of our being, to recognise it, to value it and to base our lives and actions on it. According to the Buddhist tradition, this is our Awakened Heart (Sanskrit: Bodhichitta) or Buddha Nature (Sanskrit: Tathagatagarbha).

Living the Awakened Heart training is not an academic course. Rather, it is a comprehensive training in Buddhist study, reflection and meditation – providing a sound basis for a lifetime of deep spiritual practice.

For more information and to join the training visit: www.ahs.org.uk

For weekly and archive teachings from Lama Shenpen visit: www.buddhawithin.org.uk

About the Author

Lama Shenpen Hookham is a Buddhist teacher who has trained for over fifty years in the Mahamudra and Dzogchen traditions of Tibetan Buddhism. She has spent over 12 years in meditation retreat.

Lama Shenpen spent 7 years in India after being sent there by Trungpa Rinpoche at the start of the 1970s where she was ordained as a nun by the 16th Karmapa. The Karmapa later sent her back to the West to teach where she met her main teacher, Khenpo Tsultrim Gyamtso Rinpoche, one of the foremost living masters of the Kagyu tradition of Tibetan Buddhism. She has been a student of his since the late 70s and he authorised her to teach Mahamudra.

She produced a seminal study of the profound Buddha Nature doctrines of Mahayana Buddhism, for which she was awarded a doctorate from Oxford University and which is published as 'The Buddha Within' (SUNY press, 1991).

She is also the author of 'There's More to Dying than Death' (Windhorse Publications, 2006) and the translator and editor of Khenpo Tsultrim Gyamtso Rinpoche's seminal work 'Progressive Stages of Meditation on Emptiness'.

Following advice from the teacher of all her teachers, Dilgo Khyentse Rinpoche, Lama Shenpen Hookham established the Hermitage of the Awakened Heart in north-west Wales, where she spends most of her time in semi-retreat, working with her students and on her writing.

Publisher's Note

The Shrimala Trust is the charitable organisation that supports the activities of Lama Shenpen, run by the shared effort of the Awakened Heart Sangha, the community of students under the direction of Lama Shenpen.

In accordance with Buddhist values all Awakened Heart Sangha teaching events and teaching materials are offered on a donation basis, ensuring they are available to all regardless of financial situation.

If you would like to make a donation in support or appreciation of Lama Shenpen's work and teachings, and to support the Shrimala Trust in continuing to facilitate the sharing of Lama Shenpen's teachings, please do so at:

www.ahs.org.uk/donations-and-payments

or

www.buddhawithin.org.uk/donate